The *New* New Testament

Rewritten through
Jesus
and all the
Original Authors

CONTENTS

Introduction 5

John 12

Matthew 49

Mark 77

Luke 99

Acts 127

Paul's Introduction 153

Romans 155

First Corinthians 165

Second Corinthians 175

Galatians 181

Ephesians 186

Philippians 191

Colossians 195

First Thessalonians 199

Second Thessalonians 203

First Timothy 205

Second Timothy 209

Titus 212

Philemon 214

Hebrews 215

James 224

First Peter 228

Second Peter 232

First John 234

Afterword 239

INTRODUCTION

This *New* New Testament is very different from other New Testaments. It is not the work of scholars, but of a simple believer who was asked by Jesus, and by all the original authors of the New Testament, to rewrite it as *they* want it to be heard today. Many may have trouble with this concept, with the scribe himself having been one of them. It is very hard for us to believe that **"everything is possible with God."** (Mark 10, 27)

Concerning this, the scribe would like to say as St. Paul did in Galatians: "All I want is to serve Jesus and his Message, which I received directly from him through many revelations, and not from any human person." (1, 10-12) When he asked Jesus why he had been asked to do this, the response was simply: "Because no one else would agree to do it." And the scribe clearly knows that it is Jesus using "the weak to confound the strong." (1 Cor. 1, 27)

Truth is always simple. Jesus is the Truth. Even though he was God, he was also a simple person and chose simple people to help spread the Good News to the world. He asked that his Message be rewritten now that his core Message is no longer illegal to proclaim. His core Message is very simple:

1. We are God. (John 10, 34) (We must remember that Jesus was crucified for saying that he was God.)
2. God is Love. (1 John 4, 8)
3. Love manifests as Service. (John 1, 12)

We can summarize all of this by saying simply: Our Essence is Divine Love, our Call is Human Service.

Jesus wants his simple Message presented here *to bring unity to his people and his Churches,* and ultimately to all Faiths and all Peoples! If we don't walk in unity, we don't walk with Jesus, who is God, who is Love, who is Service. We also don't live Jesus' Prayer: "That we all may be One!" (John 17, 21)

In this *New* New Testament the scribe was told to restore John's Gospel to its rightful place as the first Gospel, as reflected in ancient Aramaic Manuscripts. Thus this New Testament will begin as did the Old Testament: "In the beginning," as a sign that it is meant to supersede much of it. Revelation was to **begin again** with Jesus. This change of position of John's Gospel puts the two books of Luke—Luke's Gospel and Acts—back together as they were initially.

We must realize that Jesus was not simply to continue the Revelation of the Old Testament, but came with a radically different Message about God, Spirituality, and Community. His God was his "Dad"—"Abba" in his native language. That one word alone transcended much of the Old Testament, but all the original Apostles were Jews formed in the Judaism of the day, which had strayed a great deal from the Covenant of Abraham. Over and over Jesus upset the Jewish leaders of the time by preaching and acting a different Message. But much of his radical intimacy with God was lost on the Jewish Apostles, the authors of the original New Testament, and its translators.

For example, some scholars have pointed out that the passage usually translated, "I have not come to change the law, but to fulfill it," should actually be translated, "I have not come to change the law, but to abolish it."

The translators or scribes who changed this passage could not believe what Jesus had said, so they simply changed it to fit their own beliefs.

It should be stressed that the teaching of Jesus presented here is in no way something new. It was the core teaching in the early Church up until the fourth century when money and power overrode tradition, and to this day it is the teaching of many Eastern Churches, which never lost Jesus' real Message.

Those very close to Jesus knew this teaching and later taught it. Christianity went underground in many places because Jesus' core teaching—that we are God (John 10, 34)—continued to be illegal for a long time after Jesus was killed for preaching it, and so had to be kept secret except among members of the Communities.

Later, Jesus' teaching on love and peace became very popular with civil leaders who were tired of paying the cost of wars. The most graphic example of this was the Roman emperor Constantine. He called a meeting of the Christian Bishops of the "known" world at Nicaea to try to bring an end to the splits within Christianity, and more importantly for him, to bring peace to his realm based on Christian teachings ... which, we should mention, that were getting further and further from Jesus' real teachings.

There was some talk in this Council about which scriptures were inspired, but no decision was made as to the actual Canon. However, this decision was unofficially made after the Council by Constantine himself when he ordered fifty copies of *his* selection of books to be produced for the Christians of his area.

This was the largest commission for books in history up until that point, and has had an amazing impact on Christianity even down to our own times. Churchmen were involved in this process, but the old adage applies here, "He who pays is he who says." Most historians don't believe Constantine's conversion to Christianity was sincere, but was rather political, and that his selection of a number of the books of "his"

Canon was also political, particularly those that stress the law, when Jesus actually came to replace the law with Love.

Constantine wanted to drop all the writings of John because he thought they overemphasized love, particularly in 1 John 4, 8, which is the *only* place in the entire traditional Bible where God's essence is presented: *God is Love.* And even though love would bring peace, teaching that God is Love would do away with much of the power of Churches that often rule by threatening God's vengeance on those who do not follow the laws they have made.

And Constantine was especially concerned about John 10, 34, which talks of our being Divine. (Jesus here is quoting David who had also taught this in Psalm 82, 6, but this was never taken seriously, even though it was in the Bible.) Gods don't tend to feel a need to follow civil authority. So Jesus' main Message *that we are God* was very hard to keep alive because it was illegal, as mentioned earlier, and because it limited the power of Church leaders and civil governments. So when Constantine moved Christian Services from homes back into Temples by providing the money to build them, the main teachings of Jesus, like the pre-eminence of Family and Intimacy with God, almost completely died too. That is why Jesus asked that it be resurrected in this *New* New Testament.

It cannot be stressed enough that Jesus does not want a new Church, or a new sect to come from his Message here! He simply wants his Message of Love to be taught and believed in **all** his Churches, and all our **homes**, our most basic "*church!*" His teaching here may well radically change Christianity today everywhere except in those places, mainly in the East, were his core Message was never lost, but **it must be seen as a <u>return</u> to that Message and not a changing of it!**

Many Churches today teach that miracles died with the Apostles. Almost all Churches believe that the possibility of Scriptural Inspiration also died with the Apostles, even though Scripture itself totally negates this idea. For example, John 16, 12-15, where Jesus promises that his Spirit will continue to teach us even after he has died. There is absolutely nothing there limiting the Spirit's ability to teach us after the death of the Apostles. And there is absolutely nothing limiting Spirit's ability to inspire Scriptures after the death of the Apostles. Spirit still remains very much alive and able to do whatever (S)he feels will help Christians follow Jesus and live his teachings, even though the Apostles have long since died.

The idea of Jesus' core Message being openly proclaimed when it is no longer illegal shouts itself from all the rooftops of the world. How could he possibly not want a *New* New Testament dripping with the nectar of his core teaching, even as shocking as this may be to some?

Paul's teaching to the scribe who took down this *New* New Testament was extremely strong on this point. His own conversion to Jesus was instantaneous on the road to Damascus, but his *understanding* of Jesus took many years to sink into his Pharisaical bones. He now wanted his writings, which were still steeped in law, to be rewritten into the Love that Jesus preached. Paul cried tears of gratitude as this rewriting took place, and as the key of Jesus' Message was unlocked from the jail of the Mosaic Law. As this happened, Jesus' Message was also unlocked from the jail of Paul's prejudice against women and sexuality, and let the reverence for women and the deep respect for sexuality that Jesus had come shining through.

Jesus asks only that you read this with an open heart. Be aware of how it feels in your heart, because that is where Jesus dwells. If we feel the love of Jesus in his words here, let us share it with everyone we meet, as he did!

The mind separates things in its search for knowledge and clarity, and this can be very helpful. However, the heart unites things as it seeks oneness, and this unity is even more important. The Age of Separating has ended. The Age of the Unity of All, that Jesus taught, can finally incarnate.

Spirit has said that the problems in the world today—greed, violence, selfishness, perversion—do not come from something wrong in us, but from something wrong in our theology and spirituality. The lack of Jesus' main Message of Deification (our being God) being obvious in the original New Testament was due to it being a capital crime in that day to believe or teach it, and so it was edited out in those early centuries, and this lack has caused our Divine Energy and Identity to be twisted almost completely into these aberrations of Divinity. A main reason for this *New* New Testament is that Deification, our literally being made in the Image of God, is no longer illegal to talk about, so the Core Message of Jesus can now be openly proclaimed to the entire world. **Unfortunately, this lack has caused many to believe that Jesus' core Message is heresy!**

Jesus was the core of much of the original New Testament. He is the core of **all** of this *New* New Testament. We can say that he was its "editor in chief," since it was he who selected the books to be included here, and not Constantine, and it was he who oversaw the writing of the manuscript. He and the original authors, imparted all the Revelations that the scribe wrote down.

To believe that Revelation has ended is like believing God is dead, and that all we have is a record of what Jesus did, rather than Jesus himself present in our hearts. This belief is not consistent with what he said, as mentioned above.

When he asked the scribe in 2009 to write this down, he promised the aid of each of the original authors to help guide him. They were the authors, and Jesus' Spirit the Editor-in-Chief. If that is not possible, then the original New Testament misspoke when it says, *"Everything is possible with God!"*

All this comes down to one simple question: Can Jesus give us a New **New** *testament if he wants to? If Jesus can indeed do the impossible, it would behoove us to listen to him here with a new heart and open ears. If you believe that Jesus can do this, but you are not sure that THIS version is it, there is an easy way to find out: read it and see (you will know).*

It should be noted that the scribe who wrote this down was told not to use the word "Church" in the manuscript, since it has lost its original meaning. Originally it meant what today would be called "Community." The advent of church buildings began the decay of the original concept of Community, and the modern large church buildings have almost totally destroyed any concept or possibility of true Community.

The very early Christians, as we read in Acts, met daily in the temple for prayer and in their homes for the "Breaking of the Bread." Meeting in the temple to pray was based on their belief that they were still Jews. The gathering in homes was based on Jesus' new Ceremony of the Breaking of the Bread. This tradition has been lost in many Churches because it was seen as connected with sacrifice rather than with Deification as is very clear in John's Gospel. His "Wedding Feast of Cana" was his mystical wedding of our Humanity and Divinity, as will be clear from a reading of that section of John's Gospel.

It should also be noted that the original Scriptures were not written for personal study, but for Community sharing. The "luxury" of everyone having their own bible did not exist until fairly recently. The original belief that the *spoken* Word of God contained the Energy/Love of God has been lost. So the guidance was given that this *New* New Testament generally be seen as something to be read out loud in Community, and then discussed under the guidance of Spirit, the Spirit of Jesus. This will lead to a better, and more Spirit-filled understanding of Scripture, and a deepening sense of Community, which was the original intent of Jesus. And we all know that *Community* is something very needed in Christianity today.

There were two Introductions given to the scribe. One from all the authors together, and a special one from Paul since he wrote so much of the New Testament and has grown so much since he did that. He has evolved more into Jesus and so can better present here what Jesus has revealed to him. Paul's Introduction is placed right before his Epistles; the other authors comments are here:

A Message from the original Authors

As we look at your world today we are filled with overwhelming compassion. There are such great divisions and splits between peoples, between religions and between churches. We want this text to be a step toward real unity, and not another excuse for divisions. It is the same Tree of Life of Jesus, just with more blossoms because Christianity is now older. It is the same Word of God, only updated into modern terms and now released to present the core Message of Jesus, since it is no longer illegal to speak it openly.

A few notes about language and grammar.

Aramaic, the language that Jesus spoke, is a multi-dimensional language, whereas English generally is not. You will occasionally see words here in parentheses to try and convey multiple layers of the same Truth as does Aramaic. It should also be remembered that Eastern understanding is often very different from Western. In the East ideas and beliefs that are considered contradictions in the West are considered as complementary there. Truth is a much broader experience in the East and that should be taken into account

as we read this Testament that came from the East. As some have said, "We have forgotten that Bethlehem and Jerusalem are not in the West!"

The most graphic example of this perhaps is in dealing with the fact that Jesus' main teaching is that we are God, as already mentioned. Many of us believe we are only servants of God. The glory of Eastern understanding is that *both* these Truths can be seen as "sister and brother." Jesus, who embodies the total Truth, taught *both that we are God, and that we are servants of God.* His own life and teaching are a marvelous reflection of this.

God is generally presented here as masculine even though Divinity transcends gender. The scribe was told to try and balance this by presenting the feminine first whenever that was possible without the complicating "he/she," and to use the long tradition begun in the Old Testament of using the feminine when speaking of Spirit.

There are a number of words here that are regularly capitalized to try to stress their importance, like: Love, Community, Covenant, Faith, Light, Divine Life, Message, etc. This seems to present more clearly the emphases given in this rewriting.

It should also be noted that what you will find here is colloquial grammar. This is simply the way it came through to the scribe. And it is consistent with the fact that most all the original authors of the New Testament were simple people.

In the original *Acts of the Apostles* there are places where it appears that Luke was actually present there, (since he switches to "we") and was not simply narrating what he had heard. This was left the way it was, even though grammatically it can seem a bit confusing.

The New Testament was originally written not to be read by individuals, but to be read to Communities, as we have already mentioned. So you will find many more commas here than are "grammatically correct," in an attempt to assist in the reading aloud of this New Testament.

Jesus often talked about the value, even the need, to gather together. So we ask that we all please consider doing this in our family, and even asking our friends over and reading the *New* New Testament out loud together, as was the original intent. And then we can talk about how this can bring us closer to Jesus and one another by focusing on his Truth and not on sectarian beliefs.

And finally, it should be mentioned that an attempt was made to keep the original numbering of the chapters and verses. However, this was not always possible because of Jesus and the original authors wanting something deleted or something added.

The marvelous painting of *Jesus Laughing* was chosen for the cover of this *New* New Testament. Sometimes Jesus laughs to keep from crying about what has happened to his peoples and his Churches. And sometimes he simply likes a good joke. He even tells them occasionally in the Scriptures as he did in John 10, 32: "I have done many nice things for you. For which of these do you want to stone me?"

And also in a joke he told to the scribe: "We might say that humans love dogs because they have no theology of judgment, and so always love. And that we love cats because they have never lost their belief that they are God."

May we always remember:
God's Love is in God's Word.

The *Laughing Jesus* is by Ralph Kozak and was copyrighted by Praise Screen Prints in 1977. It is used here with permission. Please visit their web page:
www.jesuslaughing.com

JOHN

Let Us Begin Revelation Again

CHAPTER 1

1 In the beginning, before creation began, there was already Wisdom and Love. These two manifestations of God were God. *2* God extended Wisdom into the world and manifested the Son. The Son extended Love into the world and manifested Spirit. *3* From these all things were born, all Light and all Love. Light overshadowed darkness and Love transmuted fear. *4* This birthing of reality has continued and is now intensifying. *5* Old Wisdoms are being reborn into fresh ones; old Loves are being expanded into deeper ones. *6* Some birth pain continues as the illusions of darkness and fear are taught as truth. *7* But Wisdom shines brighter every day, and Love warms both the world and our hearts. *8* More and more people are realizing they are Children of God; and as such are God themselves. *9* They see that although originally born of the flesh, they are now reborn of Spirit, of God, and that together we all form the Family of God.

10 When the Son was born a new Glory entered creation, for this Glory was the Glory of God, the fullness of Wisdom and Love. *11* He came into our Dimension to bring us back to his. *12* He came with a simple Message: God is Love. God is Service. *13* This is his essence; this is our Call. *14* We are to light up the world with our Wisdom, and warm the hearts of all with our Love.

15 To do this he died in his humanity so he could more easily enter our minds and hearts with his Divinity. *16* We have come to call this Spirit, the Spirit of Jesus. *17* Without this Spirit we walk in the darkness of fear and self-centeredness. With this Spirit we walk as the continuing rebirthing of Jesus in our world. *18* The continual Good News is that God is Love; that God is Service. His Spirit is the reminder of all this.

19 When the Jewish leaders from Jerusalem sent priests and Levites to John the Baptist to ask him "Who are you?" he said, *20* "I am not the Christ you are expecting." *21* Then they asked him if he was Elijah, and he said he was not. *22* They insisted on an answer, saying they needed something to tell those who had sent them. *23* So he said, "I am someone crying in the wilderness, 'Open your hearts to God, straighten out the path to him.'" *26* He went on to say that he was baptizing with water, but that there was one coming soon who would baptize with Spirit. *28* This happened in Bethany across the Jordan River.

29 The very next day John saw Jesus coming toward him and said,

"Behold the beloved of God, who came to tell us of God's love for all. *30* He is the one I was talking about yesterday. *31* I have not yet met him, but he is the reason I came baptizing; to open your lives and hearts to him. *32* When I first saw him, I saw Spirit come down on him in the form of a dove. *33* The one who called me to this ministry told me, 'When you see the Spirit come down on a person, that is the one who will baptize with the Spirit. *34* Now I have seen him and tell you that this is a Christ."

35 The next day John was there with two of his friends, *36* and as he saw Jesus walk by he said, "Behold the Christ." *37* The two friends heard this and began to walk toward Jesus. *38* Jesus turned and saw them walking toward him and said, "What are you looking for?" They said to him, "Teacher, where do you live?" *39* He said to them, "Come and see for yourselves." So they went to where he was staying, it was about four o'clock in the afternoon.

40 Andrew, the brother of Simon, was one of these friends. *41* He went and told his brother, "We have found the Christ." *42* He then took him to Jesus. When Jesus saw him he said, "You have been called Simon, you will now be called Peter."

43 The next day they went to Galilee and saw Philip there. Jesus said to him, "Come walk with us." *44* Philip was from Bethsaida, the same town as Andrew and Peter. *45* Philip found Nathanael and told him, "We have found the one we have been awaiting: it is Jesus, son of Joseph and Mary of Nazareth." *46* Nathanael said, "I have found nothing in scripture saying anyone important is coming from Nazareth." *47* When Jesus saw Nathanael he said, "Here is a man with an open heart, who is seeking the Truth." *48* Nathanael asked him how he knew him. Jesus said to him, "Before Philip found you, I saw you sitting under a fig tree thinking about the Christ." *49* Nathanael said to him, "Teacher, I see that indeed you are a Christ." *50* Jesus replied, "Do you believe this just because I told you I saw you sitting under the fig tree? I assure you, you will see much greater things than this. *51* You will come to know where Christ lives, and come to know how you can live even as a Christ lives.

CHAPTER 2

1 Three days into Jesus' ministry there was a wedding feast in Cana of Galilee. Mary, Jesus' mother, was there. *2* Jesus and his friends were also there. *3* So when they ran out of wine Mary said to Jesus, "They have no wine." (*It should be remembered that in those days the people were much more aware of the importance of symbols. And wine was seen as the symbol of Divinity since it made people happy. So what she was really saying was: "They have no realization of their Divinity, they don't really know who they are.") *4* Jesus said, "I know, but it is not yet time for me to begin my ministry of teaching them who they really are."

5 His mother said to the servants, "Do whatever he tells you." (*Quoting here what the Pharaoh had said to the Jews who went down to Egypt to buy wheat for bread, thus bringing together symbolically bread and wine.) 6 Now there were six water jars there for the water used in the Jewish purification rituals. Each one could hold about thirty gallons. 7 Jesus told them to fill the jars with water, so they did. (*One wonders why the jars were not already full since this was a wedding feast where there would be eating and therefore the need for washing. It is obviously a symbol of a new beginning, a new ritual.)

8 Then he told them to dip out a little and take it to the person in charge of the feast. 9 And when they did, the person tasted it and went to the groom, and asked why this great wine had not been served first. 10 He said, "Usually people serve the best wine first, and the cheaper wine only when people have already become happy. 11 But you have saved the best wine till now."

12 After the feast Jesus, his mother, sisters and brothers, and his close friends, went down to Capernaum to Jesus' home and stayed there a few days.

13 Then they walked on to Jerusalem for the Passover Feast. 14 When he went to the temple to pray, he was distracted by all the business of selling animals for the sacrifice. 15 He knew that they had not heard the Prophet Hosea when he said, "God does not want sacrifice, he wants you to love one another." He decided to put a stop to all this. So he made a whip and drove all the large animals out of the temple. The money changers, who didn't leave when he told them to, had their tables turned over. 16 He shouted to everyone, "Get all this nonsense out of here, so we can pray and listen to God rather than hear the clanging of coins!"

18 The leading Jews heard of this and came and asked him what he thought he was doing. They told him that if he had the right to do this, he had to prove it with some sign. 19 Jesus said, "Destroy this temple of God and I will rebuild it in three days." 20 They mocked him and said, "It took forty-six years to build this temple, and you think you can do it in three days?" 21 But Jesus was talking about the temple of his body, his heart, where God really dwells. 22 When Jesus rose from the dead his friends remembered this and realized what he had meant.

23 While Jesus was there for the Feast, he taught many things and healed many people, so a lot of people began to believe in him. 24 But Jesus knew that their faith was still young and would need to be tested so it could grow. 25 He knew they would not really understand all that he had been teaching until the coming of the Spirit at Pentecost.

CHAPTER 3

1 A leading Pharisee named Nicodemus came to visit Jesus at night, because he was afraid to be seen with him in the daytime. *2* He said to Jesus, "Teacher, some of us realize you come from God because you do the things of God."

3 Jesus replied, "I assure you that unless a person is reborn in the Spirit, he cannot live in Divine Life." *4* Nicodemus was shocked by this and said, "Can an old man like me reenter his mother's womb and be born again?" *5* Jesus replied, "I assure you that unless people are reborn through both water and the Spirit they cannot live in the Divine Life. *6* Human birth and Divine rebirth are very different things. *7* Why are you surprised when I say you must be reborn? *8* Brother Wind blows and goes wherever he wishes. Those reborn in the Spirit do whatever they are inspired to do by God, as you have seen me do.

9 Nicodemus said, "But how can this possibly be?" *10* Jesus said, "I know that this is hard to understand, but I promise you it is true. *14* Moses lifted up the sacred snake in the desert so that anyone wounded had only to look at it to be healed. This prefigured my coming; this pointed to my Call to Heal. This is why I came: to help heal humanity into Divinity. *15* I invite all to enter fully into this Divine Life. All you have to do is really look at your Divinity to be healed in your humanity.

16 "For God's Love is so deep that he sent me, to announce that all who believe in his Message, and walk in it, will have Divine Life.

17 "God wanted the rest of his daughters and sons to know and have their Birth Right. *18* People are free to believe or not believe that they are daughters and sons of God, but what they believe does not change the reality of who they are.

19 "And this belief in Divine Life may begin with my teaching, but ultimately it comes from recognizing their very own deepest core. The Greeks say "Know yourself." I give the same advice since it explains why I have come. For me it is not a commandment, but a healing blessing. My basic healing is showing you your own Divinity, your True Identity. Know that you are Divine.

20 "If you feel like you are stumbling through Life, it is probably because you are trying to walk in the dark, trying to walk without light. The Light that I bring can hurt the eyes until it heals the heart. To walk in the light is to walk in Divinity. *21* To walk in the light is to walk in God. Those who walk in God are truly blessed. Those who believe they are only human lack the blessing of Truth."

22 After this Jesus and his friends went into Judea to minister there. *23* John was baptizing in Aenon near Salim, because there was plenty of water there. *24* John had not yet been arrested. *26* People told John that Jesus was also baptizing, and

John reminded them that he had told them he was not the Christ they were expecting, but that Jesus was.

31 Meanwhile Jesus was teaching, "I have come and shared the Words and Actions of God. God's Message is beyond Truth; his caring is beyond Love; what you see in me is simply the reflection of God. *32* You too are reflections of God. *33* Let his Truth and Love shine through you.

34 "Dad loves me and gives me Divine Life. *35* I love you and give you Divine Life through the Good News. Love others and give them Divine Life. *36* This is the Trinity of Action that reflects the Trinity of Love."

CHAPTER 4

1 As Jesus became more aware that the Pharisees were getting concerned that his ministry was expanding even more than John's, *2* he decided it was better to leave Judea and return to Galilee. *4* To do this he had to pass through Samaria. *5* There he came to a town called Sychar, which is near the plot of land that Jacob had given to Joseph. *6* Jacob's well was there and so Jesus stopped at it for a lunch break.

7 His friends had gone into town to get something for lunch, *8* when a woman came to the well to draw water. Jesus asked her for a drink. *9* The Samaritan lady asked him how he could possibly be asking her for a drink, since Jews generally won't even speak to a Samaritan. *10* Jesus answered her, "I have come to break down all these barriers and open all to Love, to God." This Living Water that I will proclaim to all will really quench your thirst.

11 The lady responded, "You don't even have a bucket and this well is deep. How are you going to give me any kind of water? *12* Are you even greater than our father Jacob, who gave us this well? (He had used it for his own family and flock.) *13* Jesus told her, "Anyone who drinks this water will eventually get thirsty again. *14* But the water I will give has eternal life, Divine Life." *15* So the lady said, "Sir, please give me this new water so I don't have to come here every day to draw water."

16 Jesus said to her, "Go and call your husband." *17* She told him she didn't have a husband. *18* He said, "That is true, for even though you have had five husbands, the one you are now living with is not your husband." *19* She responded, "Sir, I can see you are a prophet. *20* Our ancestors worshipped on this mountain, but you folks say we should worship in Jerusalem." *21* Jesus said, "The time has come to forget about where to worship God. *22* The question now is rather: 'Where is God?' *23* When we answer that question we will know that God is in our hearts, and so we need to go there to find him and love him. *24* God is Spirit and so he is not really in a place. The only "place" he is in is our hearts since he is Love." *25* The woman then said, "I know that the Christ is coming and that he will be able to explain all these things to us." 26 Jesus said, "I am he. I would love to share wisdom with you."

27 At that moment his friends returned from town and were very surprised that he was talking with a woman, since that was not generally done, but they didn't say anything. 28 The woman left her water jar there and hurried back to town. 29 She told the people what had happened at the well and told them to come and meet this person. She said she believed that he could well be the Christ. 30 So they went out with her.

31 Meanwhile his friends had returned and urged him to eat something of what they had brought. 32 But he said, "I have food that you don't know about." 33 His friends thought perhaps someone had brought him some food while they were gone. 34 But Jesus said, "What nourishes me is to do the things Dad has asked me to do. 35 That is why I came; that is what nourishes me. 36 The time is ripe for the harvest. Some sow; some harvest. 37 We need to be prepared to do both. 38 I have sent you to harvest what you did not sow. Now you must sow what others will harvest.

39 Many of the Samaritans had already begun to believe in him because of the witness of the lady: "He was able to tell me everything about my life." 40 So they invited him to stay with them, and he stayed there for a couple of days. 41 As they continued to listen to him, their belief was based on what he was

saying. 42 They thanked the lady for bringing them to him, but told her that now they believed he was the Christ not because of what she had said, but because of what they themselves had heard him say.

43 After that he continued on to Galilee. 44 He had concerns about going there since he knew prophets are not generally accepted in their native place. 45 But this time the people there accepted him, because they had been up to the Feast in Jerusalem and had seen what he did there.

46 Then he went back to Cana, where he had transformed water into wine. There was a government official in Capernaum whose son was very sick. 47 When he heard that Jesus had come back home from Jerusalem, he went to Cana to ask him to heal his son, who was near death. 48 Jesus told him, "I am always happy to heal people since it not only cures their body, it also helps cure their unbelief."

49 The official was so concerned about his son that he really didn't hear what Jesus had said. He asked him again if he would come and heal his son before he died. 50 Jesus said simply, "You may go back home. Your beloved son is going to live." 51 So the official left immediately for home. On the way there he ran into some of his servants who were coming to bring the good news that his son had recovered. 52 He asked them when he had gotten better. They told him it was the day before

around one o'clock in the afternoon. *53* He realized that was the exact time when Jesus had told him his son was going to live. So he and his whole household became believers. *54* Now this was the second sign that Jesus showed when he came to Galilee from Judea.

CHAPTER 5

1 After this there was another Feast and so Jesus went up to Jerusalem to celebrate it. *2* In Jerusalem there is a pool called the Sheep Gate. *3* Every day a lot of the sick and all those seeking healing went to the five porticos there, where a Healing Angel would sometimes stir the water. *5* One man who was there had been sick for thirty-eight years. *6* When Jesus saw him lying there and knew that he had been sick for so long, he asked him if he really wanted to be healed. *7* The man said, "Sir, I have no one to help me down to the pool after the Angel has stirred the water, so someone else always beats me there." *8* Jesus said, "Get up and take your mat and walk home." *9* He was instantly healed and went home rejoicing. This took place on a Sabbath.

10 When some Jewish leaders saw the man carrying his mat, they told him he was doing something that was not permitted on the Sabbath. *11* He said to them, "The man who healed me told me to carry my mat home." *12* So they asked him who this man was. *13* He said he had no idea who it was.

14 Later Jesus went looking for him, and told him of God's great love for him. *15* The man then went to the Jewish leaders and told them that the man who had healed him was called Jesus. *16* So the Jewish leaders began to persecute Jesus for breaking the Sabbath law. *17* Jesus told them that his Dad God healed on the Sabbath and that he was going to keep following his good example.

18 This made the Jewish leaders really angry because he seemed to be making himself equal to God. *19* Jesus said to them, "You surely know that it is good for a son to imitate his Dad; I simply watch mine and imitate him. *20* I have come to reveal his Love through imitating his actions. I do only what I see Dad do. For Dad loves me and shows me everything. Each day he shows me something even more wonderful, even more revealing, of his immense Love for us all. *21* As Dad even raises the dead and gives them new life, Divine Life, I will do the same to those who open their ears and hearts to this magnificent revelation. This revelation of love comes not only in the words I have heard from Dad's heart, but also in the actions of love that I have seen him do. You may not yet be able to see what he does, so he has sent me in a visible form to help you actually see his immense love for you. He loves you as much as he loves me. My heart burns in wanting to help you see and believe this magnificent Truth.

22 "Dad does not judge you, as you have believed. Love does not judge, but heals through acceptance. Dad is already in your deepest being. When you truly see yourself, you will truly see your God. And when you see your God, you will see love, since God is Love.

23 "I assure you that those who allow my Message into their hearts already have Divine Life in them. Those who still believe they are only human are headed only toward death, since mere humans always die. 24 Those who have heard and accepted the Good News that they are God, are already living eternal life since God(s) lives forever. Eternal life is the Divine Life of God. 25 The time has come for those headed toward human death to hear my Message and enter into Divine Life. 26 For as God has Divine Life, 27 he has given that to me to reveal to you. 28 And don't be surprised when you see the dead rise in this Divine Life, since my Message goes even beyond the grave.

30 "I can't repeat enough that Dad and I are One. I think as he thinks; I love as he loves; I will as he wills. He is not different from me, but simply the other side of me. 31 You can't reach this wisdom with your mind, and sometimes not even with your heart. 32 To find this you must be led by the torchlight of your Divinity.

33 "You sent friends to John to seek the Truth, and he shared it. 34 There is nothing more important than Truth, since it is the very

essence of God. 35 There is nothing more important to live than the Truth, since it is the very Life of God. 36 My actions show the Truth of my Life. 37 Your actions must become a scripture that all can see, a fountain from which all can drink. 38 We sometimes cannot see others' hearts, but if we can see their actions we know what is in their hearts. 39 They may slip; they may fall; but what is important is only that they get up and walk on in this Truth.

40 "Don't look for human praise, since that praise often comes from worldly values. 41 True actions never need praise, since the aroma of their love is so easy to smell. 42 Wouldn't it be wonderful if we learned to smell Divinity? 43 This would help us easily keep on the Path to God. 44 This would help us walk into ourselves. 45 This would point always to love, always to service. 46 The best teaching is done without words, 47 because its meaning is crystal clear, just as our lives should always be."

CHAPTER 6

1 After this Jesus went across the Sea of Galilee. 2 A large crowd quickly gathered, since they had heard about his miracles of healing the sick and feeding the multitudes. 3 The Jewish Feast of Passover was coming. 4 Jesus went up on the mountain with his friends. 5 When he looked back and saw how very many people were following them, he asked Philip, "Where are we going to be able to buy enough food

to feed this crowd?" 6 He asked this even though he already knew what he was going to do. 7 Philip replied, "Even a half-year's wages wouldn't be enough to buy food for all these people. 8 One of the apostles, Andrew, said to Jesus, 9 "There is a boy here who has five barley loaves and two fish, but that is not a drop in the bucket of what we need." 10 Jesus told them to have the people sit down on the grass there. So everyone sat down, about ten thousand all together. 11 Then Jesus took the five loaves and gave thanks, and gave them to all the people, together with some of the fish. 12 When everyone had eaten, Jesus asked those with him to pick up what was left. 13 When they had done this, they were amazed that there were twelve large baskets left over from the loaves and fish. 14 When the people saw this sign they said, "This is surely a Prophet." 15 They wanted to make him king, so he slipped away to pray.

16 That evening his friends went down to the sea and took a boat to row over to Capernaum. 18 A strong wind came up and the sea got very choppy. 19 When they had rowed three or four miles, they saw Jesus walking toward them on the water, and they got scared. 20 But Jesus told them not to be afraid since it was he. 21 They reached out to take him into the boat, but at that moment they arrived at the shore. 22 The next day the crowd from the previous day were confused as to what had happened to Jesus, since he was not there, but also had not gone with the others in the boat. 23 There were other boats there now, 24 and so a lot of the crowd got in them and went over to Capernaum too.

25 They finally found Jesus. He was concerned about the reason they were looking for him. 27 So he said to them, "My dear friends, I cannot stress enough the importance of keeping your priorities clean and clear. Remember the human body is going to die; only the Divine Body will live forever. So while indeed you need to nourish the human body, it is the Divine Body that gives you True Life. 28 Take care of the human body, but concentrate on the Divine Body. 29 Every day try to be a little more Divine, a little more alive, a little more Love, a little more God.

30 Let me explain my real gift to you. I have given you bread to nourish your physical body, but I have done this mainly to help you see your Divinity. As we relate with one another we become one another. You help keep me human so that I may complete my Mission here; I help you be Divine just as my Dad has made me Divine. So eat the bread that I give you knowing that I am actually giving you me. 31 His friends said, "If it is true that you are calling us to be Divine, to be God; how can we possibly learn how to act like God and to do the works of God?"

32 Jesus responded, "To do the work of God you must first believe

God. Belief is what expands humanity into Divinity. Belief changes reality. It completes creation by making it more Divine. God made creation in his own image, so when creation knows itself, it will know it is Divine. It will see God's image in itself. To do God's work you must come to believe that all of God's work is Divine, is God. This belief in unity rebirths creation for humanity. As humanity believes its own Divinity, the world will become more the Love from which it was made, and then all the birthing pains you see around you will cease and creation will be the Love it was intended to be, and has always really been."

33 Then his friends said, "Give us proof to help our belief." Jesus responded, "That is what I came to do. Dad tried to do this by giving you manna every day from Heaven, but you saw it only as nourishment for your bodies, when it was meant also to be nourishment for your Divinity. To eat food from heaven was meant to bring you into heaven, into Love. I came to help you transform your belief with a deeper understanding of this bread from heaven. I am this bread from heaven. This time the bread from heaven came in human form to help you see your divine form. He who stands before you is bread of heaven given for the world. It is given that the world may become heaven. I am revealing the link between heaven and humanity, so that humanity can return to heaven.

34 Then they began to understand and said, "Then give us this bread always, Brother!" 35 Jesus said, "I will give you this bread to reveal to you that WE can be this Bread. When we eat the Bread of Relationship we become the bridge (re)connecting God and humanity. When you eat the Divinity that I Am, you become the Divinity that You Are. When we have reached this Unity, your heart will no longer be hungry. Your eyes have seen my Divine actions simply to help your heart make the leap of faith to realize that you too can do these very same things. 36 You sometimes still see me as outside of you; that is why I want to get inside of you. You still see Divinity as outside of you; that's why I want to get Divinity inside of you. That's why I come to you as bread. Your Call is now to bring Divine Bread to the whole world so that all may finally walk into their own Divinity. We are what we eat. Eating Divinity is the Path to being Divinity.

37 "When Dad came to the Jews in the desert as manna, many still did not believe. When I tell you that I will come to you as bread, many do not believe. Lack of belief is lack of Life. I have come to bring you new Life. When you eat the Bread of God you will become God and live. When you eat the bread of fear, you will die. Dad wants all his daughters and sons to have his Divine Life.

That is why he sent me. That is why I came. You can choose to live or you can choose to die. You can choose to believe or you can choose to fear. But no matter what you do, you will remain the daughters and sons of God. And in some lifetime you will all come to believe; you will come to Life.

38 "I have come down from heaven to reveal life to all of you. I will become bread to feed your faith. 39 Faith is the leap to Reality. 40 And even if you don't believe, reality does not change; you simply aren't aware of it yet. The ceremony of Breaking the Bread and Drinking the Wine is not about me, it is about you eating and drinking in your Divine Identity."

41 The Jewish leaders were extremely upset because he said he was bread from heaven. 42 They said, "Who does he think he is?" So Jesus said, "Why are you upset? To become one with God you simply need to respond to God's invitation and walk into his Life. 43 The prophets said that God would teach those who want to learn. And everyone who listens to me listens to God. 44 You may not hear God talking to your heart, but you can hear me talking through your ears. It may be hard to see God, but it is easy to see me. 45 And to hear and believe me is to have Divine Life. 46 I am the Bread of Life. I am the glue that binds you to God. 47 Your ancestors ate manna in the desert and still died because they did not believe. 48 If you eat this Bread, if you believe this Word, you will have Divine Life and will never die. 49 Your body may fall off but your Life will walk on. 50 I am the Living Bread that came down from heaven to take you back to heaven, to union with God, to Divine Life. 51 This Bread is the Essence of God who gives His Divine Life to all who will believe and eat it."

52 The Jewish leaders scoffed at this and said, "How can we eat this man? How can we swallow what he is saying?" Jesus said, "I assure you that unless you can swallow what I say, unless you eat the Bread that I am and drink my Life's Blood, you may never realize you are Divine. You will continue to believe you are simply human. And as great as that is, it is not your true Divinity.

"But if you eat me, if you accept the Word that I am; and drink of my Life's Blood, I will be in you and you will be in me. We will be so completely one that you will never die, you will simply walk out of your body into your God. You will walk out of your humanity and into your Divinity.

"Our Divine Dad gave me life and sent me to reveal this same Divine Life to you. 53 If you eat this Bread and become this Bread, you will have Life. If you don't eat this Bread, you could well die, 54 and need to be reborn again until you have Divine Life and can live forever. 55 Those who eat my body and drink my blood welcome me into their lives, as I have already welcomed them into mine. *56* As you do this, I come into you and you come into me, and we become the same thing. *57* Just as I and Dad are the same thing. *58* Our Divine Life will come into you, and you will come into Divine Life." *59* Jesus said all these things in the synagogue in Capernaum.

60 Then many of those listening, even some of those close to him, said, "This is just too hard to swallow. Who can take this seriously?" *61* So Jesus said to his friends, "Does this shock you? I am bread to eat. *62* You are to become this bread so that others may eat of you too. *63* And remember that I am talking on a spiritual level here, not simply the physical level. *64* I know there are some of you who do not believe this. *65* That is why I have told you to ask Dad God for help with your faith."

66 Because of this, many of his friends left and went their separate ways. *67* He asked the apostles if they wanted to leave too. *68* Peter said, "To whom shall we go? You have the words that walk us into Divine Life. *69* We have come to believe that you are Christ."

CHAPTER 7

1 During this time Jesus ministered in Galilee, not wanting to go to Judea because the Jewish leaders there wanted to kill him. *2* But the Feast of Tabernacles was near, *3* and so he considered going to Jerusalem anyway. *4* His friends were leaving

for the feast and he told them to go on ahead, since he still had not made up his mind. *10* Sometime after they had left he decided finally to go himself. *11* But he went secretly to avoid the Jewish leaders. *12* They kept wondering and asking if anyone had seen him. *13* But no one wanted to talk about Jesus, fearing they would get in trouble with the Jewish leaders. *14* Finally in the middle of the Feast Jesus went up to the temple to preach. The Jewish leaders were amazed that he knew so much. *15* They asked how he knew these things when he had never studied.

16 Jesus said, "What I know did not come from studying, but from Revelation. *17* My Dad sends me Divine Energy and my heart puts it into words. *18* Those who really open their hearts will know what I say comes from Dad, *19* and will also be able to receive Revelation themselves. *20* You can all become receivers of Revelation. *21* Those who teach what they have learned by studying often try to impress people with their knowledge. *22* While those who receive Revelations, are humbled by the experience."

25 Some of those who were listening to him said, "Isn't this the one the Jewish leaders want to kill? *26* And here he is preaching openly in the temple. Do you suppose the leaders now believe he is the Christ? *27* But we know where he came from and when the Christ comes no one is to know where he came from." *28* Jesus knew this and said, "You say you know where I came from, but you don't really. *29* I came from my Dad and your Dad, to bring us all back together again." *30* At this the Jewish leaders arrived and tried to arrest him, but they couldn't because many people who were saying, *31* "Can the Christ perform miracles any greater than this one has?" *32* The Pharisees overheard this and insisted that he be arrested.

33 Then Jesus said, "I am not going to be with you much longer. I am going home, back to Dad's place, Dad's heart. *34* You will look for me but won't be able to find me. *35* You will be able to come and find me in Dad's house only when you realize he is your Dad too."

37 On the last day of the feast Jesus cried out in the temple, *38* "Those of you who are thirsty, come and drink of my Life, My Love, My Living Water. I thirst for you as much as you thirst for God. God is the only thing that will slake your thirst. Those who drink of Divinity will be filled to overflowing and even have Loving Water flowing out of them." *39* Here Jesus was referring to his Spirit, the Spirit of Love, the Spirit who was to flow more fully into them after he resurrected, and to flow out of them into the world.

40 Some of those who heard him said, "This is truly the Prophet;" others said, "this is truly the Christ." *41* Others said that he could not be the Christ because he was from Galilee, *42* when the scriptures say he is to come from the House of David and be born in Bethlehem. *43* So the crowd was divided about him. *44* Some wanted to arrest him, but no one could.

45 The guards finally went back to the high priests, who asked them why they had not arrested Jesus. *46* They said, "No one has ever spoken as he does." *47* They sneered at them for this and said, *48* "Have any of the leaders believed him? *49* The crowd doesn't know the law and so don't know what they are talking about. *50* Nicodemus, who had come to Jesus before in the night, said, *51* "Does our law condemn a person before he has been heard?" *52* They responded to him, "Check the scriptures and you will see that the Christ does not come from Galilee."

CHAPTER 8

1 Then Jesus went to the Mount of Olives to pray. *2* The next morning he again went to the temple to teach. *3* The scribes and Pharisees brought a woman who had been caught in adultery, and made her stand in front of him. *4* They said to him, "Teacher, this woman was just caught in the very act of adultery. *5* The law says that we are to stone her. What do you say?" *6* They did this to test him, and to have cause to bring charges against him. *7* But Jesus seemed lost in prayer. *8* They kept badgering him for an answer, and so finally he looked at them and said, "Let whoever has never broken a law be the first one to throw a stone at her."

9 At that they began to slowly leave, beginning with the elders. Finally she stood alone before him. *10* Jesus smiled at her and said, "Sister, has no one condemned you?" *11* She said, "No, no one." Jesus then said to her, "I have asked Dad to help you to love. Now go in peace."

12 Later Jesus began to teach again saying, "I am Light for the world. I have come to help you out of the darkness of fear. If we walk together, you can share my Light and I can share yours." *13* The Pharisees objected to this teaching. *14* Jesus responded, "Brothers, look at your hearts and see if any light is coming from them. I know you want to serve Dad, but simply haven't yet learned how. I will pray for you as I prayed for the Sister you brought to me before, since we are all one. *15* If you continue to judge, you will continue to be unhappy, and your light will not be able to shine. *16* Your invitation from Dad is to move away from the law and into the Light of Love. *17* If you can respond to this invitation, your life will change dramatically, *18* and you will begin living from your essence, from your Identity, (you're) your Divinity. *19* My only desire is that you walk out of the law into the heart of Dad. *20* That is what you long for, even though it is often so hard to see and to admit."

21 Then Jesus said to them again, "I am going home soon, but you won't be able to follow me. You may die before you realize you are Divine, because you have not believed me. As long as you believe you are only human, your only path is to die.

22 The Jewish leaders said, "Is he going to kill himself since he says we cannot go where he is going?" *23* Jesus replied, "You still believe you are only human, but I know I am God. Your views are worldly, but mine are not. *24* That is why I said to you that you will die, because if you do not believe that I am God, and that you are God; you will die in your humanity. *25* What I am telling you is what Dad has asked me to. *26* Again, remember that his is a standing invitation. I pray some day you may hear it and respond to it."

31 Then Jesus spoke to those who were beginning to believe and said, "If you believe what I have been telling you, you are on the right Path. You are on the Path to Truth, and it is the Truth that will free you from the beliefs that bind you." *32* They protested that they were daughters and sons of Abraham and had always been free. *34* Jesus said, "Unless you have walked totally out of the darkness and into the Light, out of fear and into Love; you are not really free. *37* I have come to reestablish the Covenant of Abraham, the Covenant of Love, the Family of God; and yet you are trying to kill me. *39* If you were truly daughters and sons of Abraham, you would be supporting my mission rather than trying to stop it. *42* And if you were truly daughters and sons of God, who is Love, you would love me and listen to his loving Call to rejoin the Family of God. *43* I beg you to open your hearts and your ears and hear your Dad calling you though me speaking words of Love to you, speaking words of healing to you. *51* Dad has asked me to reveal everlasting life to you, even his own Divine Life. That invitation stands forever, and all you need to do is open the door to your heart to hear it and receive it.

56 "Your Dad Abraham longed to see this day and to have his daughters and sons hear these words." *57* They said to him, "You are not yet fifty years old, so you could not possibly know that about Abraham." *58* Jesus said, "Dad has already shared his eternal, Divine Life with me. I know Abraham and all the Prophets." *59* With that they picked up rocks to stone him, but he slipped out of the temple.

CHAPTER 9

1 Later as he was walking along Jesus saw a man who had been blind all his life. *2* His friends asked him, "Is he blind for something he did, or was it something his parents did?" *3* Jesus responded, "It was nothing that he or his parents did that caused him to be blind; but now we can use his blindness to help people see Dad's Love. *4* I must do the healings that Dad has asked me to do; because when I go, many will forget that they too can heal in my Spirit. *5* While I am here, it is easier to help people see, to help people believe."

6 When he had said these things he spat on the ground and made a paste with the clay. Then he rubbed this on the blind man's eyes as he prayed. *7* Then Jesus told the man to go and wash in the pool of Siloam. So he went and washed there and came back completely healed. *8* The people were amazed at this and said, "Isn't this the blind beggar that used to sit here?" *9* Some said it was; others said it wasn't. Then the man said, "I am he." *10* They asked him who had healed his blindness. He said, *11* "A man named Jesus made a paste out of clay and spittle, and anointed my eyes. Then he told me to go wash in the pool of Siloam and I did. When I walked out of the pool, my eyes were opened." *12* Then they asked him where Jesus was and he said he had no idea.

13 They took the man who had been healed to the Jewish leaders since it was the Sabbath. *14* The leaders asked him what had happened; *15* so he related again what Jesus had done to heal him. *16* The leaders then said that Jesus was not a man of God since he did not keep the law of the Sabbath. The crowd then said, "Then how can he heal a blind man if he is not of God?" *17* So there was a dispute between them, and they asked the man who had been born blind, "What do you say about him?" The man said, "I believe he is a Prophet."

18 The Jewish leaders still did not believe that he had been born blind and had been healed; so they sent for his parents. *19* They asked them if he was born blind; and if so, how he could now see. *20* His parents said it was true that he had been born blind, but that they had no idea how he could now see. *21* They told the leaders to ask him since he was an adult because they did not want to get into trouble. *22* They knew the leaders would expel anyone from the synagogue who said Jesus was the Christ.

24 The Jewish leaders called back the man who had been healed and told him to admit that Jesus was a sinner. *25* The man said, "I don't know if he is a sinner or not; but I do know I had been blind from birth and now I can see." *26* They asked him to repeat again what had happened. *27* He said, "I have already told you everything. Why do you want to hear it again? Do you want to become his followers?" *28* They called him an idiot and then said, "You may be his follower, but we are Moses' disciples. *29* We know God spoke to Moses, but as for this fellow, we don't know where he is from."

30 The man answered saying, "I find it amazing that you don't know where he is from when he opened my eyes. *31* We all know God does not listen to sinners, but only to those who follow him. *32* Never in the history of the world has anyone opened the eyes of someone born blind. *33* If this man were not from God, he could not do the works of God." *34* They were furious and said,

"You are a dirty sinner and you dare to teach us?" Then they had him thrown out of the synagogue.

35 Jesus heard about this and went looking for him. *36* When he found him, he said, "I would now like to help open the eyes of your heart. Our Dad God asked me to come and tell everyone that they are his daughters and sons. Do you believe this?" The man replied, "I would like to, but I don't understand it." *37* Jesus said, "I have opened your eyes, but the eyes of the heart are often even harder to open. Sometimes we just have to believe, knowing we will later understand it." *38* The man bowed down saying. "I do believe it." *39* Jesus said, "Dad sent me into the world to fill it with this Truth. Those with open hearts will have their eyes truly opened. And those who keep their hearts closed; already have their eyes closed."

40 Some of the Jewish leaders overheard this and came up to Jesus and said, "Are you saying that our eyes are closed, that we are blind?" *41* Jesus said to them, "If you were simply blind, it would not be so bad, but you believe you are the only ones who see, who know the Truth; when in reality you are soaked in lies.

CHAPTER 10

1 "I assure you that the person who does not go into the sheep corral through the gate, but sneaks over the fence, is a thief. *2* The one who comes in through the gate is the shepherd of the sheep. *3* The gatekeeper knows him and opens the gate to him. His sheep recognize his voice and follow him out when he calls to them. *4* He leads them and chats with them as friends. *5* They would never follow a stranger because they would not trust him. Trust develops through friendship."

6 Jesus used this illustration to teach them the importance of shepherding the people; but they did not understand him. *7* So Jesus tried again and said, "I assure you that I am the gate to the sheep. I am the example of how to be a Shepherd. *8* The spiritual leaders who have come before were not really interested in the people and the people knew that. *9* I am the gate. I am the Way. If you walk through me, you will find pasture; you will find true nourishment for your life. *10* The path of the others often leads to death; but I have come to give Life, Divine Life. Anyone who doesn't know his sheep, is not a true pastor but either a lazy man or a business man. *11* I am the Good Shepherd, and the Good Shepherd gives his Life for (to) his sheep.

12 "On the other hand a hireling, who is simply paid to take care of another's sheep, will run off when a wolf comes. He does not want to risk his life for something that is not his. *13* He runs away and lets the wolf ravage the sheep because he has no real commitment to them. *14* I am the Good Shepherd. I know all my sheep, and all my sheep know me. *15* My Dad knows and loves me; and

I know and love my Dad. And so I give my life for my sheep, and I give Life to my sheep because you are my true sisters and brothers. *16* I want to be very clear that I am not speaking here of only my Jewish sisters and brothers, but about All my sisters and brothers throughout the world and throughout the universe. *17* As Dad's Word spreads and people follow it, there will eventually be only one sheepfold and one shepherd. Until that day there will be wolves that come and scatter his flock. Do not follow them. Follow only those who teach the Word of Love and Unity. My prayer for Unity will happen, and blessed are those who help to bring it about. I am going to give my own Life to realize this prayer. Dad has asked me to do this and I do it with Love. I give up Life that you may receive Life. *18* My main concern is that you be open to the Life I freely give you. The wolf has come and scattered Hearts, and Hearts are the door I want to walk through. Help my Heart and your Heart become One Heart. Please help me fulfill what Dad has asked me to do." *19* All of this caused an uproar among the Jewish leaders. *20* Many said, "He is a lunatic! Why do you listen to him?" *21* Others responded, "His words may sound crazy, but his actions are of God. Who else could heal a blind person?"

22 It was the Feast of Dedication, and it was cold in Jerusalem. *23* Jesus went into the temple and was walking in Solomon's Porch.

24 The Jewish leaders surrounded him and said, "How long are you going to keep us in suspense? If you are really the Christ, tell us."

25 Jesus said, "I have already told you, but you would not believe me. What good are words when you don't even believe my actions? Dad told me to do the works of God to help you believe that I am God. 26 But you don't even believe the actions of God, so how can you believe God? Your closed hearts have closed your eyes and even your ears. To follow me you need an open heart, so you can hear what I say and see what I do. 27 My friends are so close they can even hear my heart beat, as I can hear theirs. 28 And I give them Divine Life, and they shall never leave it. Once your heart starts beating with Divinity you are home and don't ever want to leave. 29 My Dad who has given them to me has a Heart big enough for all to enter, and once you are in his hand and in his heart, there is no way to escape his Love. 30 Dad and I are so intimate that we are One."

31 Then the Jewish leaders picked up stones to kill him. 32 Jesus said, "I have done many marvelous works for you that my Dad asked me to do. For which of these works do you want to kill me?" 33 The Jewish leaders replied, "It is not for any marvelous works that we are going to kill you, but for your blasphemous words. You are only a man and you claim to be God." 34 Jesus raised his Spirit and Heart and almost shouted, "Can't you see that even your own scriptures say, 'You are God!' 35 I am not only saying that I am God; I am saying that **you all are God**, as do your own scriptures. Don't you even believe your own scriptures? 36 If you did really believe your own scriptures which say that you are God, you would not be upset when I say that I am God, and that you are God. 37 If I don't do the works of my Dad and your Dad, my God and your God, do not believe me. 38 But since I indeed do my Dad's works, even if you have trouble believing my words, believe my works so that you will know that Dad is in me and I am in Dad."

39 The Jewish leaders were now so furious that they tried to grab him, but he slipped away and went out of the temple. 40 He then went again up beyond the Jordan River where John had baptized and stayed there in prayer.

41 Then many people discovered he was there and came to him and said, "John did not perform any works like you have; but we can see that all the words he said about you were true." 42 And many began to walk with him.

CHAPTER 11

1 Lazarus of Bethany, where Mary and her sister Martha lived, was very sick. 2 This was the same Mary who anointed Jesus with fragrant oil, whose brother Lazarus was sick. 3 So the sisters sent word to him saying, "Your dear friend Lazarus is

very sick." *4* When Jesus heard this he said, "The sickness is not to take his life but to demonstrate the power of God, and also the power of the daughters and sons of God." *5* Jesus loved Mary, Martha and Lazarus very much. *6* But when he got this news he stayed on where he was. *7* Then he said to his friends, "Let's go to Judea again." *8* His friends were shocked at this and said, "Teacher, we were just there and the Jewish leaders were trying to kill you. Do you think it is really wise to go back there?" *9* Jesus replied, "If you walk in the Light there is no darkness to be afraid of. *10* But if you walk in the dark you are going to trip up because there is no Light there." *11* Then he said, "Our friend Lazarus is asleep and I am going to go there and wake him up." *12* His friends said, "If he is sleeping he must be getting better." *13* But Jesus had been speaking of the sleep of death. *14* So he said plainly, "Lazarus is dead. *15* I am glad for your sakes we were not there because you would have been sad. Now I have an opportunity to increase your faith. So let's go."

16 Thomas said to the other friends, "Let's all go with him that we may die with him." *17* So when they all finally got to Bethany, Jesus was told that Lazarus had already been in the tomb four days. *18* Now Bethany was only about two miles from Jerusalem. *19* And some of the Jewish leaders had come to help comfort Mary and Martha over their brother's death. *21* Martha said to Jesus, "Teacher, if you had come earlier my brother would not have died. *22* But I know that even now whatever you ask Dad, he will do for you." *23* Jesus said, "Your brother will come back to life." *24* Martha said, "I know he will come back to life in the resurrection at the end of the world." *25* Jesus said to her, "We are Resurrection; We are Life. Belief bridges Realities. Those who can walk over the Bridge of Faith into Life will never die, even when their bodies slip away. *26* Those who truly believe in Life can never die. Do you believe this?" *27* She said to him, "Yes, I believe *you* are a Christ, a Son of God, Who was prophesized to come."

28 Then she went back to the house and quietly said to her sister Mary, "The Teacher has come and wants to see you." *29* As soon as Mary heard this she ran out to meet him. *30* Jesus had not gotten into town yet, but was still where he had talked to Martha. *31* When Mary's friends realized she had gone out, they went after her, thinking that she was going to the tomb to cry. *32* When Mary got to where Jesus was, she hugged him and said, "If you had been here my brother would not have died."

33 When Jesus saw her crying and her friends also crying, his heart was about to break. *34* He asked where they had laid him out. They said to him, "Teacher, come and see." *35* Then he too began to cry. *36* Those close enough to see this said, "See how much he loves them!" *37* And some of them said, "We know this man opened the eyes of the blind; couldn't he have kept this man from dying?" *38* Then Jesus, with his heart breaking, came to the tomb. It was a cave with a stone used as the door. *39* Jesus told the people to take away the stone. Martha said, "Teacher, he has been there four days, there is going to be a stench."

40 Jesus said to her. "Didn't I tell you that true Life comes from believing?" *41* Then they took the stone door away from the tomb. Jesus lifted his eyes to heaven and said, "Dad, thanks for hearing me. *42* I know you always hear me. So I say this to help those here believe that you are the One who sent me."

43 Then he shouted out, "Lazarus, come out here." *44* And the dead man hobbled out bound head and foot with grave wrappings, and his face was wrapped with a cloth too. Jesus said, "Unwrap him and let him go free." *45* Then many of the Jews who had followed Mary to the tomb and seen what Jesus had done began to believe him.

46 Some went to the Jewish leaders and told them what Jesus had done. *47* Then the high priests and Jewish leaders held a council and talked about what they could possibly do since Jesus worked so many signs. *48* They said, "If we don't do something, soon everyone will be believing him. Then the Romans will come and take our temple and destroy our nation. *49* Caiaphas,

who was high priest that year said, *50* "Don't you realize it is better to have one man die than the whole nation?" *51* This was not simply his idea, but as high priest that year he was able to prophesy that Jesus was going to die for the nation. *52* And not simply for the Jewish Nation, but for all the people of the world; for all the daughters and sons of God. *53* From that day on the high priests were plotting ways to kill Jesus. *54* Jesus knew this and so no longer walked openly among the Jews, but went to the desert city of Ephraim and stayed there with his friends.

55 Later when the Jewish Feast of Passover was coming up, many were going to Jerusalem to purify themselves for the Feast. *56* Many of them were looking for Jesus and wondering if he was going to come to the Feast. *57* The chief priests and all the Jewish leaders had put out the word that anyone who knew where Jesus was must report this to them so they could arrest him.

CHAPTER 12

1 Six days before Passover Jesus came back to Bethany where he had raised Lazarus from the dead. *2* Jesus had supper with his friends. Lazarus was there and Martha served. *3* Mary took a lot of expensive oil and anointed Jesus. This filled the house with a wonderful fragrance. *4* But Judas Iscariot, the friend plotting against Jesus, said, *5* "Why wasn't this oil sold so we could give the money to the poor?"

6 He wasn't really concerned about the poor. He was in charge of their money and would often steal some.

7 Jesus said to him, "Relax, she is upset about my coming death and wanted to do something very special for me to show her love. 8 There will be plenty of opportunities to give to the poor, but the time to give to me is coming to an end." 9 Word spread that Jesus was there and so many came to see him. And not only him but also Lazarus, whom Jesus had raised from the dead. 10 The chief priests were plotting to kill Lazarus too because many became believers in Jesus, 11 because of what Lazarus shared about his experience of being reborn.

12 The next day a huge crowd came to the Feast because they had heard that Jesus was coming to Jerusalem. 13 Some of them took palm branches and went out to meet him. 14 They kept shouting: "Hosanna! God has appeared among us! This is our true King!"

15 Jesus saw a donkey's colt there and got on it. This was to fulfill the prophecy: "Don't be afraid daughter of Zion, your king is coming riding a donkey's colt." 16 The friends did not understand all of this as it was happening. But after the Resurrection they thought back on this and realized the prophecies had all come true.

17 As all this was going on, those who had seen Jesus raise Lazarus from the dead were talking about the experience. 18 Hearing about this astounding sign many more began to believe Jesus. 19 The Jewish leaders were talking among themselves about what was happening. They were very upset that it seemed the whole world was beginning to follow Jesus.

20 Now there were some Greeks who came up to worship at the Feast. 21 They came to Philip, who was from Bethsaida in Galilee, and told him they wanted to meet Jesus. 22 Philip came to Andrew and told him this, and they together went to Jesus and told him. 23 But Jesus chose not to deal with them because he had already started dealing with his upcoming death and resurrection. So he began teaching again.

24 "I assure you, that unless a grain of wheat falls into the ground and dies, it remains just a grain of wheat; but if it dies, it produces much more wheat. 25 Those who are not willing to give their lives in love will lose them. Those who give their human lives will then live in their Divine Life, which lasts forever. 26 Those who believe me can follow me into this Divine Life so that as I am they also will be. Those who believe me will also be as Dad is.

27 "I am really stressed, but what should I say? 'Dad, I don't want to go through with this.' But I know that I have come to do this. 28 'Dad, open your heart to me.'" Then his Dad spoke to him: "My son, you are always in my heart. Now you are becoming my heart." 29 The people nearby who heard this thought it was thunder. Others thought an Angel

had spoken to him. *30* Jesus said, "This voice did not come simply for me, but also for you. *31* Now the judgment of God's total love for us has come, and fear has been cast out. *32* As I am lifted up, I will draw everyone in the world with me." *33* Jesus used this expression to proclaim how when he was raised up on the cross to open the gates out of fear, he would invite all to leave fear with him.

34 The people were confused and said, "As we understand scripture the Christ is to remain with us forever. Yet you imply that you will be crucified. Aren't you the Christ?" *35* So Jesus said to them, "A little while longer my Light will shine on you. Learn to walk in this Light, otherwise your old fears, your darkness, will overshadow you again. And there is no possibility of really finding your way when you walk under the shadow of fear. *36* While my Light is shining on you, begin to believe that you too can become this Light."

37 As soon as Jesus had said this they couldn't see him anymore. But even though he had worked many miracles before them; they still did not believe in him. *38* This was so that the prophesy of Isaiah might be fulfilled: "Lord, who has believed what I have said? *39* Who has come to believe that you are Love? *40* Instead they walk around with their eyes and hearts closed. I know how you long for them to open their eyes and open their hearts so that you may heal them." *41* These things Isaiah said after he himself had opened his eyes and seen God, and opened his heart and heard God.

42 Even with so much disbelief around. many were beginning to open their hearts and believe Jesus. But they were so afraid of being kicked out of the synagogue that they often kept their belief hidden. *43* This was because what people thought of them was still more important than what they thought of God.

44 Then Jesus shouted out, "Those who believe in me are really believing in the one who sent me. *45* Whoever sees me sees the one who sent me. You keep looking for God while he is standing right in front of you, and even more, he is already living in your hearts.

46 "I am the new Light that has come into the world. Believing me opens your eyes and hearts to this new Light. *47* And even if you hear my Message and don't follow it, I will not judge you; because I did not come into this world to judge, but simply to Love. *48* Whoever does not believe me and follow my Message; does not follow their own heart— because we are all One. Those who do not see and experience this oneness will feel judged, because judgment tries to separate unity. *49* I speak to you from my Unity with Dad. He has told me everything I should say. *50* His words bring Divine Life; that is why I say just what he told me to."

CHAPTER 13

1 Right before the Passover Feast, Jesus knew that it was time for him to go home to his Dad, so he wanted to show his friends one last time how very much he loved them. *2* On the other hand, Judas Iscariot was about to show his lack of love. *3* Jesus was very conscious of that fact. He knew that his Dad had placed everything in his hands and that he had come from God, and was now about to go back to God. *4* So at supper he got up and took off his robe and picked up a towel and wrapped it around himself. *5* He poured water into a basin and began to wash his friends' feet. *6* When he came to Peter; Peter asked him, "Teacher, are you going to wash my feet?" *7* Jesus answered him, "Just now you don't know what I am doing, but you will soon." *8* Peter said, "You are never going to wash my feet!" Jesus replied, "If I do not wash your feet, you will not really understand my Message." *9* So Peter said, "Then wash not only my feet, but also my hands and face." *10* Jesus said, "All I have to wash is your feet since the rest of you is already clean."

12 After he had washed all their feet, he put his robe back on and sat back down. Then he said, "Do you know what I have done to you?" *13* You call me teacher, and that is what I am. *14* So if I, your teacher, can still wash your feet, how much more should you wash one another's feet. *15* For I have given you an example (of ministry) that you might do for others what I have done for you. *16* I solemnly assure you, a servant is not better than the master. *17* If you understand what I have just tried to teach you, you will be very happy if you live by it.

18 "I am not talking about all of you, because I know each of your hearts. The scripture has to be fulfilled which says: 'One who has eaten at my very table has betrayed me.' *19* I am telling you this now so that when it happens you may believe that I am Christ, the one spoken of in the scriptures. *20* I assure you that anyone who welcomes the ones I have sent welcomes me, and whoever welcomes me welcomes the one who sent me."

21 When Jesus said these things he became very thoughtful. He said, "I assure you that one of you is going to betray me." *22* The friends looked at each other wondering who he was talking about. *23* One of the friends whom Jesus had a special love for, was reclined next to him. *24* So Peter motioned to him to ask Jesus who it was. *25* The beloved friend leaned back against Jesus' breast (*The breast was the part of the offering to God that was given to the priests in the temple. John is saying here that priests and ministers are to eat of the breast of Jesus, the Love of Jesus, as John symbolically is doing here.) and whispered, "Who is it?" *26* Jesus said, "The one I give this bit of bread to after I dip it in the sauce." Then he took a bit of bread and dipped it and he gave it to Judas Iscariot.

At that time Judas decided to go through with his betrayal. *27* Then Jesus said to him, "Do quickly what you are going to do." *28* None of the others at the table knew why Jesus had said this to him. *29* Some thought perhaps that since he was in charge of the money, Jesus wanted him to buy something for the feast; others thought maybe Jesus wanted him to go give alms to the poor. *30* Judas ate the bit of bread and left. It was dark out.

31 After he had left, Jesus said, "Now the Son of Man has shown his utmost Love, just as Dad always shows me. *32* As Dad has always shown me the utmost Love; he will shortly manifest this Love to everyone. *33* My dear friends, I will be leaving you soon. You will look for me, but as I told the Jewish leaders, you cannot follow me yet. *34* I give you a new command, 'Love one another.' As much as I have loved you; you are to love one another. *35* Everyone will recognize you are my friends if you love one another as much as I have loved you."

36 Peter said, "I want to know where you are going." Jesus responded, "Where I am going now you can't come until later." *37* Peter said, "I don't understand why I can't follow you now. I am willing to give my life for you." *38* Jesus said, "You will give your life for me? I assure you that before the cock crows you will have denied me three times.

CHAPTER 14

1 "Take all the worry and fear from your heart by believing in God and believing in yourself. *2* My Dad's heart is huge, as I have already told you. I am changing your heart that you may understand God's heart. *3* And when that is done our hearts will be One, so that as *I am* you also will be. *4* The Way I am is the way you already are, if you could only see that. Please understand the Unity that we are, the Unity we are called to proclaim to the world." *5* Thomas said, "Lord, we don't really understand you, so how can we become (like) you?"

6 Jesus said, "As I am you already are. No one reaches their Divinity without knowing their Identity. *7* As you have come to know me, you have come to know God. From now on you will know God and be God."

8 Philip said, "Show us the Way to God. That is all we ask." *9* Jesus said, "Have I been with you all this time and you still do not realize that you are already God? How can you ask me to show you God when you are already God? *10* Don't you see that I am in God and God is in me; and that you are in God and God is in you? *11* I am simply repeating what I have said so many times before. I speak as God because I am God. You are to speak as God because you **are** God.

12 "Don't you see that God is in me and I am in God? Otherwise how can I do the works of God? When you understand this you too will do the works of God, and even greater works than what I have done. *13* The reason you will be able to do this is that my core teaching will someday no longer be illegal and so you can proclaim it from the house tops. Tomorrow I will transition completely into my Divinity so I can help you transition into your own Divinity. *14* When you are in this Divine Unity; what you ask for is what God asks for. And what God asks for always is fulfilled. Love must always direct all our actions and all our thoughts.

15 "All you need to do is realize that as I transition out of this world tomorrow, I will transition into your hearts and become your Spirit. *16* This Spirit will bring you to the Truth that the world cannot understand, because it does not realize that it too is Divine. *17* But you will, because I will live in you and become you. *18* You will never be alone again because we will always be One, always together. *19* Tomorrow the world will believe that I have died, but you will know that my Spirit has simply transitioned into you. My rebirth in you will be your rebirth in me. *20* Tomorrow you will know that the Spirit of God has become my Spirit, and my Spirit has become your Spirit. *21* Those who really love have already become me, and those who have become me have become God. Now you will know that to be yourself is to know you're (your) God.

22 Judas (not Iscariot) said to him, "Are you only just going to come to us and not to everyone?" *23* Jesus responded, "Anyone who opens to Love and the Truth of their Divinity will rest in this Identity, this Divine Union. It will be living with God, in God and as God.

24 "I am a gentle Lover. Those who do not open their hearts and being to Love remain lost in the illusion of limitation. I don't force anyone to open to (my) Love, but since everyone *is* Love, to close your heart is to cease to really live. This is not simply my idea, it is the simple Truth.

25 "I have told you all of this before, but it has been too much for you. I may be limited in my teaching but not in my Being. *26* That is why I have decided to transition tomorrow into your Being. There I can tickle your heart into accepting your Divine Identity. *27* As you accept and realize your true Identity, you will experience true Peace. Peace comes when we stop fighting Truth. This is way beyond present human wisdom.

28 "I have told you I am transitioning tomorrow. If you really understood what that means, you would be really happy. You have enjoyed being with me, now you can enjoy being me. *29* Being God is so much better than simply being taught by God. I have told you this before it happens so that when it does happen you will understand what is going on. *30* I do not have much more time to be with you since things are already in motion for my transition.

31 "Remember that I have always acted out of Love and I invite you to continue on this Path.

CHAPTER 15

1 "I am True Life that flows into you. *2* As you open to Love, you open to True Life, Divine Life. *3* You can count on my help in this by remembering and living what I have taught you. *4* Live in my life as I live in your life. Unless we are joined in Life and Love; neither of us really has Life and neither of us really is Love. *5* I am Life, the Life that lives your Life. Together we can accomplish a lot, separated we can do nothing. *6* If you cut yourself off from Life you will die, even if you continue to walk around. If this has already happened, you need the fire of transformation to be reborn.

7 "If you live in me and my Words live in you, we can move mountains. Moving mountains shows our Divine Unity and glorifies the whole universe. *8* As God loves me, so I love you. *9* May our Divine Unity blossom! Open your heart to Love as I have opened my heart to Life. *10* This gives True Light to the world. *11* I share these Truths with you that my joy may completely fill your hearts and overflow onto the world.

12 "The most important thing is that you love each other as much and as deeply as I have loved you. *13* Tomorrow I will show you how very much I love you. *14* You have become my true friends. Let that never change. *15* You don't work for me, we work together. We now have the very same Call. *16* I have shared with you everything I know so we can work together as friends, as equals.

17 "Remember that I am the one who asked you to share my Divine Call. I now ask you to walk into your Divinity and then out into the world. What your heart wants, your Divinity will manifest. Again I say: Love one another. Everything else is superfluous.

18 "People who see only the material world may hate you as they have hated me. *19* If you walk in their world they will love you. But you now know the deeper Truths and this frightens them. 'You hate only what you fear.'

20 "It is extremely important to remember what I said about us all being equal, that we are all exactly the same (thing). So don't be surprised when they persecute you, because they persecuted me; nor when they welcome your teaching since many have welcomed mine. *21* When they persecute you, know that it is because they don't recognize their own Divinity. They are jealous because they see something in you that they want and don't realize they already have it, already *are* it. *22* What I have shared with them has scared them. They believe the chasm between their fear and my love is too wide for them to jump over; but it only looks that way when you are weighed down with materiality.

23 "To hate God is to hate yourself. To hate my teachings is to hate your own inner wisdom. It is to start a war between your mind and your heart. This is the deepest pain of humankind today. The fire of love is the only thing that will melt this into Peace.

24 "My performing Healings and Miracles set them on fire with fear. They saw a power greater than their humanity at work. And since they are convinced they are only human, this power made them afraid. They feared they would lose themselves in this power, when in reality this power, this Divinity, *is* themselves. 25 This all happened to fulfill the prophesy that pointed out humankind's struggle to transition into their Divinity. Before only death could open the door to this transition; but now Love can open that door, since to really Love is to be Divine.

26 "When my Spirit, the Spirit of Love, enters your Heart, you will be opened to this Truth. 27 This infused wisdom will be God's Loving Presence in you. This is my greatest Gift to you who have walked with me. Share it!

CHAPTER 16

1 "I have shared these things to help you walk in the Light. 2 You will be kicked out of synagogues and those who kill you will be thought holy. 3 They will do these things since they know neither the God in

me nor the God in themselves. 4 I tell you these things so you won't be surprised when they happen. 5 I did not tell you these things in the beginning because then you believed that only I was God. Now that you are beginning to see your own inner Divinity you are better prepared to understand these things.

6 "Since I am leaving tomorrow, this is our last time to talk about these things. I know in your hearts you want to ask me where I am going, but most don't yet have the courage to ask, even though what I have said has made you very sad. 7 But I tell you the Truth—it is better that I go away, because if I don't, you will continue to fall back on your old belief that I am God and you are not. My Spirit, the Spirit of Love, can only come after I have left. 8 I can only really transition into your Spirit after I have left my human Spirit. 9 I will transition out of my Life into your Life. I will die to me and become you. 10 Not a new you, but the True You. Your union with God will shift from an outer connection to an inner Reality. 11 As your outer God dies your inner God can finally be reborn. It is for this that I have come.

12 "I have a lot more I would like to tell you but they are already preparing to come and get me. I do not judge them for this since it is their part in my transition. 13 However, remember that when our hearts and minds and souls have become truly One, your inner Divinity, your

inner Spirit, will remind you of what I have said tonight, and continue to reveal Truth and Reality to you. *14* Then you will know that all the Glory that you believe is mine will be yours too. *15* You may stumble in accepting this new glorious Reality so I intend to come back to you in a very special way fairly soon. *16* So don't become discouraged, simply stay open, simply love the best you can until we melt together completely into One. *17* All that is God's is mine and all that is mine is yours, especially the Divine Identity. *18* You are daughters and sons of God, and daughters and sons of God are God, and they inherit all that belongs to our Dad God, our Mom God.

19 "Again, tomorrow it will seem as though I have gone. But all that will be gone is the illusion that I am simply human. I will return in my Divinity and then the entire universe will join me to celebrate your commission of Proclaiming the Good News of Universal Divinity. I know you will be sad for a while, because we have become great friends. *20* But the sadness you will feel will simply expand your heart so you can accept more Love when I return.

21 "You will be like a lady who is sad that her labor pains are coming. But know that your sadness only points to the birth of your True Identity, your rebirth into the God you have always been. *22* Then even in the midst of the trials of life there will always be the underlying Divine Joy in you.

23 "And when that happens you won't have to ask me for anything anymore, you will be able to go directly to God yourselves since you are God. And remember that there are two sides to God: The Outer and the Inner. These are moving closer to one another as you understand my Message more fully. I am your mediator with God only in the sense of sharing the Good News that the "two" Gods are one. I am fully God and I am fully human. You are fully God and you are fully human. *24* Humankind will reach equality with God as you soak in this Truth. Humankind's evolution is simply toward this Truth. Your preaching of this Good News moves Humankind closer to their own Divinity.

25 "I have told you these things in Words, but the Time of Infused Wisdom is coming when I can reveal things to you without words. True Wisdom comes from True Identity. You have not known who you are and so haven't known how to act. When you realize that you are God, that you are Love; it will be easy to know what to do. Doing always flows freely from Being. Your Divinity has always been your Identity. Words speak to the mind. Being speaks to the Heart. Love is Who we are and Love is how we are to act.

26 "When you truly understand this, you will see that you can do what I have done. You will know that you can always pray directly to God. You will know that your purity of heart is your way of Praying from your Divinity. *27* For Dad loves you himself because you believe I am a manifestation of him. This is the perpetual Circle of Love. It has no beginning and no end. It simply loves and in so doing moves the world. I am God's Eternal Creation. *28* I come from God as did all Creation. Now I am leading it back to God so it will understand and believe it is Sacred, that it too is God. I became human so that humans could become God."

29 His friends said, "It is now obvious to us that you have all Wisdom. We truly believe that you came from God. Our struggle is to believe we can fully return to (be) God. *30* We believe you are the Way back to God. But it is hard to believe that we are to accompany you on this journey back to (be) God."

31 Jesus said in reply, "I know what I say is hard to believe, and even harder to live. I know you will be tempted to run away when things get tough. But I have seen our Dad's Heart. I have seen your hearts, and I know they are exactly the same thing. And this Truth will indeed manifest as we walk together down this Path back to Divinity.

"Tomorrow many of you will be scattered, and it will seem that I am alone. But I am never alone, for Dad and I are One. And even though you will run away, you will still be with me because **We Are One!** So when you feel you cannot possibly do what

you are called to, remember that the Resurrected Me, the Spirit, has already done it all. So simply awaken from the dream of inadequacy into the Reality of everything already having been done.

32 "This knowledge and wisdom will bring great peace to you. The true change is never the doing; it is always the Being, and you are already God! There will still be struggles in your life, but your Divinity can now handle them. Remember, problems are never really outside, they are always inside. You may look out into the world and see problems, but if you look deeply inside you will see only Divinity. *33* And your Call is to take this Divinity out into these problems. Incarnate Love into the Chaos!"

CHAPTER 17

1 After Jesus said these things, he lifted his heart to heaven and said, "Dad, I know you love me, and you know I love you. You asked me to tell everyone about their Divinity—their Divine Life. And I have shown them what Divine Life is by living it. *2* Divine Life is your Life. You are my Dad. You are their Dad. They are beginning to see this even though it is so hard for them to make the jump of believing that not only I, but even they are Divine. *3* Their faith grew as their Gifts from Spirit manifested. I am about finished doing what is possible now. After I have transitioned, I will complete what you asked me to do. *4* They understand with their minds at times, but when I have incarnated in them in My Spirit, their hearts will also open to this Truth. And this Truth will give them Life and show them the Way.

5 "As I showed them how to love, they learned that God is Love. When I showed them they are God, they began to understand that they are Love. They have taken a few glorious peeks into this new Reality and have answered your Call to spread your Love. But you and I and Spirit will have to fully enter their hearts and fully become them before they can transition out of their purely human way of believing.

6 "With their background of believing you wanted sacrifice, it is a huge leap for them to realize that what you really want is Love—for them to love you, for them to love one another, for them to love themselves. As they have come to realize that you and I love them completely and unconditionally, they have glimpsed the reality that they are Love(d).

7 "Now they realize that these new ideas do not come simply from me, but that they come from you too. Their image of you, Dad, is changing immensely as they have seen what I have done in your name. I had told them everything you have told me in prayer. I have taught them how they too can listen to you in prayer and that you will speak to and with them. They are beginning

to feel you are "Dad" rather than a distant potentate.

8 "They understand that I came as your voice of Love and that their Call is to take this to the entire world. They are still intimidated by the immensity of the Call, so our work of instilling Faith will need to continue. You giving me Faith, me giving them Faith, and they giving Faith to those they minister to. We will need to include them in our Trinity, in our Life. *9* This Bond of Oneness is the only way they can fulfill what we have asked them to do. This Trinitarian Life, this life of total Love, is the only bedrock that can support Your Plan of Love. All that is mine is yours; all that is yours is mine, and all that is ours is theirs.

10 "Tomorrow I leave the material world and will come home to you, Dad. Now it will be more important than ever that we keep them in our hearts and support them with our Love. That we bring them into our Trinitarian Life and Live as One in Love! Otherwise they will slip back into thinking they live alone rather than in our Love. *11* To be One with God is such a new idea to them that every day they will need to feel our Love and Presence, our Oneness with them. Our Essence is Presence. They need more experience of this in order to preach it.

12 "I tried very hard to do this as I walked with them. Sadly one of them could not open to this marvel. But we will continue to love him until he feels the love that he is. Love always succeeds because everything *is* Love. Love is the only thing we are not free from. Our essence always eventually enters our hearts and understanding.

13 "As I come to you, I say these things so that the Joy we have together, Dad, will spill over into them, and from them into the world. They will need a heavy dose of Joy these days ahead. But we have enough Joy to fill the world.

14 "I have taught them everything you have taught me. But many in the world are locked into feelings of separation and the fear of being close to you. I have taught unity and oneness and some have chosen to continue living in hell, and refuse the invitation into heaven. But since they **are** Love, they **are** God; and will eventually end up in heaven. Then we can truly be All One!

15 "We do not have to force them out of their beliefs, since we can love them into ours. Love attracts; Love conquers, not by power, but by continuous invitation and openness. Eventually their pain, the fires of hell, will move their hearts to walk into heaven where our gates are always open and our hearts always accepting. Lost sheep are always welcomed back by the Good Shepherd.

16 "Those you have given me to walk with are responding to this Invitation. Bring them into your Divinity by infusing them with (your) Truth. *17* Share your Truth with those who seek Truth. Because

just as you sent me into the world, I am sending them into the world. *18* The World is thirsting for (your) Truth. The world is hungering for your truth. *19* I have always tried to walk in the Truth with Love, as an example to them, and as an example of what they too can do.

20 "My heart goes out to all those who will be drawn into their own Divinity by the ministry of my dear friends. The need for our Love will expand as the preaching of your Word, your Truth expands, until the whole world is drenched in our Love.

21 "Dad, I want them to be as much in love as we are. I want them to be as much at One as we are. **That we all may be One!** You in me, me in you, we in them and they in us. This unity will prove their Divinity and our Divinity. Then I will have accomplished what you sent me here to do.

22 "The Divinity you gave me I have given to them that they may be One just as much as we are one. I in them, and you in me, forming the perfect Trinity. *23* And, Dad, I want the world to know that the Love I was asked to teach them came from the Love that you **are**. I want them to know that you love them as much as you love me!

24 "Dad, I want all those you have asked me to walk with to be exactly as I am. Fully human, totally Divine! I want them not only to see (my) Divinity, but also to *be* (my) Divinity! The very Divinity you gave me at the beginning!

25 "My beloved Dad, the world has not known you are Love. 26 But I have and these I have walked with have. 27 I have told everyone who would listen that you are Love, and I will continue to do this forever through those who have seen and believed this truth. 28 That this same exact Love that you have for me may be in them, and that I may be in them **as their Divinity**, as their very Life."

CHAPTER 18

1 When Jesus had finished saying these things he went out across the Kidron Valley to a garden with his friends. 2 Judas knew where they were going, 3 so he got a detachment of soldiers and some attendants from the high priests and went there with torches and weapons. 4 Jesus was aware of everything that was going on and so he went out and asked them, "Who are you looking for?" 5 They said, "Jesus of Nazareth." Jesus told them, "I am he." Judas was standing with them. 6 When Jesus said to them, "I am he," they fell backwards and some even to the ground. 7 He asked them again, "Who are you looking for?" and they replied, "Jesus of Nazareth." 8 Jesus said, "I told you I am he, so if you are after me, let these others go."

10 Then Peter drew his sword and struck the high priests slave and cut off his right ear—the slave's name was Malchus. 11 But Jesus said to Peter, "Put your sword away. Shall I not do what Dad asked me?"

12 Then those who had come after him grabbed him and tied him up. 13 They took him first to Annas who was the father-in-law of Caiaphas, the high priest that year. 14 This is the same Caiaphas who told the Jewish Leaders that one man's death would benefit the whole Jewish people. 15 Peter followed Jesus with another friend who knew the high priest. That friend went into the high priest's courtyard. 16 Then he went back out to get Peter who couldn't get through the gate. He spoke to the high priest's slave girl who was in charge of the gate and brought Peter in.

17 The doorkeeper said to Peter, "Aren't you one of that man's friends too?" He replied, "No, I am not." 18 The slaves had made a charcoal fire and were warming themselves, because it was cold out. Peter was standing with them to get warm too. 19 Meanwhile the high priest was asking Jesus about his teaching. 20 Jesus answered him, "I have spoken openly to anyone who would listen. I have been teaching regularly in the synagogues and even in the Temple, where all the Jews gather. I have not tried to hide my Message. 21 So why do you ask me? Ask those who have heard me since they know what I teach."

22 When Jesus said this one of the attendants standing nearby slapped him in the face and said, "Is that any way to talk to the high priest?" 23 Jesus answered back, "If I said something wrong, prove it; but if

I didn't, why did you slap me?" 24 Then Annas sent him still bound to the high priest, Caiaphas.

25 Peter was still standing by the fire getting warm himself. Those standing around him said, "Aren't you one of his too?" 26 He denied it and said, "I am not." 27 One of the high priest's slaves, a relative of the one whose ear Peter had cut off said, "Didn't I see you in the garden with him tonight?" Peter again denied it and just then a rooster crowed.

28 Then they took Jesus from Caiaphas to the Praetorium. It was already early morning so the Jews did not enter the palace for fear of being defiled which would make them unable to eat the Passover. 29 So Pilate came out to them and asked what charge they had against this man. 30 They answered, "If he were not a criminal, we would not have brought him here to you." 31 Pilate said, "You deal with him according to your law." The Jewish leaders said to him, "But we have no legal right to execute anyone." 32 This happened so that what Jesus said about the type of death he would die would be fulfilled.

33 Then Pilate went back into the Praetorium and asked Jesus, "Are you the King of the Jews?" 34 Jesus replied, "Do you ask me this of your own accord or have others told you about me?" 35 Pilate answered him, "I am not a Jew, am I? Your own people and the chief priests have handed you over to me. What have you done to cause this?" 36 Jesus answered, "My kingdom is not of this world. If it were, my attendants would have made sure I was not turned over to the Jewish leaders. But for now my kingdom is not of this world." 37 So Pilate said, "Then you are a king?" Jesus replied, "You may say that. The reason I was born, the reason I came into the world was that I might preach the real Truth." 38 Pilate scoffed at this and said, "What is the real Truth?" 39 When he had said this, he went back out to the Jews and said to them, "I don't find him guilty of anything, and since it is your custom to have me free one person for you at Passover, I am wondering if you would like me to free for you the King of the Jews?" 40 But they shouted, "Not this man, but Barabbas." Barabbas was a thief.

CHAPTER 19

1 Then Pilate took Jesus and had him flogged. 2 And the soldiers wove a crown of thorns and set it down hard on his head. They put a purple robe on him to mock him and said, 3 "Hail to the King of the Jews," and they slapped him in the face.

4 Once more Pilate came out and addressed them. "Look, I am bringing him back out to show you I don't find him guilty." 5 Then Jesus came out wearing the crown of thorns and the purple robe. Pilate said to them, "Here he is!"

6 When the chief priests and their attendants saw Jesus, they shouted, "Crucify him! Crucify him!" Pilate

said, "Take him yourselves and crucify him because I do not find him guilty." *7* The Jewish leaders replied, "According to our law he must be killed because he claims to be God." *8* When Pilate heard this he was alarmed, *9* so he went back into the Praetorium and asked Jesus, "Where are you from?" But Jesus would not answer him. *10* Pilate was shocked and said, "Don't you realize I have the power to release you or to crucify you?" *11* Jesus replied, "You have no power whatever of your own, but only what is given to you by God. Because of this the one who handed me over to you has the greater responsibility."

12 From that point on Pilate kept trying to find a way to release him; but the Jewish leaders kept shouting, "If you free him you will betray Caesar. Anyone who says he is a king is a rebel against Caesar." *13* When he heard this, Pilate led Jesus out and sat down in the judgment seat. *14* It was about noon the day of preparation for the Passover. He said to the Jews, "This is your king." *15* But they shouted, "Get him out of here. Crucify him!" Pilate asked them, "Do you really want me to crucify your king?" The chief priests answered, "We have no king but Caesar." *16* Then he handed Jesus over to be crucified.

17 So they took Jesus out carrying his own cross to a place called Skull, where they crucified him. *18* Two others were crucified with him, one on each side with Jesus

in the middle. *19* Pilate had a sign made and he had put it on the cross. It read "Jesus of Nazareth, King of the Jews." *20* Many Jews read the sign because the place where Jesus was crucified was near the city, and it was written in Hebrew, Greek and Latin.

21 The chief priests protested and asked Pilate to change the sign to say, "He said he was the King of the Jews" *22* but Pilate said, "The sign stays as written."

23 When the soldiers had crucified Jesus, they took his clothes and divided them into four parts, one for each soldier. *24* But they decided to cast lots for his tunic since it was one piece woven all the way from top to bottom. This fulfilled scripture which says: "They divided my clothes among themselves and cast lots for it."

25 By the cross of Jesus stood his mother Mary, his wife Mary Magdalene, and his sister Mary. *26* When Jesus saw his mother and the friend he had a special love for, he said to his mother, "Mom, this is your son." *27* Then he said to his friend, "This is your Mom." From that day on Mary lived with John.

28 After this Jesus knew there was only one thing left to do, so to fulfill the scripture he said, "I am thirsty." *29* There was a jar full of vinegar there, so a guard dipped a sponge in it and held it up to Jesus' mouth. *30* When Jesus had sipped a bit of vinegar he said, "It's all over." Then be bowed his head and went back to his Dad.

31 Now since it was Preparation Day, the Jewish leaders asked Pilate to have their legs broken so they would die soon and not be hanging on the crosses on the Feast Day. *32* So the soldiers came and broke the legs of the two crucified with Jesus. *33* But when they came to him he was already dead so they did not break his legs, *34* but one of the soldiers threw his spear into his side and blood and water flowed out. *35* The one who saw this and gave testimony to it is trustworthy so you can believe what he said. *36* These things happened that the scripture may be fulfilled: "Not a bone of his shall be broken." *37* And another scripture that says, "They will look at the one they have pierced."

38 After this Joseph of Arimathea, a secret friend of Jesus, asked Pilate if he could take the body of Jesus and bury it; and Pilate gave him permission to do this. *39* Nicodemus, who had come to Jesus at night, also came and brought about a hundred pounds of a burial mixture of myrrh and aloes. *40* They then took the body of Jesus and wrapped it with this mixture in the traditional linen burial clothes. *41* There was a brand new tomb in a garden near where Jesus had been crucified. *42* They laid Jesus' body there since it was already Preparation Day.

CHAPTER 20

1 Early that Sunday morning, while it was still dark, Jesus' wife, Mary Magdalene came to the tomb with some other family members, and saw that the stone covering the entrance had been moved. *2* She couldn't figure out what had happened and just stood outside the tomb crying. *3* She finally bent down and looked into the tomb, and saw that it was empty.

4 Then she turned around and saw Jesus standing there, but she did not recognize him through her tears. *5* Jesus said to her, "Mary, why are you crying? Don't you see what has happened?" *6* She still didn't understand and so Jesus simply said to her lovingly, "Mary!" *7* Then Mary turned completely toward Jesus and said, "My beloved!" and went to him and was overcome with tears as they hugged.

8 Jesus said, "I know my body is different, but my heart is the same." *9* They held each other and talked for a while and then Jesus said, "Please go now and tell my friends that I am going to ascend to my Dad and their Dad; to my God and their God." *10* So Mary Magdalene hurried to the friends and told them all that had happened and what Jesus had said.

11 Peter and John didn't believe her and started off immediately for the tomb. *12* They were both running, but John was faster and reached the tomb first. *13* He bent down and looked in and saw the linen burial clothes lying there, but he did not go in. *14* Peter ran up and went right into the tomb. He saw the linen burial clothes lying there and the cloth that had been around his head lying off by itself. *15* Then John finally went into the tomb. *16* He looked around and realized it was true that Jesus had risen. *17* Before this they had not understood what Jesus had said about rising. *18* Then they went back to where they had been hiding.

19 That very evening the same friends were gathered with the doors locked for fear of the Jewish leaders. Jesus came to them and said, "Peace, my sisters and brothers!" *20* Then he showed them his hands and side. The friends were overjoyed to see him. *21* He said to them again, "Peace."

Then he said, "Just as my Dad has sent me, so I send you." *22* He breathed on them and said, "Receive my Spirit. I have given you Peace and Spirit to take to the whole world. Tell everyone that they are beloved by God, and are in fact God! *23* Otherwise they will continue to believe they are sinners, and those who believe they are sinners tend to sin, while those who believe they are loved tend to love!"

24 Thomas, one of the twelve, was not with them when Jesus came, so the other friends told him they had seen the Teacher. *25* But Thomas said, "Unless I put my own fingers in the nail holes in his hands and my hand in his side, I cannot believe you saw him."

26 The next Sunday the same friends had gathered again and locked the doors, and this time Thomas was with them. Jesus came and stood before them and said, "Peace to you." *27* He then said to Thomas, "Come here and put your fingers in my hands and your hand in my side, so that you can really believe." *28* Thomas did that and said, "My Teacher." *29* Jesus said, "You have done this to help those believe who will not see me as you have."

30 Jesus did many other wonderful signs so that his friends could understand who he was and who they are. Most of these are not written in this Gospel; *31* but these are written so you may come to believe that Jesus is Christ, and also your brother. So that knowing and believing this, you may realize that your Divine Life comes through (his) Divine Life and that his Brotherhood makes you daughters and sons of God too!

CHAPTER 21

1 After this Jesus appeared to the friends by the sea of Tiberius and this is the way it happened. *2* Now Peter, Thomas, Nathanael, James, John and two other friends were gathered together. *3* Peter said, "I am going out to fish." The rest said they would go with him. So they went off and got into their boat, but that whole night they did not catch anything.

4 When it was daybreak Jesus appeared on the shore. However, the friends did not recognize him. *5* Then Jesus said to them, "Brothers, have you caught anything?" They answered him, "No." *6* He said to them, "Cast your net to your right of the boat and you will catch some." So they cast the net there and could almost not draw it up because of all the fish in it.

7 Then John said to Peter, "It is the Teacher!" When Peter heard this he wrapped his clothes around himself and jumped into the sea. *8* The other friends rowed the boat to shore since it was only about a hundred yards away, dragging the net full of fish. *9* When they got out of the boat, they saw a charcoal fire there with fish cooking on it, with bread. *10* Jesus said to them, "Bring some of the fish you have just caught." *11* Peter got back in the boat and brought the net to shore. The net was filled with a hundred fifty three large fish and still did not tear.

12 Jesus said, "Come and have breakfast." They were too shaken by Jesus' presence to say anything. *13* Jesus came and gave them bread and also the fish. *14* This was the third time Jesus had appeared to the friends after he had risen from the dead.

15 After breakfast Jesus asked Peter three different times if he loved him. Each time Peter said he did. And each time he said he loved Jesus; Jesus gave him instructions for the ministry of Love. *16* The last time Jesus asked, Peter was upset and said, "Teacher, you know everything. You know I love you." *17* All this happened to give Peter a chance to erase his three denials of Jesus the night before the crucifixion. Not because Jesus needed this, but because Peter did.

18 Finally Jesus said to Peter, "I assure you that when you were young you clothed yourself and went wherever you wanted; but when you are old you will hold out your hands and another will clothe you and take you where you don't want to go." *19* He said this to indicate by what type of death Peter would transition to God.

20 After this he said to Peter, "Follow me." Peter turned around and saw John following him, the same friend who had leaned on Jesus' breast at the Last Supper. *21* Noticing him Peter asked Jesus, "Teacher, what about him?" *22* Jesus told him, "If I want him to stay until I come back, what is that to you?"

24 This is the same friend who testifies here to all these facts, and he can be believed because he was there. *25* There are besides what is written here, many other things that Jesus did. But if we wrote about all of them not even the whole world could hold the books that would have to be written.

MATTHEW

CHAPTER 1

18 We begin with the birth of Jesus. Shortly after Mary and Joseph were married, she became pregnant with Jesus. *19* Then an Angel appeared to Joseph in a dream and said, "Joseph, son of David, your wife Mary will give birth to a son, and you are to call him Jesus (God is in us.)" *22* All this happened to fulfill the prophesy of Isaiah: *23* "The young girl will bear a son to show that God is in us."

CHAPTER 2

1 Right after Jesus was born in Bethlehem of Judea, spiritual men from India arrived. *2* They asked where the newborn spiritual leader of the Jews was, since they had seen his star in their country and had come to honor him. *3* When King Herod heard this he was greatly troubled by this possible rival. *4* So he called together all the chief priests and Jewish leaders, and asked them where this newborn was. *5* They told him of the prophesy, *6* that a special leader was to be born in Bethlehem. *7* Herod then called a meeting with the spiritual men from India to find out exactly when the star had appeared. *8* He then sent them to Bethlehem and told them to come and tell him when they found the child so that he too might go and honor him. *9* When they left the king, the star guided them to the place where Jesus was. *10* On seeing this they were ecstatic. *11* They went in and found Jesus and his parents Mary and Joseph, and bowed down to honor him. They gave him the gifts they had brought of gold, incense and myrrh. *12* Then, being warned in a dream not to return to Herod, they took another route home.

13 After they had left, an Angel appeared to Joseph in a dream telling him to take Jesus and Mary and escape to Egypt; for Herod was about to kill all the young boys of the area. *14* So he got up in the middle of the night and they left for Egypt. *15* They stayed there until Herod died.

16 When Herod realized he had been outwitted by the spiritual men from India, he became furious and sent soldiers to kill all the boys under the age of two in and around Bethlehem. He did this based on what the Spiritual men had told him about the time of the star's appearance.

19 When Herod died, an Angel appeared to Joseph, *20* and told him to go home since the one who had wanted to kill Jesus had died. *21* So he got up and started for home. *22* But hearing that Archelaus had succeeded his father Herod, he was afraid to go to Judea. Then an Angel told him to go instead to Galilee, which he did. *23* They settled there to fulfill the prophesy: "He shall be called a Nazarene."

CHAPTER 3

1 In those days John the Baptist appeared in the Judean desert. *2* He said, "Rethink your lives and find where God is." *3* Some said, "John is the one spoken of by the Prophet Isaiah: 'He is the one crying in the desert, to help people find their way to God.'" *4* John believed the way to encounter God was to leave the world, so he had his clothes made of camel's hair and ate only locusts and wild honey.

5 The hunger for God in the people had become so strong that they came from Jerusalem, *6* all of Judea, and the entire Jordan region to hear him and be baptized by him in the Jordan River. *7* When he saw the rich and powerful coming, he warned them that they were trying to see God in the external world, but that he could only be found inside their hearts. *8* He told them that their actions must come from their hearts, from their love, and not from arrogance or a desire for money or power. *11* John said, "I baptize you with water to help you cleanse and rethink your lives. But there is one coming who will baptize you with fire and Spirit which will transform your lives. I am here to help you cleanse your hearts; he is coming to give you new hearts and new eyes!"

13 Then Jesus came from Galilee to John at the Jordan to be baptized by him. *14* John recognized who he was and asked to be baptized by him. *15* But Jesus responded, "For now I wish to be baptized by you." And so John baptized him. *16* Immediately after Jesus was baptized and had come up out of the water, the heavens opened and Jesus saw the Spirit of God descend on him like a dove. *17* And a voice from heaven said, "You are my beloved Son, I really love you!"

CHAPTER 4

1 Then an Angel came and led him into the desert to face his fears before he began his ministry. There were three false beliefs he had to deal with to keep his Message pure. So he spent forty days and forty nights in prayer and fasting as preparation for this. *2* When he finished, he was hungry. *3* He heard this voice say, "You are God, so change the stones into bread." *4* He replied, "We don't live on bread alone, but on God alone."

5 Then in Vision he looked down from the top of the temple and the voice said, *6* "Jump! Show you are God by showing your power." *7* But Jesus said in return, "Being God is not for show, but for service and love."

8 Next in Vision he was on the highest mountain and could see forever. *9* The voice said, "This is your kingdom, take it and be proud." *10* Jesus responded, "My kingdom is in the hearts of women and men. I don't rule there; I simply live there."

11 Then the voice was silent and Jesus went back to his friends.

12 When Jesus heard that John had been arrested, he went back up into Galilee; *13* and moved from Nazareth to Capernaum by the sea. *16* It was there that Jesus began to show his great light to those lost in darkness. *17* From then on he began to preach saying: "Rethink your lives and find where God is."

18 Shortly after this Jesus was walking by the Sea of Galilee and saw two brothers, Peter and Andrew, casting a net into the sea, for they were fishermen. *19* He said to them, "Come, and I will make you fishers of men." *20* And they left everything and followed him. *21* Walking a little farther he saw two other brothers, James and John, in a boat with their father Zebedee, mending their nets. *22* He called them too, and so they left their boat and followed him.

23 Jesus walked all over Galilee, teaching in the synagogues, announcing the Good News, and healing all kinds of disease and illness among the people. *24* News of this spread to all of Syria, and they brought all those suffering from pain and illness to him, and he healed them all. *25* Great throngs began to follow him everywhere.

CHAPTER 5

1 One day seeing the huge crowd he went up the side of a mountain with his apostles to share with them. *2* Then he sat down and said:

3 "Blessed are the poor, for they know where God lives.

4 "Blessed are they who are sad, for they will have reason to rejoice.

5 "Blessed are the gentle, for they have already won their world.

6 "Blessed are those who are hungry and thirsty for God, for he has come to live in them.

7 "Blessed are those who love, for they shall be loved.

8 "Blessed are the pure of heart, for they shall soon be God.

9 "Blessed are the peacemakers, for they are God's daughters and sons.

10 "Blessed are those who are persecuted for their love of God, for God is already in them.

11 "Blessed are you when they slander and persecute and defame you because of me; *12* for these are the same birth pains into heaven that the prophets experienced, and there you will be just like them.

"Before you were born into the world; now you are being born into God."

13 Jesus paused to allow people time to absorb these amazing Truths. Then he went on to say, "When you realize God is in you; you will realize your call to add this flavor to the lives of those around you. If you don't, who will? And a great opportunity will be lost.

14 "You are to funnel the light of Divine Love onto every person you meet and to everything you do. *15* This light of Love must shine so brightly from your heart and from your eyes that every shadow of fear is reborn into love. *16* Open your hearts to love and then help others walk this path with you to God.

21 "The old commandment was: do not kill anyone. My new Commandment is: do not hate anyone. Hate comes from anger, anger comes from fear; fear comes from a lack of love, and God is Love. *22* If your heart starts to turn to anger or hate, turn it instead to God. In this way even those you consider enemies can point you to God. *23* So when you begin to pray, and remember that your sister or brother holds something against you, *24* go and be reconciled with that person, and then begin your prayer again. *25* Because we pray to come closer to God, we must realize that our sisters and brothers are God too. *26* Let this Truth flow into all your life so that you treat everyone the way you would treat God.

27 "The old commandment was: don't commit adultery. My new commandment is: respect everyone as you respect God. *28* Sexual attraction comes naturally and is to be honored; but sexual action must always be a decision based on respect and love, and founded on the God it manifests.

31 "The old law was that anyone who wanted to divorce should issue a divorce certificate. *32* My new law is that no one should ever divorce unless the life of the marriage has been fought for, but has died.

33 "God is Truth, so always speak the truth. *34* Say 'yes' when you mean yes, *35* and 'no' when you mean no. *36* Anything else is not of God.

38 "The old law said 'An eye for an eye and a tooth for a tooth.' *39* My new law is, don't try to hurt those who hurt you. *41* If someone asks you to walk with them a mile, walk two miles. *42* Realize that everything is of God, and you are simply stewards of what you believe you own; so be very generous with those who beg from you, or ask to borrow from you. And if you have more than you need, you must give it to those in need. And at times you must give even what you believe you need, knowing that Dad will always provide.

43 "The old belief was that we should 'Love our neighbors, and hate our enemies.' *44* But what I want you to do is love your enemies, and pray for those who persecute you. *45* This will show that you are daughters and sons of our Dad, whose light shines on everyone and whose rain refreshes the just and those considered unjust. *46* For everyone loves their friends, and that does not reflect the depth of God's love. *47* And if you greet only your family and friends, do not even those who don't believe in Dad do that? So strive to love everyone, just as Dad does.

CHAPTER 6

1 "Be sure to do your good works in secret, so you do not do them for the wrong reason. *2* You must give for the benefit of others and not for the benefit of your own glory. *3* When you practice charity, don't let your left hand know what your right hand is doing. *4* Your heart is the only part of you that needs to know.

5 "And when you pray, do this too in private, so your heart keeps centered on God and not on what others are thinking of you. *6* When you pray, close your door and go into your heart and just listen to and talk to Dad. *7* When you pray, talk as simply as you do with your human Dad and Mom. *8* After all your God already knows all about you and what is in your heart.

9 "When you pray, say something like this: 'Dad, father of all, we really love you. *10* May we feel you in our hearts and see you in our actions. *11* Please give us what we need today, and help us share what we don't. *12* May we treat others with the same love and gentleness as you treat us. *13* And keep us always on the Path to you.

14 "Forgiveness is always the key to peace in your hearts. *15* Since God forgives everyone, how can you do any less? *16* When you fast you should be the only one who knows it. *17* This keeps you centered on God and not on what others think of you.

19 "Keep your heart pure and your values straight, so as not to believe that material things can bring you happiness, for all these things will pass away. *20* Only spiritual treasure lasts forever. *21* And remember that where you believe your treasure is, that is where your heart will be.

22 "The eye is the lamp of the body. So if your eye is clear, your whole body is light; *23* but if your eye is clouded, your whole being is in the dark. And there is no greater darkness than the darkness within.

24 "No one can follow two bosses with different ideas. You cannot serve God and money, for they have very different ideas.

25 "So I say to you: don't worry about what you are to eat, or what you are to drink, or what you are to wear. Is not life more important than its nourishment, and the body than its clothing? *26* Look at the birds, how they neither sow nor reap nor store their food in barns; but our heavenly Dad takes care of them. So why would you think he won't take care of you?

27 "Furthermore, who of you through worrying can add a minute to your life? *28* And why do you worry about clothes? Look at how the lilies in the fields live. *29* They don't spin to make their clothes but even Solomon in all his splendor was never dressed so beautifully as one of these. *30* So if God clothes the grass of the fields, that is here today and gone tomorrow, will he not do even more for you?

31 "So don't worry about what you are going to eat or drink or wear. *32* Those who don't trust Dad worry about these things. *33* I want you to look for God in your hearts; and when you find his reflection there, you will know all these things will be taken care of. *34* So don't worry about tomorrow, live in the now, for that is where God is found.

CHAPTER 7

1 "Be very aware of how you judge others so you can learn how you judge yourselves. *2* What we do to others simply mirrors what we do to ourselves. *3* If you see something in your brother's eye, *4* look in the mirror first at your own eyes before you offer to do anything to his. *5* For ultimately there is no 'other' since we are all one.

7 "Ask and it will be given to you; seek and your will find; knock and it will be opened to you. *8* For anyone who asks will receive; anyone who seeks will find; and anyone who knocks will have it opened. *9* Who among you, whose daughter or son asks for bread, would give them a stone; *10* or if they ask for a fish, would give them a snake? *11* So if you know enough to give your children what is good for them, imagine what your heavenly Dad will give those who ask him. *12* We can simplify all this to a simple phrase: How you want to be treated is how you need to treat others.

15 "If you want to know if people are trustworthy, look at what they do. *16* You will know the kind of person you are dealing with much more by what they do than by what they say.

21 "Be sure to align your will with the will of God, otherwise you will always be divided within. *22* For God dwells in the deepest part of your heart; and your heart is the deepest

part of you. *23* To struggle against the will of God is to struggle against yourself, because at your deepest level you are God. *24* Those who align their will with the will of God are like those who build their home on rock. *25* There will always be things in life that feel like storms, but a house built on stone can stand straight in a storm. *26* Those who fight the will of God are like those who build their home on sand; when the storms come, the rain washes their homes away. *27* To resist God who is love, is to resist love, and this never brings us the happiness we all seek."

28 When Jesus finished talking, the crowd was amazed at his teaching, *29* for he taught with his own authority, and not like the scribes who simply parrot what they have heard from others.

CHAPTER 8

1 When Jesus came down from the mountain great crowds followed him. A leper came up and knelt before him, *2* and said, "Teacher, if you are willing, you can cleanse me." *3* Reaching out his hand Jesus touched him saying, "I am willing, be cleansed." And instantly his leprosy was cleansed. *4* Jesus said to him, "Don't tell anyone about this. Go into the deepest recesses of your heart and thank the God who cleansed you."

5 Later he went to Capernaum and while he was there a centurion came to him and said, *6* "Teacher, my servant boy is at home paralyzed and in great agony." *7* Jesus said, "I will come and heal him." *8* The centurion replied, "I don't feel worthy to have you come into my home. Just say the word and my boy will be healed. *9* For I am under authority and have authority over others. I say to a soldier 'Go!' and he goes; and to my servant, "Do this!' and he does it." *10* As Jesus listened to him he marveled and said, "Rarely have I met anyone with such faith as this Roman. *11* Many like him will sit at the table of Abraham in heaven. *13* Then Jesus said to the centurion, "You have believed, and so your boy will be healed." And at that exact moment the servant boy was healed.

14 Then Jesus went to Peter's house. His mother-in-law was sick in bed. *15* So he went in and touched her hand and she was healed. She got up and started to serve them. *16* That evening they brought many possessed and sick people to him and he healed them all.

18 Shortly after that they went down to the lake, but there were so many people there that Jesus decided to go to the other side. *19* Just then a scribe came up to him and said, "Teacher, I want to follow you wherever you go." *20* Jesus replied, "The foxes have dens, the birds have nests, but I have no real place in this world. *21* If you really want to follow me, *22* you will have to look way beyond the things of this world."

23 Then he got into the boat with his friends. *24* A severe storm came up on the lake and the waves were tossing the boat all around. *25* Jesus was asleep during all of this; so they woke him up and said, "Teacher, we are going to drown; save us." *26* Jesus replied, "Your faith is still weak. There is nothing to be afraid of." Then he stood up and talked to the wind and the waves, and there came a great calm. *27* Those with him said, "What kind of man is this that he can even calm the wind and the sea?"

28 When they reached the other side of the lake, two men who lived among the tombs came out to meet him. *29* They both had troubling energies, and they started shouting at Jesus. *30* So he healed them and sent them on their way.

CHAPTER 9

1 Jesus went home again by boat. *2* There they brought him a paralyzed man on a stretcher. When Jesus saw their faith in him, he said, "Cheer up, my son, you are precious in the eyes of God." *3* Some scribes who were there thought to themselves, "This man blasphemes! How can he know God's heart?" *4* Jesus knew this and said, "Why do you think these things; *5* for which is easier, to know God's heart or to say to this man, 'Get up and walk?' *6* But to show you that I know God's heart (he then said to the paralyzed man), 'Get up and walk home.'" *7* The man got up and walked home. *8* And when the crowd saw this they were utterly amazed, and they gave thanks to God for what they had seen Jesus do.

9 Then Jesus walked on and saw a man named Matthew sitting collecting taxes. He said to him, "Come with me." So he got up and went with him. *10* They went and sat in another tax collector's patio. More tax collectors and others not-well-thought-of came and sat down with them. *11* When the Pharisees saw this, they said to Jesus' friends, "Why does your teacher eat with this kind of people?" *12* Jesus overheard this and said, "It is not the healthy who need a doctor, but the hurting. *13* Try to understand what the prophet said, 'It is love that I want and not sacrifice.' for I did not come just to call those close to God, but to call those who feel abandoned by God."

14 Then those who were with John came and said, "Why do we and the Pharisees fast and your friends do not?" *15* Jesus answered, "Didn't you just hear me say, 'It is love that I want and not sacrifice?' You fast to sacrifice; it would help you more to fast to open your hearts more fully to God.

16 "Remember that you cannot patch an old coat with a piece of un-shrunken cloth. If you do, the patch will shrink and make an even bigger hole. *17* And you cannot store new wine that is still fermenting in dry wineskins because it will burst the skins. So please don't try to sew what I am teaching you onto your old beliefs, or put it into them. You need to start with fresh beliefs to absorb what I am teaching."

18 While he was still speaking, a ruler came up to him and said, "My daughter has just died. Please come and lay your hands on her and bring her back to me." *19* Jesus and his friends got up and followed him. *20* On their way to the house a woman, who had suffered from a vaginal hemorrhage for twelve years, (which made her unclean according to the Jewish law, and unable to touch anyone) came up behind Jesus and touched the fringe of his robe. *21* For she said to herself, "If I can only touch his robe I will be healed." *22* Jesus felt her do this and turned around and said to her, "Cheer up, your faith has healed you." And the woman was completely healed.

23 When they got to the ruler's home, there was a large group of mourners there. *24* Jesus told them to go outside; that the girl was not dead, but just sleeping. They made some snide remarks as they went outside. *25* After they had left, he went into her bedroom and took her hand and raised her up. *26* News of this spread all over the country.

27 As Jesus was walking away from there, two blind men shouted at him, "If you can raise her from the dead, you can surely cure our blindness." *28* He went into their place and asked them, "Do you really believe I can heal you?" They responded, "Yes we do!" *29* He walked over to them and touched their eyes and said, "As you believe, so it shall happen." *30* And their eyes were opened and they could see. *31* He told them not to tell anyone about this, but they went out and told everyone.

32 As they were leaving, a dumb man with a negative presence came up to Jesus. *33* Jesus told the presence to leave and the man began to speak. The crowds saw this and said, "Nothing like this has ever been seen." *34* Some Pharisees were there and said, "He can deal with these negative presences because he deals with the prince of negativity."

35 Jesus went among all the towns and villages announcing the Good News and healing all who were sick. *36* When he saw all the others who needed the Good News and to be healed, he felt pity and love for them since they seemed like sheep without a shepherd. *37* He said to his friends there, "Pray that Dad sends more shepherds, more pastors, and that more receive this Call and answer it. *38* For the possibilities of love are tremendous if people will only answer their Call."

CHAPTER 10

1 Jesus called his twelve apostles together and gave them the ability to cast out negative energies, and to heal every disease. *2* These are their names: Peter and his brother Andrew, James and his brother John; *3* Philip and Bartholomew, Thomas and Matthew, the tax collector; *4* James and Thaddeus, Simon the Zealot, and Judas Iscariot, who later betrayed him.

5 Jesus sent these twelve out with these instructions: *7* "As you go along, tell people that God lives in their hearts. *8* Heal the sick; raise the dead; cleanse the lepers, and cast out negative energies. I give you the ability to do this without charge, so exercise these gifts without charge. *9* Don't take any money, extra clothes, or anything else with you; *10* so you will learn that I will take care of you.

11 "Whenever you enter a town or village, follow your heart to the home of someone you believe will be open to our Message; *12* and stay with that family as long as you are in that Community. *13* Those who are open will sense the peace that your presence brings. *14* If people don't receive you, bless them and move on.

16 "You need to be well aware that I am sending you out as sheep among wolves. *17* So be as subtle as snakes and as innocent as doves. *18* You will be brought before government officials, and beaten by synagogue members. *19* But don't worry about any of these things. *20* If you are brought to court, don't worry either, for the Spirit of God will speak through you and help you.

23 "If they persecute you in one town go on to the next. I assure you that you will not have gone to all the towns around before the seeds of Truth you are planting begin to take root and bear fruit.

24 "You need to remember that a student is not greater than the teacher. *25* They have called me the devil, so don't expect everyone to call you a saint. *26* Nevertheless, don't be afraid to preach openly the Truth about God that has been hidden until now. *27* What I have taught you in the night you are to speak out in the day, and what I have whispered in your ear, you must proclaim from the rooftops.

28 "Don't be afraid of those who want to kill your body, because your spirit will live on forever. *29* Even the hairs on your head have been counted by Dad, so great is his love for you. *30* And you will always have life from the love in his heart. You may lose your life, but never his love. *31* So there is absolutely nothing to be afraid of.

34 "I have come to bring Truth to the world, and Truth does not always bring peace at first because many resist it; others even oppose it. *35* So there will be divisions even in families, between those who accept the Truth and those who reject it. *36* There may even be daughter against mother, son against father. Don't let this discourage you, *37* for Truth always finds a home in our hearts, even if our ears initially reject it. *38* So set your heart on the Truth, and you will find the Path to life. *39* Truth always ends in life, even if the body ends in death.

40 "The main Message I want you to teach is that everyone is a daughter or son of God, absolutely everyone has been (re)born into God's Life, Divine life. *41* Tell people that if they let God into their hearts they will discover he has always been there. And this seed of Divine Life that is planted in the heart will grow and encompass the whole person. *42* This is the Truth that gives life. This is the Truth that eventually brings peace, for if all are Divine, there are no distinctions between people and so no need for any type of conflict."

CHAPTER 11

1 When Jesus finished giving his instructions to the apostles, he sent them out to preach and heal in the surrounding towns.

2 When John heard in prison about all this, *3* he sent friends to Jesus to ask him if he was the Christ. *4* Jesus told them to relay to John what they were seeing and hearing: *5* the blind could now see; the lame could now walk; lepers are cleansed; the deaf could now hear; the dead are raised to life; and the poor are hearing the Good News. *6* "This will answer John's question for him."

7 As John's friends were getting ready to go back, Jesus began to talk about him to those close by. *8* "John is the prophet that you were really looking for when you went out to the desert. *9* I tell you he is even more than a prophet. *10* He is the one about whom it is written: 'Listen carefully. This is the Messenger I have sent to help you prepare the Road to Divinity. *11* I assure you that he is a marvelous man, but those who will walk into their Divinity will be even greater than he is now!

25 "Dad, thank you for revealing

these things to the little ones and not to the learned ones. *26* I know this is the way you like things."

28 Then he said to the crowd gathered there, "Come all of you who have hard work to do, or who feel heavily burdened, and I will show you where you can rest. *29* Accept my teaching and learn from my example, for I am gentle and humble of heart. *30* Once you take this Truth into your heart and find God there, you will have found your true resting place."

CHAPTER 12

1 Then one Sabbath Jesus was walking through the wheat fields. His friends were hungry and so they began to pick the heads of wheat and eat them. *2* The Pharisees noticed this and said to Jesus, "Your friends are doing things that are not allowed on the Sabbath." *3* Jesus replied, "Have you not read what David did when he and his men were hungry— *4* how he entered the temple and ate the bread that only the priests were allowed to eat? *5* Or have you never read how the law permits priests to do things on the Sabbath? *6* But I tell you we are talking about something more important than the temple here. *7* And if you can come to understand that God wants love and not law, you would not condemn us."

9 He left them and went into the synagogue. *10* There was a man there with a paralyzed hand. So to trap him they said, "Is it lawful to heal on the Sabbath?" *11* Jesus replied,

"Is there anyone of you who would not save his sheep if it fell into a pit on the Sabbath? *12* If it is all right to help a sheep on a Sabbath, surely it is all right to help a person on the Sabbath." *13* Then he said to the man, "Stretch out your hand." He stretched out his paralyzed hand, and everyone saw that it was as perfect as the other hand. *14* But the Pharisees were very upset and so began to plot to kill him.

15 Jesus knew this and left that place. *16* Many followed him and he healed them all, *22* even a man who was both blind and dumb. He healed him so that he could see and speak, but he told them not to tell anyone about it. *23* All the crowds were completely amazed at this.

33 Jesus said, "We know that a mature tree can bear good fruit, but a young one can't. We know a tree by its fruit."

46 While he was still speaking, his mother, sisters and brothers, came to see him. *47* Someone told him they were there. He thanked the person for telling him this, and said to the crowd, *48* "I need to go visit with my family, *49* but before I do that I want all of you to know that you too are my sisters and brothers. *50* We are all the Family of God."

CHAPTER 13

1 That same day Jesus went down and sat on the beach near his home. *2* So many people gathered around him that he finally stepped into a boat so he could more easily talk to them on the shore. *3* He began to teach them in parables.

4 "A farmer went out to sow, and as he sowed, some seeds landed near the road, and the birds came and ate them. *5* Some seed fell on rocky soil and although they sprouted, there was not enough soil for them to put down roots, *6* so the sun scorched them and they died. *7* Some seeds fell among the thorns, and the thorns grew up and choked them. *8* But most of the seeds fell on good soil so they grew and produced a nice crop—some a hundred-fold, some sixty and some thirty. *9* Open your ears wide to hear what I am saying."

10 His friends came up and asked him why he was teaching in parables. *11* Jesus replied, "Parables are stories of Truth. *11* It is often easier to remember a story than it is to remember a Truth. *12* And parables can carry a number of Truths at the same time.

16 "So keep your eyes and ears very open, *17* for I assure you that many prophets and saints have longed to see what you see, and to hear what you hear. *18* Now let me help you understand the parable of the farmer. *19* When people hear the Good News but do not understand it, negative energy can snatch away the seed sown in their hearts. This represents the sowing along the road. *20* And what was sown on rocky soil refers to those who hear the Good News and accept it immediately; *21* but it doesn't put down roots in their hearts, and so when trouble or persecution comes, they turn away from it. *22* And what is sown among thorns refers to those who hear the Good News, but worldly cares and the enticement of money choke the Good News, and it never bears fruit in their hearts. *23* But what is sown on good ground refers to those who hear the Good News, understand it, and begin to really live it. These are the ones who bear fruit, some a hundred-fold, some sixty and some thirty."

24 Then Jesus told them another set of parables, "The Divine Life in us is like those who sow good seed in their fields; *25* but while they *are* asleep their enemy *came* and sowed weeds among the wheat. *26* So the wheat and the weeds grew together. *27* The owner's workers came and said, 'Wasn't that good, clean seed that was sowed in your field? So where did these weeds come from?' *28* The owner said, 'An enemy has done this.' So they asked him if he wanted them to root out the weeds. *29* He said, 'No, because if you did that, you would also uproot a lot of wheat.'"

31 Then he told them another parable, "The Divine Life in us is like a mustard seed. *32* It is the smallest seed, but when it grows, it becomes a tree so large that the birds can rest in it." *33* Then he told them this parable: "The Divine Life in us is like yeast that is put in a batch of flour until it has all raised."

34 Jesus told all these things to the crowd in parables. *36* One of them then asked him to explain the meaning of the parable about the weeds. *37* So he said, "The sower of the good seed is the Son of Man. *38* The field is our hearts. *39* The good seed is his Divine Life. *40* The weed seed is sowed by fear. *41* Fear can keep the Divine Life from growing strong when it is planted. *42* Its roots sometimes intertwine with the roots of Divine Life. *43* But at the final Harvest fear will die because it is ultimately nothing."

44 Jesus then went on with another set of parables. "Divine Life is like a precious treasure that a person finds in a field. He is so happy that he found it that he goes and sells all he has and buys the field where it is. *45* Again, Divine Life is like a merchant looking for beautiful pearls. *46* Having found one of exceptional value, he went out and sold all he owned and bought it."

51 Jesus then said, "Have you understood all of this?" They said they had. *52* So he said to them, "Every teacher of this Divine life must be very creative and use all sorts of ways to help people understand it."

53 When Jesus finished preaching all these parables, he went back home. *54* There he taught in the synagogues in such a way that everyone was amazed. They wondered how he came by all this wisdom and all the miracles. *55* They said to one another, "Isn't this the son of Joseph, the carpenter? Isn't his mother called Mary, and his brothers James, Joseph, Simon and Judas? *56* And don't we know his sisters Mary and Joanna? Where did he get all this wisdom?" *57* And they refused to accept him. Jesus then said to them, "A prophet is not without honor except in his own hometown." *58* And because of their disbelief he did not perform many miracles there.

CHAPTER 14

1 At that time King Herod heard of Jesus' fame and said to his attendants, *2* "This must be John the Baptist reincarnated with all these powers at work in him." *3* For Herod had arrested and imprisoned John on account of Herodias, the wife of his brother Philip. *4* John had told him, "You have no right to marry her." *5* Herod wanted to kill him but was afraid to because the people considered him a prophet.

6 On Herod's birthday the daughter of Herodias danced before them and pleased Herod so much, *7* that he promised her anything she wanted up to half his Kingdom. *8* Prompted by her mother, she asked for the head of John the Baptist on a platter. *9* Herod was upset by this request, but complied because of his promise. *10* He sent orders to the prison to behead John. *11* His head was brought to her on a platter, and she gave it to her mother. *12* His friends came and buried his body and went and told Jesus. *13* When Jesus heard this news, he went off to a deserted place to pray, but the crowds found him. *14* When he came back, he saw a great mass of people there and had pity on them. He healed all their sick.

15 As evening arrived, the apostles came to Jesus and said, "It is getting close to dark and this is a deserted place. Why don't you dismiss the crowd so they can go to the villages around and buy food for supper? *16* But Jesus said to them, "They don't need to leave. You can feed them." *17* They answered, "All we have here are five loaves and two fish." *18* He said, "Bring them here to me, and have the people sit down on the grass." *19* Then he took the five loaves and the two fish, prayed and gave thanks, and broke the loaves and handed them to the apostles, who gave them to the people. *20* They all ate what they wanted and then they gathered up what was left. *21* It was twelve full baskets, and there had been over ten thousand who had eaten.

22 He then told his apostles to sail to the other side while he dismissed the crowd. *23* And after he had dismissed the people, he walked up the hill to pray. Night had come and he was there alone. *24* But the boat by that time was a long way from shore and was being tossed about by the waves; for the wind was very strong. *25* In the wee hours of the morning he came walking to them on the water. *26* When the apostles saw him walking on the sea, they shouted out in terror, "It is a ghost!" *27* But Jesus said, "Don't be afraid! It's me!" *28* Peter answered, "If it is

you, command me to come to you on the water!" *29* Jesus said, "Come!" Peter was startled at this but got out of the boat and began to walk on the water toward Jesus; *30* but when he looked at the waves, he got frightened and began to sink. He cried out to Jesus, "Save me!" *31* Immediately Jesus reached out his hand and took hold of him and said, "You were doing so well. Why did you stop believing?" *32* After they had gotten into the boat, the wind quieted down. *33* Then those in the boat knelt before him and said, "Truly you are the Christ." Jesus said, "Get up! You can do what I have done if you just believe!"

34 When they reached Gennesaret, *35* the people there recognized him and sent word to all the surrounding country; and they brought all their sick to him. *36* They begged him to let them touch the fringe of his robe, and all who did were healed.

CHAPTER 15

1 Then the Pharisees and scribes from Jerusalem came and asked Jesus, *2* "Why do your friends not follow the law about washing their hands before they eat?" *10* He asked the people to gather around and he said to them, "Please listen closely to this. *11* It is not what enters the mouth that pollutes a person, but what comes out of a person's mouth that pollutes him." *15* Peter then asked Jesus to explain this. *16* Jesus said, "Even you do not understand? *17* Do you not know that what enters the mouth passes through the stomach and then is purged? *18* But what comes out of the mouth comes from the mind and heart, and that is what pollutes a person. *19* For out of the mind comes negative thoughts and plans, dishonesty and slanders; and what comes out of the heart is hatred, pettiness and greed. *20* These are what pollute a person, and not eating with unwashed hands."

21 Then he said to the Pharisees and scribes, "Now let me ask you something. Why do you not keep the commandment to honor your mother and father? Rather than taking care of them, you tell them that you are going to use that money to offer sacrifice in the temple. Remember what Hosea said, 'It is love that I want and not sacrifice.'"

22 Later Jesus' friends came and said, "Are you aware that the Pharisees and scribes were shocked by what you said?" *23* Jesus replied, "Every plant that Dad did not plant must be uprooted." *24* They asked him to explain that, so he said, "People make up things and say they are from God. All these weeds must be uprooted from our traditions. Be careful of these people. *25* They are lost in a field of these weeds. It has made them blind to what God really wants, and they lead others who are also blind."

26 Jesus left there and withdrew to the region of Tyre and Sidon. *27* There a Canaanite woman came to Jesus and cried out, "Teacher, take pity on me; my daughter is badly possessed." *28* Jesus answered her, "Woman, your faith is great. I will do what you ask." And at that very moment her daughter was healed.

29 Jesus went from there to the Sea of Galilee and climbed a nearby hill and sat down to teach. *30* Great crowds kept coming to him with people who had all sorts of physical ailments. *31* He healed them all; and amazed the crowds when they saw the dumb speaking, the lame walking and the blind seeing. They all gave thanks to God.

32 Jesus called his apostles and said, "I am very concerned about all these people. They have been with me three days now and have nothing to eat. I don't want to send them away hungry for they may faint on their way home." *33* The apostles said to him, "Where are we possibly going to get enough food to feed such a huge crowd?" *34* Jesus asked them if they had any food at all. They said they had seven small loaves of bread and a few little fish. *35* Jesus asked the crowds to sit down. *36* Then he took the seven loaves and the few fish, gave thanks for them, and passed them to the apostles, who passed them out to all the crowd. *37* After they had all eaten well, they gathered up what was left over and it filled seven baskets. *38* More than eight thousand people had eaten their fill. *39* Then Jesus dismissed the crowds and sailed to the Magadan region.

CHAPTER 16

1 There the Pharisees and Sadducees came up and asked him for a sign of his calling from God. *2* He told them the only sign they would have would be the sign of Jonah *3* (referring to his three days in the tomb). *4* Then he left them and moved on.

5 When they all got to the other side of the lake, the apostles realized that they had forgotten to bring bread along. *6* Jesus said to them, "Beware of the yeast of the Pharisees and Sadducees." *7* The apostles thought he was concerned that they had forgotten to bring along bread. *9* He reminded them of the ten thousand they fed with five loaves, *10* and the eight thousand they had fed with the seven loaves, so that not having bread was not a problem. *11* He told them that instead they should have more faith because of what they had already seen. *12* Then he told them that the yeast of the Pharisees and Sadducees that he was referring to was their teachings.

13 When they were entering the region of Caesarea Philippi, Jesus asked his friends who people thought he was. *14* They said, "Some say John the Baptist; others Elijah, others Jeremiah, or one of the prophets." *15* He then asked them, "But you, who do *you* believe I am?"*16* Peter answered, "You are the Christ." *17* Jesus answered him, "Blessed are you, Peter, for it was no human person who revealed this to you, but our Dad. *18* I say to you Peter that you are one of the rocks on which I will build my Mission of Love. *19* The Key to this Mission is Divine Life, Divine Love. *20* Be sure you tell everyone that Dad is Love."

21 From then on Jesus began to prepare his apostles for his death in Jerusalem. He also told them that he would rise from the tomb on the third day, as Jonah had come out of the whale's mouth on the third day. *22* Then Peter pulled him aside and said, "This must never happen to you!" *23* Jesus said to him, "Peter, sometimes you are a little devil. To help spread my Mission you must learn to think like a God and not like a man." *24* Then Jesus said to his apostles, "If you are really going to follow me; you have to follow me all the way, all the time; and not just when convenient. *25* Dad's way can be very hard, but it is the only way to the Truth. You may even lose your life, but you will find yourself.

26 "But what good is it to acquire the whole world? For you will lose it when you die. Strive simply to become the Divine that you already are. *27* For I came to teach you to be daughters and sons of God. *28* And you can do this without even dying."

CHAPTER 17

1 Six days later Jesus invited Peter, James, and John to go up a high mountain with him. *2* There he was transfigured before them. His face shone as the sun and his clothes became as white as the light. *3* Isaiah and Elijah also appeared to them and they were talking with Jesus. *4* Then Peter said to Jesus, "Teacher, it is so wonderful being here. If it is all right with you we can make a place for you and Isaiah and Elijah."

5 While he was saying this a bright cloud overshadowed them and a voice said, "This is my beloved Son, whom I really love. Listen carefully to him." *6* As the three heard this, they fell on their faces in great fear; *7* but Jesus came over to them, touched them and said, "Get up and don't be afraid." *8* And when they opened their eyes, they saw only Jesus.

9 As they were coming back down the mountain, Jesus told them not to tell anyone about the Vision until he rose from the dead. *10* The three said, "We now know you are Christ, but many say that Elijah must come first. Is that what just happened?" *11* Jesus replied, "No, Elijah has already come back to help straighten out things, but people didn't recognize him. *12* In fact they killed him just as they will kill me." *13* Then the three realized he was talking about John the Baptist.

14 When they got back down the mountain, a crowd came. One of them said, *15* "Teacher, please take pity on my son. He is an epileptic and suffers terribly. He often falls into the fire and often into water. *16* I brought him to your apostles, but they could not heal him. *17* Jesus replied, "Bring him here to me!" *18* Jesus put his hand on him, and at that moment the boy was completely healed.

19 Then the three came up next to Jesus and said, "Why could we not heal him? Jesus replied, "Because you do not believe enough. Why do you think I took you up the mountain and showed you clearly that I am God? I am not simply your teacher; I am your mirror! What you see in me is what is in you. What you see me do is what you are to do. From now on believe, and you will do what I do. *20* For I assure you, if you have faith the size of a mustard seed, you can say to this mountain, 'Move over there' and it will move. And nothing will be impossible for you. *21* To heal as I just did, you need to know and believe you are God.

22 They all gathered back in Galilee and Jesus said to them, "I am about to be betrayed and killed; *23* and be raised on the third day." They were all very distressed at this news.

24 They went to Capernaum, and the tax collectors came to Peter and asked, "Does your teacher pay taxes?" *25* Peter said, "Yes." Later Peter asked Jesus what he thought of their paying taxes. He said, "Who do the kings tax, their daughters and sons or foreigners?" *26* Peter responded "Foreigners." Jesus said, "So we daughters and sons (of the king) are exempt. *27* However, so as not to offend them, go down to the sea and catch a fish. In the fish's mouth will be a coin. Take it and pay our tax."

CHAPTER 18

1 Then the apostles came to him and asked him who were the most important people in heaven. *2* Jesus called a little child over, and asked him to stand with them. *3* He then said to them, "There is no one more important to this child than those who love him. *4* You are going to have to know the importance of love to understand heaven. *5* If you want to be important in heaven, become humble like this child; become loving like this child. *6* Then you will finally realize that everyone is important in heaven."

12 Then Jesus taught them with a story. He said, "If a shepherd has a hundred sheep and one gets lost, doesn't he leave the ninety-nine and go looking for the one who is lost? *13* And if he is able to find the one that is lost, isn't he happier over that one than over the ninety-nine that weren't lost? *14* Your heavenly Dad is like that shepherd; he doesn't want anyone to get lost. And I have come to find the lost.

15 "If a sister or brother has done something against you, go privately and talk to them. If they listen, you have made a friend. If they don't listen, ask another person or two to go with you to talk to them. *16* Perhaps with these witnesses you can get the dispute resolved. *17* If that doesn't work, it is probably better not to deal with that person, *18* but continue to treat the person with respect when you do meet them.

19 "I assure you that if two of you agree about anything for which you pray, our heavenly Dad will do it. *20* For where two or three gather in my name, I am with you."

21 Then Peter came up and said to him, "Teacher, if a person offends me, how many times should I forgive him? Even seven times?" *22* Jesus said to him, "Not seven, but seventy times seven."

CHAPTER 19

1 Then Jesus left Galilee and went to the Judean territory across the Jordan. *2* Large crowds came to him and he healed them all.

3 Then the Pharisees came to him and asked if it was ever right to get a divorce. *4* Jesus said, "Since the beginning of creation marriage has been the joining of husband and wife into one flesh, *5* so they are no longer two but one. *6* The only possible reason for divorce is if the marriage has already died."

13 People were bringing their little children to Jesus so he might lay hands on them and pray for them. *14* His friends tried to stop this, but Jesus said, "Let the little children come to me, for they remind me of the kingdom of heaven." *15* And after laying hands on them he left.

16 A young man came up to Jesus and said, "Teacher, what should I do to live the Life of God?" *17* Jesus said, "You know the commandments, follow them. *18* And love your neighbor as yourself."

20 The young man replied, "I have done all these things. Is there anything else I should do?" *21* Jesus said, "There in one more thing you can do. You can sell everything you have and give the money to the needy and come walk with me." *22* When he heard that, he went away sad because he owned a lot of property.

23 Then Jesus remarked to the apostles, "I assure you that it is extremely hard for rich people to live the Life of God. *24* In fact it is impossible unless they realize they are simply stewards and not owners of the property. Dad didn't create the world for people to possess it, but rather to use it for the benefit of all his daughters and sons." *25* The apostles were amazed when he said that. They wondered who possibly could live that way. *26* So Jesus said, "The only way to live the life of God is to be God. That is what I came to teach."

27 Peter then said, "We have left everything to follow you: *28* What is in this for us?" *29* Jesus replied, "You who have left everything to follow me will have everything that I have and everything that I am. *30* You will know the Way; You will know the Truth, and you will live as God.

CHAPTER 20

1 "For the kingdom of heaven resembles the owner of an estate. He went out early in the morning to hire people to work in his vineyard. *2* They agreed on the usual daily wage, and he sent them off to his vineyard. *3* At about nine o'clock

he went out and saw other people looking for work. *4* He told them to go and work and he would pay them whatever was fair. So they went to work. *5* He went out at twelve and three and did the same thing. *6* When he went out at five he found still others there seeking work. He asked them why they weren't working. *7* They said, 'Because no one has hired us.' So he told them to go to his vineyard and work.

8 "As evening fell he said to his foreman, 'Call the workers and pay them starting with those who came last and work back to those who came first.' *9* When those who started work at five came, they received a full day's wage, *10* so when those who started first came, they thought they would get more, but they got the same daily wage.

11 "They grumbled against the owner and said, *12* 'These last ones have worked only one hour and you gave them the same pay as us who worked all day in the hot sun.' *13* But the owner said, 'My friend, I have done no wrong to you. I have paid you what we agreed to in the morning. *14* Take what you received and go on home. I choose to pay those who came last the same as you. *15* Do I not have a right to be generous with my own money?' *16* So the last can be first and the first can be last."

17 As they were all walking to Jerusalem, Jesus took the apostles aside and said to them, *18* "I want you to know that when we get to

Jerusalem, I will be betrayed to the chief priests. *19* They will sentence me to death and hand me over to the civil authorities, to be mocked, scourged and crucified; but on the third day I will be raised.

25 "Before that happens I want to remind you that even though the civil rulers lord it over other people, it is not to be that way with you. *26* Whoever among you who wishes to be great must learn to serve. *27* And whoever wants to be first must act like a servant. *28* Remember, I did not come to be served but to serve, and to give my life as an example of this."

29 As they were leaving Jericho, a great crowd followed them. *30* Two blind men who were sitting by the side of the road heard that Jesus was walking by; so they shouted, "Teacher, have pity on us." *31* The crowd told them to be quiet, but they shouted even louder, "Teacher, have pity on us!" *32* Jesus stopped and asked them what they wanted him to do. *33* They said, "Teacher, we want you to open our eyes." *34* Jesus took pity on them and touched their eyes. They were cured instantly and got up and followed him.

CHAPTER 21

1 When Jesus drew near to Jerusalem, he was very tired from his journey. *2* A friend offered him a donkey to ride so he got up on it. *3* As the people saw him coming on the donkey they began to put their coats down in the road to honor him.

4 Others brought branches and did the same. *10* The people of Jerusalem who didn't know who he was wondered what was happening. *11* The crowds leading him kept singing, "Blessed is he who comes in the name of God."

12 Jesus went into the temple and drove out those selling things. *13* He shouted "Our Dad's house is for prayer, not for business." *14* The blind and lame came to him in the temple, and he cured them all. *15* When the chief priests saw the amazing things he was doing, they were very upset. *17* That night he went outside the city to Bethany and spent the night there. *22* The next morning he went back to the temple and taught again about the importance and the power of belief. He said, "Everything you ask for in prayer with faith will happen, if you believe."

23 Then the chief priests came to him and asked him by what authority he was doing the things he was doing. *24* Jesus responded, "Let me ask you a question too; and if you answer it, I will answer your question: *25* 'Where did John's baptism come from; from God or from *us humans*?'" They realized they were trapped because if they said "from God," he would ask them why they didn't believe in it. *26* And if they said "from us humans" they had reason to fear the people's reaction, since they considered him to be a prophet. *27* So they answered, "We do not know." He responded,

"Neither do I tell you by what authority I do these things."

42 Jesus went on to say, "But there is one thing I will tell you. The people whom you look down upon, the prostitutes and tax collectors, are going to beat you to heaven. *43* Have you not read in your scripture, 'The stone that the builders rejected has become the chief cornerstone?' *44* All the people who feel rejected by religious leaders will be welcome in Dad's house."

45 When the chief priests and Pharisees realized that Jesus was talking about them, they wanted to arrest him but were afraid to because the crowds considered Jesus a prophet.

CHAPTER 22

1 Jesus began to teach again in parables. *2* "The Kingdom of Heaven is similar to a king who was preparing a wedding feast for his daughter. *3* He sent out his servants to let those invited know that the feast was ready; but they would not come. *4* Again he sent out his servants with a stronger message that the dinner was ready and everything prepared and urging them to come. *5* But they disregarded the invitation and went on with their own plans. *7* The king decided instead to invite to his banquet those who were hungry. *8* So he sent his servants out a third time to invite everyone who wanted to come, *9* the bad and the good; *10* and so the banquet hall was filled completely with those who were hungry."

15 When the Pharisees heard this, they realized he was again talking about them, so they decided to trap him and disgrace him in the eyes of the crowd. *16* To do this they sent followers of theirs and emissaries from Herod to him who said, *17* "Do you think it is right to pay taxes to Caesar or not?" *18* But Jesus saw the trap and so said, "Why do you try to trap me. Show me a coin." *19* And they gave him a coin. *20* He said to them, "Whose image is this?" *21* They said, "It is Caesar's." So he told them, "Then give it to Caesar, and give to God what is God's." *22* They were amazed at his answer and left him alone.

33 The Pharisees came back later with another idea about how to discredit him before the crowd. *34* So one of them, a teacher of the law said, *36* "Teacher what is the greatest commandment in the law?" *37* Jesus said to him, "You shall love God with your whole heart, with your whole soul, and your whole mind. *38* This is the greatest commandment. *39* The second is like it: 'You shall love your neighbor as yourself.' *40* On these two commandments the whole law rests."

46 No one was able to say anything else, and from that day on no one tried to trap him with questions.

CHAPTER 24

1 After Jesus had left the temple, his apostles were pointing out how beautiful it was. He said to them, "Yes, it is very beautiful, but it will not last. 2 I assure you that there won't be even one stone left on top of another." 3 They all walked to the Mount of Olives and when they were alone, his apostles asked him to explain what he had meant about the temple.

Jesus said, "My dear friends, what I will say today will shock you. What I will say today will be ignored by many who claim to be following what I have preached. There is no way around that; and there is nothing to fear about that. God's Heart is patient and kind. He knows his children are passing through their teenage years of rebellion; but also that they will eventually return to him; because they were created to *be* him, and won't really be happy until they are back with him. Teenagers often revolt and believe they can only be themselves by proving they are not like their parents. After they have passed through this phase they return to their inheritance and admit, and then rejoice, that they are indeed daughters and sons of Dad, daughters and sons of God, Goddesses and Gods.

"In the meantime there will be the chaos of rebellion. During this time many immature believers will try to act like mature believers and say, 'I am God,' even before they know who or what God is. Don't be swayed by them; and don't worry about them. In time they will mature into their own Divinity and be the God of Love and Service that a deep part of them already knows they are.

"During this time mature believers will be persecuted by immature believers because of jealousy. So when you are persecuted for being a believer in your own Divinity, love those who believe they have to destroy your Divinity to be themselves. The human Heart knows innately that we are all Divine, but until the time when this Truth really incarnates, there will be wars and all sorts of calamities. Don't worry about this, it is simply the rebirthing pains of humanity returning to its Divinity.

"We spoke earlier of the temple, and you were shocked to hear that it will be destroyed. I came to teach that the Temple of God is in your hearts. For people to believe this, the external Temple of God has to fall.

"You now believe that Divinity rests in me. And even though this is true, you have not yet realized that Divinity also rests in you. And this is exactly what I came to teach. I am soon going to be killed. Don't worry about that. It is simply another step in taking away the mirror so you can see your real selves. Now you see Divinity only in me; then you will see your own Divinity face to face in yourselves.

"It will take longer for the temple to fall than it will for me to seem to fall. But I will rise from the dead by becoming alive again in you. The external temple that we recently walked out of will need to come back to life in your hearts as well.

"Dad does not need to be honored by buildings, but by love; for he **is** Love. The great prophets from this day forth will amplify Hosea's wonderful Truth and say in God's Voice: 'It is love I want and not honor!' Honor can often separate us if we don't see that the person we honor is one with us.

"So the sign of my coming back will be love growing in each heart; God growing in each heart. Please teach this to the people. Please tell all my sisters and brothers that together we are one Divine Celebration!"

CHAPTER 26

The apostles were amazed at what Jesus had said. So they asked him, "Then what are we to do? What is our Call?" Jesus replied, "Your Call is very simple: Treat everyone as you would treat God. Teach everyone that they are God. Be the God you believe in. For I will return as the believers mature.

2 "You must know that in two days the Passover will be celebrated and I will be handed over to be crucified."

3 Meanwhile the chief priests and the elders met in Caiaphas' house 4 and plotted about how to arrest Jesus secretly and to kill him. 5 They said, "But not during the Feast or we could have a riot among the people."

6 While Jesus was in Bethany, 7 Mary Magdalene anointed his head with special perfume. 8 Some apostles were upset with this interruption. 9 Jesus noticed this and said, "Mary is very upset that I am going to die soon and wanted to do something special for me. 10 So why do you embarrass her with your jealousy, when she is doing something lovely for me? 12 By pouring this perfume on me she has prepared me for burial. 13 Wherever you preach about my life, I want you to talk about my wife."

14 Then Judas left and went to the chief priests and said, "What are you willing to give me if I hand Jesus over to you?" 15 They offered him thirty silver coins, each worth a day's wage. 16 And from that day on he looked for an opportunity to betray Jesus.

17 On the first day of unleavened bread the apostles asked Jesus where he wanted to eat the Passover Meal. 18 He told them to go to his friend in Jerusalem, and ask about using his place for this ceremony. 19 So they went there and got things prepared for the Passover.

20 In the evening Jesus sat with his friends at the table. 21 He said to them, "I tell you, one of you is going to betray me." 22 They were really upset by this and asked him who he was talking about. 23 He replied, "He who has dipped his hand with me in the dish will betray me." 25 Judas then said, "Surely it is not me you are talking about." Jesus said, "Yes it is."

26 As they were eating Jesus took

bread and broke it and gave it to those there saying, "Take this and eat it; it is my body." 27 Then he took a cup of wine and gave thanks, then he passed it to them and said, "Take this and drink it, for it is my blood. 28 When you drink my blood, we will consummate our New Covenant, and you will have (my very) Life in you. 29 I tell you this is the last time I will eat before I go home to Dad."

30 Then they sang a hymn together and went out to the Mount of Olives. 31 When they got there, Jesus said, "Tonight you will desert me. 32 After I have been raised up, I will go ahead of you back to Galilee."

33 Peter said, "Even if all the others desert you, I will not." 34 Jesus said, "This very night before the cock crows you will deny me three times. 35 Peter said to him, "Even if I must die with you, I will never deny you." And everyone else said the same thing.

36 Then they went to a place called Gethsemane and he told his friends, "Sit down here while I go over there and pray." 37 Taking Peter, James and John with him, he became very distressed. 38 He said to them, "Stay here and pray with me." 39 And going on a little farther he began to pray. He said, "Dad, I am ready to come home, but I don't look forward to tomorrow. Help me!"

40 He came back to the three and found them asleep. He said to Peter, "So you could not pray with me even for an hour? 41 Your spirit is willing, but you body is weak."

42 He went back again to pray and said, "Dad, I am ready. I will do what we have agreed to." 43 He went back to the three and found them asleep again. 44 So he just went back to talk to his Dad again. 45 When he came back to the three again, he woke them up and said, "It's time to go. 46 They have come for me."

47 He had just finished saying this when Judas arrived with a crowd from the chief priests and elders. They were carrying clubs and spears. 48 His betrayer had told them, "The one I kiss is the one you want." 49 He went right up to Jesus and said, "Greetings, Teacher," and kissed him. 50 Jesus said, "My friend, why have you come here?" Then they came forward and took hold of Jesus and arrested him. 51 Peter drew his sword and swung at the high priest's servant and cut off his ear. 52 Jesus said to Peter, "Put your sword away. Haven't I told you that I do not believe in violence?"

55 Then Jesus said to the crowd, "Why have you come with clubs and swords to arrest me, when I have been sitting in the temple teaching every day?" 56 At this all the apostles deserted him and fled.

57 They took Jesus and led him away to Caiaphas who was high priest that year. The scribes and elders had gathered there. 58 Peter followed them at a distance and went into the high priest's courtyard and sat down to see what would happen. 59 The chief priest and the entire Sanhedrin were trying to get enough

false testimony so they could get him executed. *60* And although many false witnesses did come forward, there was really no proof of anything deserving the death penalty. *61* Then finally two witnesses came forward and said, "He said, 'I have the power to destroy the temple and to build it up again in three days.'"

62 So the high priest got up and said to Jesus, "Do you have anything to say in rebuttal of these witnesses?" But Jesus remained silent. *63* The chief priest said, "I command you under oath to the living God to tell us whether you are the Christ." *64* Jesus said to him, "Yes, I Am Christ."

65 At this the high priest tore his clothes and said, "He has blasphemed! What further need do we have of witnesses? *66* What do you think?" They answered, "He deserves death!" *67* Then they spat in his face and beat him. *68* Others slapped him and said, "Prophesy, oh Christ! What is my name?"

69 Now Peter was still sitting outside in the courtyard. A servant girl came up to him and said, "You were with Jesus the Galilean." *70* But Peter denied this and said, "I don't know what you are talking about." *71* As he was going out the gate another servant said to those around, "This fellow was with Jesus the Nazarene." *72* Again Peter denied this and said, "I don't even know him." *73* Shortly after that the bystanders came up to him and said, "We are sure you were with this man. You have the same accent." *74* Then he began to curse and swear, "I don't know him!" Then a cock crowed. *75* Peter remembered what Jesus had predicted, and went out and cried bitterly.

CHAPTER 27

1 At dawn all the chief priests and elders of the people held a consultation over the execution of Jesus. *2* They bound him and handed him over to Pilate, the governor.

3 When Judas saw that Jesus was condemned, he felt such remorse that he returned the thirty silver coins to the chief priests. *4* He said, "I have sinned in betraying an innocent man." But they said, "What is that to us? That's your problem." *5* So he flung down the silver coins in the temple and went and hanged himself. *6* The chief priests picked up the coins and said, "It is not right for us to put this back in the treasury since it is blood money. *7* So they bought the Potter's Field as a cemetery for foreigners; *8* which is still called, "The Field of Blood."

11 Now Jesus was standing before the governor, being questioned. Pilate asked him, "Are you the King of the Jews." Jesus replied, "Yes I am." *12* But to the accusations of the chief priests he gave no reply. *13* Then Pilate said to him. "Don't you hear what they are saying against you?" *14* The governor was very surprised when he still said nothing.

15 It was a custom for the governor to release a prisoner that the people wanted at the time of the Feast. *16* At that time there was a notorious convict named Barabbas in jail. *17* So when they had assembled before him, Pilate said, "Do you want me to release to you Barabbas or Jesus, who is called the Christ," *18* because he knew they had delivered Jesus over to him simply because of jealousy.

19 When he was seated on the tribunal, his wife sent him a message to have nothing to do with Jesus, "For he is an innocent man." She said that because she had had a bad dream about the situation. *20* But the chief priests and elders convinced the crowd to ask for Barabbas' release and for Jesus' execution. *21* The governor asked them again who they wanted him to release. They shouted, "Barabbas!" *22* He said, "Then what shall I do with Jesus?" They all shouted, "Crucify him!" *23* But then Pilate said, "But what has he done wrong?" But they just shouted even louder, "Crucify him!"

24 When Pilate realized he was getting nowhere, and that the crowd was about to riot; he took water and washed his hands before the crowd and said, "I am innocent of this man's death. Take him and see to it yourselves." *25* The crowd responded, "His blood be on us and on our children." *26* He then released Barabbas to the crowd, and had Jesus flogged and handed over to them to be crucified.

27 Then Pilate's solders took Jesus into the palace and the whole cohort gathered around him. *28* They stripped him and put a scarlet robe on him. *29* They put a crown of thorns on his head, and a reed in his hand. Then they knelt before him and mocked him saying, "Long live the King of the Jews." *30* They spat on him and hit him on the head. *31* And after mocking him, they took off the robe and put his own clothes back on him. Then they led him out to be crucified.

32 On the way they found a Cyrenian and forced him to carry the cross for Jesus, since he had kept falling down from fatigue. *33* When they got to Golgotha, which means "Place of the Skull," *34* they gave him wine mixed with gall to drink; but after tasting it, he did not drink it. *35* And after they had crucified him, they divided up his clothes, *36* and then sat down and watched him. *37* Over his head they nailed a plaque: Jesus, King of the Jews.

38 Then two robbers where crucified and placed on either side of him. *39* Those walking by insulted him and shook their heads and said, *40* "You said you could destroy the temple and rebuild it in three days. If you really are the Christ, come down from the cross." *41* Likewise, the chief priests with the scribes and the Jewish elders mocked him and said, *42* "He saved others, now let him save himself. *43* If he really is the King of the Jews, let him come down from the cross and we will believe him." *44* Even the robbers crucified with him mocked him.

45 About noon it started to get very dark, and this lasted until about three o'clock. *46* Then Jesus cried out, "Dad! Dad! Help me!"

47 Some of those around said, "He is calling for God. *48* One of the soldiers dipped a sponge in vinegar and putting it on a reed, started to offer it up to Jesus to drink. *49* But the others there said, "Wait a minute. Let's see if God comes to save him."

50 Jesus once more cried out to Dad, and then went to him. *51* At this the veil in the temple was ripped in two from top to bottom, and there was an earthquake. *52* Some tombs were opened and many saints were raised from the dead. *53* And after Jesus' own resurrection they entered the holy city and were seen by many.

54 When the centurion and all his men there saw the earthquake and everything else that happened, they were dreadfully frightened and said, "Truly, this was God's Son." *55* There were a lot of women looking on from a distance. They were the ones who had walked with Jesus from Galilee. *56* These included Mary Magdalene his wife, Mary his mother, (who was also the mother of James and Joseph,) and Mary the mother of James and John.

57 It was now getting close to evening, and a rich man from Arimathea called Joseph, who was a believer in what Jesus said, *58* went and asked Pilate for the body of Jesus. Pilate gave orders that it be given to him. *59* Joseph took the body and wrapped it in a new linen and laid it in his own tomb, which he had had hewn out of rock. *60* Then a large rock was rolled across the door and he went away. *61* But Mary Magdalene and Mary, his mother, stayed watching at the tomb.

62 The next day, which was the day after the Preparation, the chief priests and Pharisees went to Pilate, *63* and reminded him that Jesus had said he would rise after three days. *64* They asked him to have the tomb watched for three days so that his believers could not steal the body and say that he had risen, indicating that this would be disastrous. *65* So Pilate gave them soldiers and told them to go and make the tomb as secure as possible. *66* So they went and sealed the tomb and set a guard outside.

CHAPTER 28

1 That Sunday morning, after the Sabbath rest was over, Mary Magdalene, his wife, and Mary, his Mother, went to the tomb for the family annointing of the body. *2* They found the stone rolled away from the entrance to the tomb. *3* This really upset them and they leaned down and looked into the tomb and saw that it was empty. *4* The guards then woke up, and also saw that the tomb was empty, and so ran away.

5 Then Jesus appeared to his family and said, "Don't be afraid, it is really me! *6* I have risen like I said I would." *7* They approached him slowly, and gradually began to believe it was really him. *8* They were overcome with joy and peace and began to hug him. *9* After they had talked a while, Jesus asked them to go and tell his friends that he was indeed alive, that he had risen from the dead. *10* So they left quickly, to go tell the wonderful news to his friends.

11 While they were on their way, the soldiers went to the chief priests and told them everything that had happened. *12* The chief priests talked things over, *13* and then gave the soldiers a lot of money to say that the believers had come in the night while they were asleep and had stolen the body. *14* "And if this word gets to the governor we will take care of it for you." *15* So the soldiers took the money and did as they were told.

This is the story that many believe even until this day.

16 When Jesus appeared to the eleven and the others, they were very excited, although some had trouble believing what was happening. *17* Jesus said to them, "My work here is done. Now I send you to continue it. *18* Go, therefore, to the whole world, baptizing them in the Spirit, **baptizing them into themselves!** *19* Teach them what I have taught you: that they are all daughters and sons of Dad, that Love is the most important thing, and always manifests as service. *20* And remember always that I am with you until the end of time, and even more, that *I am* you for ever!"

MARK

CHAPTER 1

1 The beginning of the Good News of Jesus, a Christ, a Son of God.

2 The prophet Isaiah wrote, "I send my Messenger before you to prepare your way; *3* a voice crying in the desert to help people find their way to God." *4* John the Baptist appeared in the desert and baptized people to help them cleanse themselves and their lives. *5* And many people from Judea and Jerusalem came and were baptized by him in the Jordan River.

6 John's clothes were woven of camel's hair, with a leather belt around his waist. He ate only locusts and wild honey. *7* He kept saying, "There is someone coming after me who is greater than me. *8* I baptize with water, but he will baptize with Spirit."

9 Then Jesus came from Nazareth in Galilee and was baptized by John in the Jordan. *10* And the moment he came up out of the water, he saw the heavens open and Spirit come down on him like a dove. *11* Then a voice came from heaven, "You are my beloved son. I really love you!"

12 Then he was lead by Spirit into the desert to face his fears before he began his public ministry. *13* He stayed there forty days in prayer.

14 After John had been arrested, Jesus went up to Galilee preaching the Good News of God. *15* He would say, "The time has come to learn that God is in your hearts. Rethink your lives and believe this Good News."

16 As Jesus was walking along the Sea of Galilee, he saw Peter, and his brother Andrew, casting a net into the sea, because they were fishermen. *17* Jesus said to them, "Come walk with me, and I will teach you how to fish for people." *18* They immediately left their net and went with him. *19* Going a little further he saw James and his brother John, the sons of Zebedee, who were in their boat, mending their nets. *20* He called them and they left their father and their boat and followed him.

21 They went to Capernaum and the next Sabbath Jesus went to the synagogue and began to teach. *22* They were amazed at his teaching since he seemed to teach from experience and not just talk about what he had read, as the scribes do.

23 There was a man in the synagogue with a negative energy. *26* Jesus expelled the negative energy, and it came out of the man. *27* The people who witnessed this were amazed. Here was a man who taught with real authority, and could expel negative energies. *28* Because of things like this, his fame quickly spread throughout all of Galilee.

29 That same day Jesus went with James and John to the house of Peter and Andrew. *30* Peter's mother-in-law was sick in bed. *31* They told Jesus this, and he went in and took her hand and raised her up. She felt so good that she began to wait on them.

32 That evening as the sun was setting they brought all the sick and possessed to him, *33* until it seemed the whole city was at their door. *34* He cured many people who were sick with different diseases, and healed many possessed.

35 Jesus got up before dawn the next morning, and went out to a deserted place to pray. *36* Jesus' friends went looking for him, *37* and when they found him they said, "Everybody is looking for you." *38* Jesus said to them, "Let us continue on to the neighboring towns so I can preach and heal there too, for that is why I came." *39* So he went preaching in their synagogues and casting out negative energies throughout all of Galilee.

40 A leper came to Jesus and begged him to heal him. He said, "If you want to, I know you can heal me." *41* Jesus was deeply moved and put out his hands and touched him, and said, "I do want to! Be cleansed." *42* Immediately the leprosy left him and he was completely cleansed. *43* Jesus sent him off and said, *44* "Don't tell anyone about this." *45* But he went off and told everyone he met; so that Jesus could no longer enter a town openly, but had to stay in deserted places. And even then people kept coming to him in droves.

CHAPTER 2

1 Some days later he returned to Capernaum and people soon learned that he was home. *2* So many congregated that before long you couldn't even get in the house. *3* Jesus was preaching the Good News, when four men came carrying a paralytic for him to heal. *4* Since they could not get in the door they went up on the roof and took off part of it. Then they lowered the man on the cot to where Jesus was sitting. *5* Jesus was very impressed with their great faith and so said to the paralytic, "You are very loved by God." *6* Some of those there mumbled, "This man is a sinner. How can he be loved by God? *7* And how can Jesus know the heart of God? It is blasphemy to presume that you can." *8* Jesus knew what they were thinking and so said, *9* "Which is easier to do? Know the heart of God or to say to a paralytic 'Get up and walk home?' *10* But to show you that I do know the heart of God, *11* I now say to this paralytic, 'Get up and take your cot and walk home!'"

12 At once the man got up, picked up his cot and walked out the door and went home. Everyone was amazed to see this. They said, "We have never seen anything like this." *13* Then Jesus walked out again by the seashore; and the crowd followed him; and he taught them.

14 Later as he walked along he noticed Levi, the son of Alpheus, sitting at the tax office. He said to him, "Walk with me." He got up and they walked off together. *15* And so it was that at Jesus' table there were regularly many tax collectors and others not-well-thought-of. *16* The Pharisees noticed this and asked Jesus' friends why he ate with such people. *17* When he heard this he said, "It is not the well that need a doctor, but sick people. I did not come to call just those well thought of, but mainly the lowly. *22* I know this is a new concept for you, so put it in a new mind-set, just as you put new wine into new wineskins."

23 Jesus was walking through a wheat field on a Sabbath and his friends began to pick the heads of wheat and eat them. *24* The Pharisees saw this and said to him, "Why are your friends doing what is not allowed on a Sabbath?" *25* Jesus said to them, "Why do you always ask me about the law? *26* God is Love; *27* God is not law. *28* If you want to get closer to God get closer to love, and don't worry so much about law."

CHAPTER 3

1 Jesus went into the synagogue on a Sabbath and there was a man there with a withered hand. *2* They watched him to see if he would heal on the Sabbath, so they could accuse him of breaking the law. *3* He told the man with the withered hand to stand in the center. *4* Then he said to them, "Is it all right to help a person on the Sabbath?" But they would not answer him. *5* Looking around at them and being concerned about their hard hearts, he said to the man,

"Hold out your hand!" He held it out and it was completely restored. *6* And at this the Pharisees left and began to plot how to kill him.

7 Then Jesus and his friends went down to the seashore, and many people followed him from Galilee, Judea, Jerusalem, and all over. *8* They came because they had heard what he had done. *9* He told his friends to have a boat ready so he could be out on the water and teach without the crowd crushing him. *10* For he had healed so many that anyone with ailments wanted to touch him. *11* And he drove out the negative energies.

13 Then Jesus went up a hill and selected his apostles. *14* He appointed twelve who would be sent out to heal the sick, rid people of the negative energies, and preach the Good News. *15* He appointed these twelve: *16* Simon, whom he called Peter, *17* James and John, the sons of Zebedee (Thunder); *18* Andrew and Philip; Bartholomew and Matthew; Thomas and James, the son of Alpheus; Thaddeus and Simon from Cana; *19* and Judas Iscariot.

20 Then they went back down to eat, but so many crowded around that they couldn't. *22* Scribes had come down from Jerusalem and said that Jesus himself was possessed. *23* They believed the negative energies were actual beings, and said that Jesus was using their leader to drive the rest out. *24* So Jesus called them together and said, "How can it be that the leader of the negative energies drives the others out? If a kingdom is divided against itself, it cannot last. *25* Just as a family divided against itself will not last. *26* So if the leader of the negative energies is driving them out, they are about to come to an end."

31 Jesus' mother, sisters and brothers came to see him, but they could not even get into the house where he was, so they sent a message in to him. *32* The message was: "Your mother, sisters and brothers are outside asking for you." *33* Jesus said, "Tell them I will be out in a minute. *34* But first I want to explain to you that we are all sisters and brothers, daughters and sons of God our Dad. *35* We who acknowledge God as our Dad all have this special bond of Family."

CHAPTER 4

1 Later on he went down to the seashore again to teach. He got into the boat there and sat down. *2* As was his custom, he taught them with a parable: *3* "A farmer went out to sow and as he did some seeds fell along the road, *4* and the birds came and ate them. *5* Some seeds fell on rocky soil and although they sprouted, there was not enough soil for them to put down roots. *6* So the sun scorched them and they died. *7* Some seeds fell among the thorns, and the thorns grew up and choked them. *8* But most of them fell on good soil, so they grew and produced a nice crop—some thirty-fold, some

sixty, and some a hundred. *9* Open your ears wide to what I am saying."

10 Later when the crowd had left, the twelve asked him about the parable. Jesus said, "Parables are Stories of Truth. *11* It is often easier to remember a story than it is to remember a Truth. *12* And Parables can carry a lot of Truths at the same time."

13 He then asked them, "How do you believe you can teach people if you can't understand and work with Parables? *14* At the present time I am the sower of the Good News, but soon you will be, for that is your calling. You are to preach the Good News and then prove its Truth by healing. Healing is the physical side of preaching the Good News.

15 "So let me help you understand how to work with parables. When people hear the Good News but do not understand it, negative energy can snatch away the seed from down in their hearts. This represents the sowing along the road. *16* And the seed sown on rocky soil refers to those who hear the Good News and accept it immediately; *17* but it doesn't put down roots in their hearts, so when persecution or trouble comes, they abandon it. *18* And what is sown among thorns refers to those who hear the Good News, *19* but worldly cares and the enticement of wealth choke the Good News and it never bears fruit in their hearts. *20* And those sown on good soil refer to those who hear the Good News, understand it, and welcome it into their lives. These are the ones who bear good fruit; some yield thirty, sixty or even a hundred-fold."

21 He then said to them, "Is a lamp brought into a house to be put under a bushel basket or under the bed? Don't we put it out in the open or on a stand? *22* For nothing is hidden that will not be known and nothing kept secret except to be revealed. *23* Open your ears wide so you can understand what I am saying."

24 He then said, "Be very careful to learn this Truth. The way you treat others is the way you treat yourself, and the way they will treat you. *25* And those who believe they are blessed will be blessed; and those who do not feel blessed usually aren't blessed. We attract to ourselves what we believe about ourselves."

26 And he said, "The Divine Life in us is like the farmer who scatters seed on the ground, *27* then he goes to sleep that night and the next morning the seeds are sprouting, but he doesn't know all that happens. *28* Then he sees the blade come out and it forms a head. *28* Finally there is the mature head of wheat. *29* And when it is ready, he gets his sickle for the harvest.

30 "Or again, the Divine Life in us is like the tiny mustard seed, *31* that when it is planted grows to be larger than any plant. *32* So large that the birds can nest in its branches."

33 With parables like these he shared the Good News of God's Divine Life in us. *34* And later when they were alone he always explained it more, so the apostles could learn to teach it better.

35 That very evening he said to the apostles, "Let's go across to the other side of the lake." *36* Some people in other boats joined them. *37* After he went to sleep, a heavy squall came up and the waves grew very dangerous. *38* They woke him up and said they were about to sink. *39* He got up and asked them, "Why are you so afraid? *40* Don't you have any faith?" He then calmed the wind and said to the sea, "Relax, it is all right." Then the wind slowed, and there was a great calm. *41* They were still terribly frightened and said to one another, "Who is he anyway, for even the wind and the sea listen to him?"

CHAPTER 5

1 In the morning they arrived at the opposite shore in the country of the Gerasenes. *2* Just as they arrived, a man came out from among the tombs who had a negative energy. *3* He made his home among the tombs and was completely out of control. *5* He always remained among the tombs and in the mountains shrieking and cutting himself with stones.

6 Everyone tried to avoid him, but Jesus went up to him and calmed the negative energy. *15* The man calmed down and became himself again. *16* When people realized what Jesus had done, they were filled with awe.

17 They were also afraid of his power and so asked him to leave the area.

18 As Jesus was getting back into the boat the man who had been healed came up to him and asked to go along with him. 19 But Jesus said to him, "Go back to your family and friends and tell them what happened, how the Love of God has been manifested in your life." 20 And the man went off and went through all the Ten Cities around, telling the marvels of what Jesus had done for him, and all who heard his story were astonished.

21 Jesus crossed to the other side again, trying to avoid the crush of the crowd. 22 However, as soon as they arrived there, one of the synagogue leaders came up to him and begged him to come to his house. 23 He said, "My daughter is almost dead. 24 Please come and lay your hands on her that she may recover and live."

25 On their way they met a woman who for twelve years had suffered from vaginal hemorrhages. 26 She had been treated by all the doctors of the area to no avail, and had spent all her money. (We must remember that this ailment made her always unclean in the eyes of the law.) 27 But she came up behind Jesus anyway and said to herself, 28 "If only I can touch his robe, I will be healed." 29 As she did this, her hemorrhage stopped, and she knew she was healed.

30 Jesus was aware that this had happened and turned around and asked, "Who touched me?" 31 His friends said, "You see how the crowd is pressing around and yet you ask, 'Who touched me?'" 32 But Jesus looked around to see who had done it. 33 The woman came up to Jesus trembling because she knew she had broken the law; but she also knew she had been healed. 34 He said to her, "My daughter, your faith has healed you. Go in peace."

35 While he was still talking to her, servants from the ruler's house arrived and told him he did not need to bother Jesus anymore because his daughter had already died. 36 But Jesus said to the ruler of the synagogue, "Don't worry! Just have faith."

37 From there on he didn't allow anyone to go with him except Peter, James and John. 38 When they got to the ruler's home, there was loud weeping and wailing. 39 He went in the house and said, "Why all this turmoil and weeping? The child is not dead, but just sleeping." 40 They ridiculed him for saying this, but he asked them all to leave. Then he took the child's mother and father and went into the room where the child was. 41 He took the girl's hand and said, "Little girl, get up." 42 And instantly the little girl got up and walked around. She was twelve years old. They were all astonished beyond expression. 43 He then charged them not to tell anyone what had happened there. Then he told them to get her something to eat.

CHAPTER 6

1 He left there and went back to his hometown with his friends. *2* That Sabbath he went to the synagogue to teach. Many who were there were utterly amazed at what he taught. They began to ask, "Where did he get all this wisdom? And how does he work all these miracles? *3* Isn't this the carpenter's son, the son of Mary and Joseph? Aren't his brothers James and Joseph and Jude and Simon? And don't his sisters Mary and Joanna live here with us?" They were shocked by what he was doing.

4 He knew what they were thinking and saying, and so he said, "It is sad that a prophet is never accepted where he grew up." *5* He could do no great work there because of their lack of belief; and so he laid his hands on a few sick people and healed them. *6* Then he left and went around the nearby villages teaching.

7 Then he called the twelve and began to send them out two by two. He gave them power over negative energies. *8* And gave them instructions for their ministry. They were to take nothing at all along with them except a staff. This was so that they would learn that he would always take care of them.

10 He also told them to be respectful of the people who gave them hospitality. *11* And that if a community was not hospitable, they were to move on to one that was willing to listen to the Good News. *12* So they went out and preached

that people should rethink their lives and their priorities and put God first. *13* They also dealt with many negative energies, and anointed the sick and healed them.

14 King Herod heard about this since Jesus had become well known. He believed that John the Baptist had risen from the dead and was doing these miracles. *15* Others said he was Elijah, and still others said that he was a prophet like they used to have long ago. *16* But Herod was convinced he was John the Baptist. *17* For Herod had had John arrested and put into prison because of Herodias. *18* She had been his brother Philip's wife before he married her; and John had told him he had no right to marry her. *19* So Herodias held a grudge against him and wanted him killed but saw no way to do it. *20* For Herod stood in awe of John because he believed him to be an upright and holy man, and enjoyed listening to him. *21* An opportune time for Herodias's revenge came on Herod's birthday. *22* He gave a banquet to his nobles and prominent Galileans, at which Herodias' daughter came in and danced for him. *23* He was so pleased with this that he swore to her that he would give her anything she asked for, even half his kingdom. *24* She went and asked her mother what she should ask for. Herodias said, "The head of John the Baptist." *25* She went back to the hall and told the king that she wanted the head of John the Baptist brought to her on a platter.

26 The king was very saddened by this request, but because of his oath, and his guests, he did not want to refuse her. 27 So he sent a guardsman with the order to bring John's head. 28 He went and beheaded him in prison and brought his head and presented it on a platter to the girl, and she took it to her mother. 29 When John's friends heard about this, they came and took his body and laid it in a tomb.

30 The apostles came back from their missions and reported to Jesus everything they had done. 31 He said to them, "Come away with me to a place where you can rest for a while." For so many people were coming and going that they didn't even have time to eat. 32 So they left by boat to a lonely place to be by themselves. 33 But the people saw them leaving and knew where they were going and so ran there and got there first. 34 When Jesus landed, he saw the crowd and took pity on them, for they were like sheep without a shepherd. And he began to teach them.

35 It got late so the apostles came to Jesus and suggested he dismiss the people, 36 so they could go and get something to eat. 37 But he answered them, "You give them something to eat." They said, "Shall we go and spend a half year's wages on food to feed them?" 38 He asked them, "How many loaves do you have? Go and find out." They came back and reported that there were five loaves and two fish.

39 He then asked all the people to sit down on the grass 40 in groups of about a hundred. 41 Then taking the five loaves and the two fish he looked up to heaven and gave thanks. Then he broke the bread and gave it to the apostles who passed it out to the people. He also divided the two fish for them all. 42 They all ate what they wanted. 43 Then the apostles picked up twelve full baskets of leftovers of the bread and the fish. 44 This was after some ten thousand people had eaten.

45 Then he urged the apostles to get into the boat and cross over to Bethsaida. 46 Jesus then dismissed the crowd and walked up the mountain to pray.

47 When it got dark, the boat was in the middle of the sea, and Jesus was alone on the shore. 48 Seeing them still struggling and rowing hard because the wind was against them, he went to them about three o'clock in the morning, walking on the sea. 49 They thought he was a ghost and so cried out. 50 But he said, "Don't be afraid. It's me." 51 He then got into the boat, and the wind calmed down. 52 They seemed more amazed at this than they did at the feeding of the ten thousand with five loaves and two fish.

53 After they had finished crossing the lake, they docked at Gennesaret. 54 As soon as they got out of the boat people recognized Jesus, 55 and spread the news to the

entire region. So everyone with any kind of ailment was brought to him wherever he went. *56* And wherever he went, whether in the towns or in the country, people brought those who were sick and begged him to allow them to even touch the hem of his robe. And all who touched him were healed.

CHAPTER 7

1 Then Pharisees and scribes came from Jerusalem and asked Jesus why his friends did not follow the law, *2* and wash their hands before they ate. *3* Jesus asked them why they were teaching human regulations as though they were doctrines from God, *4* and why they broke the commandment about honoring their mothers and fathers. *5* Jesus said, "Rather than taking care of them, you tell them that you are going to offer sacrifice in the temple. *6* Do you not remember what the prophet Hosea said, 'It is love that I want and not sacrifice?'"

14 Jesus asked the people to gather round, and he told them, "Please listen to what I have to say. *15* Nothing that enters a person from the outside can make that person unclean, but it is the things that come out of a person which makes that person unclean. *16* Please open your ears wide so you can understand me."

17 When he had gone inside away from the crowd, his friends asked him about the parable. *18* He said to them, "Do you not realize that whatever enters from the outside cannot defile a person, *19* because it does not enter his heart but rather his stomach, and passes through and is passed on?" (In saying this he declared all food to be clean.) *20* He then said, "What comes out of a person's mouth comes out of his heart, *21* and that is what can pollute a person. *22* For out of the heart come negative ideas and plans. *23* And it is all these negative things that come from the heart that defile a person."

24 Then he got up and went to the district of Tyre. There he went into a home to get away from the crowds for a bit; but that was now impossible. *25* A lady who had a daughter with a negative energy came to him as soon as she heard he was there. *26* She was a Gentile from Syro-Phoenicia with great faith. *27* Jesus showed God's universal love and healed her daughter. *30* When she got back home she found her daughter perfectly healed.

31 Coming back from the district of Tyre he passed through Sidon on the Sea of Galilee and went up the center of the region of the Ten Cities. *32* They brought him a deaf man with a speech impediment and asked him to lay hands on him. *33* Taking him off by himself, Jesus put his finger into his ears and touched his tongue with saliva. *34* Then looking up to heaven he sighed and said, "Be opened." *35* And at once his ears were opened and he could speak clearly.

36 He told him not to tell anyone, but he told everyone. *37* Those who heard of this were amazed and said, *38* "He can even make the deaf hear and the mute talk!"

CHAPTER 8

1 Later another huge crowd gathered to hear Jesus teach. *2* After teaching for three days he called his apostles and said, "I feel very sorry for these people since they have been listening to me for three days and now have nothing more to eat. *3* I am concerned that if I simply send them away, they will faint on their way home, since most of them live a long way from here."

4 His apostles responded, "Where in this desert could we possibly find enough food for such a huge crowd?" *5* Jesus asked them how many loaves they had. They said they had seven. *6* So he asked the crowd to sit down on the ground. Then he took the loaves, gave thanks, broke them, and gave them to the apostles to give to the people. *7* They also had a few small fish; and so Jesus gave thanks and gave them to the apostles to pass them out to all the people. *8* All the people ate what they wanted and they picked up seven baskets of what was left over. *9* About eight thousand people had eaten. *10* He then dismissed them and set off for the region of Dalmantha.

14 After a bit they crossed the lake again, but the apostles forgot to bring along bread. *15* Jesus said, "Beware of the yeast of the Pharisees and Herod." *16* They thought Jesus was hinting about their having forgotten bread. *17* So he said to them, "Why are you worrying about bread? *18* Have you not seen what has taken place? *19* When I broke the five loaves for the ten thousand, how many baskets were left?" They answered, "Twelve." *20* "When there were seven loaves for the eight thousand, how many baskets did you pick up?" They said, "Seven." *21* And he said to them, "Don't you see that having bread is not our problem?"

22 When they reached Bethsaida they brought a blind man to him and asked Jesus to touch him. *23* So Jesus took him by the hand and led him out of the village. After anointing his eyes with saliva, he laid hands on him; and then asked him if he saw anything. *24* The man looked and said, "I see people, but they look like trees walking around." *25* Then Jesus laid hands on his eyes again. This time he looked more intently and saw everything distinctly. *26* Jesus then told him to go home and not go back into the village.

27 Jesus and the apostles went to the villages around Caesarea Philippi, and as they were walking, he asked them, "Who do people say that I am?" *28* They said to him, "Some say John the Baptist, others say Elijah, and still others say one of the prophets." Jesus then asked them, *29* "But you, who do you say that I am?" Peter said, "You are a Christ." *30* And he told them not to tell anyone this.

31 He then began to tell them that he was going to suffer and be rejected by the elders, chief priests, and the scribes, and be executed. Then after three days he would rise. 32 He emphasized this to them. Then Peter took him aside and began to remonstrate with him. 33 Jesus looked at him and said, "Peter, you just said I am a Christ, and now you want to straighten me out? I am going to do what Dad tells me, and not what you tell me!"

34 A crowd gathered and so he said to everyone there, "Those who want to walk the Path that I have taught will have to give up everything: what you think, what you believe, especially believing that you own what you have. 35 This is not an easy Path, but it is the Path to happiness and peace. 36 Hanging on to what you now believe will cost you what is really important. 37 What is more important for you, your illusions or your real life?

38 "Follow my footsteps back home to Dad."

CHAPTER 9

1 He also said, "I also want to make it very clear that before I came, death was thought to be the only door to Divine Life. Now you have my Good News to open this door to your own Divine Life any time you want to open it. I have not come only to lead you back home to Dad; but also to lead you back home to the Divine in your own heart. And ultimately show you that you and I and Dad are the exact same thing; the exact same person. We are simply different manifestations of the same person, the *only* person, the One!

2 To help them understand this, three days later he took Peter, James and John with him up a high mountain where they could be alone. And there he showed them his Divinity, to help them see their own Divinity. 3 His clothes became a pure natural white before them. 4 And Elijah and Isaiah appeared to them and talked with Jesus.

5 Peter said to Jesus, "Teacher, we are ecstatic to be here with you and see this. Let us build three booths, 6 one for you, one for Elijah, and one for Isaiah." He really did not know what to say in his astonishment.

7 Then a cloud came over them and a voice from it said, "This is my son, my beloved. Listen closely to him." 8 Then suddenly all they saw was Jesus. 9 And as they were walking down from the mountain, Jesus told them not to tell anyone about this until he rose from the dead, because the others would not believe it until he had risen. 10 They didn't tell anyone, but talked among themselves about what "rise from the dead" must mean.

11 Then they asked him why the scribes say that Elijah must come first. 12 He answered them, "Elijah had indeed to come first and you have just witnessed that, as you witnessed it with John the Baptist. Now the deeper question is 'Why do I have to suffer and be treated

with contempt?'" In saying this Jesus connected the Transfiguration on the mountain and the "Transfiguration" on the cross. *13* He went on to explain, "I tell you that Elijah has also already come in human form too, and they treated him as they will treat me." In saying this Jesus showed how John the Baptist was connected with Elijah and also with himself.

14 When they got back to the other apostles, they noticed a large crowd around them and the scribes arguing with them. *15* On seeing Jesus, the whole crowd was in awe from the afterglow of the Transfiguration, that could still be seen on him. So they all ran to him and greeted him. *16* He asked them what they were discussing. *17* One of the crowd answered him, "Teacher, I have brought my son to you. He has a negative energy in him. Whenever it takes hold of him, it throws him to the ground and he foams at the mouth. *18* He grinds his teeth and becomes rigid. I asked your friends here to heal him, but they couldn't."

19 He turned to his apostles and said, "You are going to have to believe more." He then said to the boy's father, "Bring your son here to me." *20* So they brought him to Jesus. As they did, the negative energy began to move violently in the boy. He fell to the ground and had convulsions, rolling around and foaming at the mouth. *21* Jesus asked the father how long this had been going on. The father said, "Since he was a little boy. *22* Often it has thrown him into the fire or in the water to hurt him. If you can do anything, please help us."

23 Jesus said to him, "If I can do anything? Everything is possible for the person who believes." *24* Immediately the father cried out, "I do believe, please help me believe even more!" *25* Jesus, noticing that a mob was gathering, dismissed the negative energy saying, "Come out of him and never enter him again." *26* After throwing another fit, the boy collapsed. He looked like a corpse, so many said he was dead. *27* But Jesus, taking him by the hand, raised him up.

28 After he had gone inside, the apostles asked him privately, "Why couldn't we do that?" *29* He told them, "This kind cannot be healed unless you believe you are Divine, as I have been teaching you. You need to be Transfigured into your Divinity to heal this type."

30 They left there and went through Galilee. Jesus was very preoccupied about telling the apostles that he was going to be arrested and executed. *31* He said they were not to worry because on the third day he would rise again. *32* They still didn't understand what "rise again" meant; but were so upset at the thought of his being executed that they didn't ask him to explain it.

33 They went on to Capernaum and to Jesus' home. He then asked then what they were arguing about on the road. *34* They kept quiet because on the road they had been arguing about who was the most important, about who would become first when Jesus was no longer there.

35 Jesus sat down and asked the twelve to join him. He said, "If anyone wants to be first, he must make himself last, the servant of all." 36 Then he called the neighbor's little girl over and took her on his lap. 37 He said, "Whoever loves a child like this, loves me; and whoever loves me, loves the one who sent me. Because we are all one. There is no first. There is no last. We are all one, we are all the same!

38 John said to Jesus, "We saw someone healing in your name, someone who is not in our company, and we forbade him, because he is not one of us." 39 Jesus told him, "Do not forbid him; we are all one. 40 He who is not against us is part of us. 50 Let us all live together in peace."

CHAPTER 10

1 Jesus left there and went to the farther side of the Jordan. Crowds flocked to him and, as was his custom, he taught them. 2 Pharisees came to trap him and asked him if it was lawful to divorce. 3 He told them it was not lawful, unless the marriage was already dead. 4 "God made women and men and when they have joined in marriage, 5 they are no longer two but one. 6 One cannot be divided."

10 When they were back together inside, the apostles asked him again about this. 11 He told them,

"Whoever divorces and marries again commits adultery. 12 Marriage only ends with the death of the spouse or the death of the marriage."

13 Some parents brought their children to Jesus for him to bless, but the apostles stopped them. 14 Jesus noticed this and said, "Let the little children come to me, for they are the presence of God. 15 They teach us the Love and Openness that Dad has for all. Let them remind you what it is like being with God." 16 Then he hugged them and gave them a blessing.

17 As he started off on his journey, a man came running up to him and asked, 18 "Teacher, what should I do to have Divine Life?"19 Jesus said to him, "You know the commandments: Do not kill; do not commit adultery; do not steal: do not lie; honor your mother and father."

20 He replied, "Teacher, I have done these things all my life." Jesus looked at his heart and saw an openness there, and said, "There is one more thing that will bring you fully into Divine Life. 21 Go and sell everything that you have and give the money to the poor; and then come and walk along with me" 22 The man was appalled at this and went away sad, because he was very wealthy.

23 Jesus looked at the apostles and said, "It is extremely hard for the wealthy to live the Divine Life!" 24 The apostles were amazed at this since the belief was that wealth was a blessing from God. Jesus said again, "How very difficult it is for

the wealthy to live in the presence of God; they often believe that wealth is presence enough; and that wealth is theirs, rather than simply something they are stewards over." 25 It is easier for the large camels to kneel down and crawl through the low city entrance gates than for a rich person to struggle into the presence of God."

26 The apostles continued to be astonished at this and said among themselves, "Then who can possibly do this?" 27 Jesus said, "It is not humanly possible, only divinely possible. For everything is possible with God."

28 Peter said, "Then what about us? We have left everything to be with you." 29 Jesus said, "I assure you there is no one who has left home or family or fields to walk with me and spread the Good News, who will not receive a hundred times over what they have given up. 30 Many will receive material things in this life. All will receive Divine Life in the next. They will also have more sisters and brothers, mothers and fathers, than before. And theirs will be the blessing of purifying persecution to help open the gates of their Divine Life. 31 And many who are thought to be last will be seen as first. And many who are thought to be first will be seen as last.

32 Then they began walking to Jerusalem with Jesus in front. They were all in a daze and filled with apprehension over what he had been telling them. So he called them all together and began once more to tell them what was going to happen.

33 "We are going up to Jerusalem, and there I will be handed over to the chief priests and the scribes. They will condemn me to death and hand me over to the civil authorities. 34 They will mock me, spit on me, flog me, and then execute me. But three days later I will rise again; so there is really nothing to worry about.

42 "When you become leaders in the spreading of the Good News, do not lord your Call over those who walk with you. 43 Those who are leaders must be servants. 44 And those who want to be first must consider themselves last. 45 For even I did not come to be served, but to serve, and to give my life to show the immensity of God's love for all."

46 They went through Jericho, and as they were leaving it, a great crowd walked with them. 47 Bartimaeus, a blind beggar was sitting by the side of the road. Hearing that it was Jesus who was passing, he cried out, "Jesus, take pity on me!" 48 Those around him told him to keep still; but he shouted even louder, "Jesus, take pity on me!" 49 Jesus stopped and asked the people to call him over. So they called to the blind man, "Take courage! Get up, he is calling you."

50 He threw off his coat, jumped up and went to Jesus. 51 Jesus said to him, "What do you want me to do for you?" The blind man said, "Teacher, let me see again." 52 Jesus said to

him, "Go, your faith has healed you." And he instantly recovered his sight and began to walk with Jesus.

CHAPTER 11

1 When they got near Jerusalem, near the Mount of Olives; Jesus sent two of the apostles into the village. *2* He told them, "Go into the village and you will see a colt tethered there which no one has ridden. *3* Bring it back here. And if anyone questions you, tell them the Teacher needs it."

4 The two went into the village and found the colt just as Jesus had said. *5* They untied it and started back. Some of those standing there asked them what they were doing. *6* They told the people that the Teacher needed it, and they let them go. *7* They took the colt to Jesus and put their coats on it. Then Jesus mounted it. *8* As Jesus rode along, many people laid down their coats, and some put palm branches down to honor him. He rode into Jerusalem and went right to the temple. That night he went out to Bethany. *15* The next morning he went back to the temple. He began to drive out the sellers and buyers of animals for sacrifice, *16* and did not allow anyone to carry things through the temple to sell. *17* He said, "Is this not a house of prayer? You are making it a den of thieves."

18 The chief priests and scribes heard of this and looked even harder for ways to destroy him, for they were afraid of him, knowing that the people were amazed at his teaching. *19* That evening he went back to Bethany.

20 The next morning he met up with his friends as he was walking back to the temple. *21* Peter commented on the marvels that were happening. *22* Jesus said, "Have faith in God. For I tell you that whoever has faith and says to a mountain 'Jump into the sea,' *23* if he does not waiver in his faith, the mountain will jump into the sea. *24* I tell you that whatever you ask for with complete faith will be yours.

25 "And whenever you are praying and remember something against a sister or brother, forgive that person in your heart. This will open your heart more to God also and facilitate your prayer. *26* It is impossible to really be open to God when you are closed to your sisters and brothers."

27 They entered Jerusalem and while Jesus was walking in the temple, the chief priests and scribes came up to him and asked him, *28* "By what authority are you doing the things you are doing?" *29* Jesus responded, "I will ask you a question and if you answer it, I will answer your question. *30* 'Was John's baptism from God or from us humans?'"

31 They realized if they said, "It was from God," that he would ask them why they didn't believe it. *32* But if they said "From us humans," the people could well riot since they considered John to be a prophet. *33* So they said they had no answer. Jesus then told them that he had no answer for them either.

CHAPTER 12

13 Then they sent some Pharisees to trap Jesus. *14* Coming up to him they said, "Teacher, we know that you are an honest and upright man who teaches the way of God. Tell us, is it lawful for us to pay tax to Caesar? *15* Shall we pay it or not?" Jesus knew the trap that was in their hearts so he said, "Why do you try to trick me? Let me see a coin." *16* They handed him one, even though their Jewish law forbade them to carry coins with images. He asked them, "Whose image is this?" They said, "Caesar's." *17* Jesus said, "Then give to Caesar what belongs to Caesar, and to God what belongs to God." They left amazed at how skillfully Jesus avoided their trap.

28 Then one of the scribes who had heard this realized the wisdom of Jesus. *29* So he came to Jesus and asked him, "Which is the most important commandment?" *30* Jesus answered him, "The most important commandment is: 'Love God with all your heart, with all your soul, and with all your strength.' *31* The second most important one is: 'Love your neighbor as yourself.' There is no other commandment greater than these."

32 The scribe said, "I believe what you say, Teacher. *33* We are indeed to love God with all our heart, with all our soul, and with all our strength. And we are to love our neighbor as ourselves. These two are worth more than all the burnt offerings and sacrifices." *34* Jesus appreciated his response and said to him, "I can see that you have God in your heart." After that no one ventured to ask him any more questions.

41 Jesus then sat down across from the temple treasury and watched those who were putting in money. Many of the rich put in a lot of money. *42* But one poor woman came and put in two pennies. *43* He called the apostles over and told them, "I assure you that this poor woman has put in more than all the rich together. *44* For they put in out of their excess, while she put in all she had to live on."

CHAPTER 13

1 As they were leaving the temple one of the apostles said to Jesus, "Teacher, look how beautiful these buildings are." *2* Jesus replied, "You see these great buildings? They will all be destroyed with not one stone left on another."

3 They walked over to the Mount of Olives, which is opposite from the temple. *4* Sitting there Peter, James, John and Andrew asked him privately, "Tell us when this is going to happen." So Jesus began to explain, "Remember what I have been telling you about Dad God. He is not to be found in external temples, but in the internal temples of our hearts. To help people learn this and experience this, the external temple will be destroyed. This will be a shock for many people, but it is a birth pain into the Good News. I have been preaching that we are all God. *5* Some will try to fight this by proclaiming that only they are the new Christ. *6* Don't be deceived by this. From now on everyone can be a Christ who walks into her or his Divinity. The external God is dying so that the internal God may rise. Stop looking for the external God, for he is already in your hearts.

7 "Don't be alarmed when you hear about wars and violence, because it will take some time for everyone to hear and to live the Good News of Universal Love. We are all God, and God is Love; so when this Good News spreads, wars and violence will end. We can fight our Divinity, but we can't change it. We have free will, but we don't have free Identity. Whether we like it or not, whether we live it or not, we are all Love; we are all God. *8* So wars and violence are simply signs that we have not yet understood who we really are. We are like teenagers rebelling against being members of the Family of God, the Family of Love. When we grow into Love, all these things will stop. You can help all this by ending the wars and violence in yourselves, in your hearts.

9 "In the meantime you will still need to look out for yourselves. For there will be those who will turn you over to the councils, and you will be flogged in the synagogues. You will stand before governors and kings because of preaching the Good News, in order that you may bear witness to it. *10* And the Good News must be preached to all nations

and believed, before Love will truly incarnate.

11 "And when they arrest you and take you to court, don't worry about what you are going to say. *12* Just speak from your heart; for it will not really be you who are speaking but Spirit, who is speaking. After I rise fully into my Divinity, I will return and help you rise into your Divinity through the indwelling of (my) Spirit in your hearts. *13* So don't let fights, even family fights, bother you. Love will win in the end simply because Love is what ultimately we all are.

28 "Learn from this parable of the fig tree. Whenever its branches grow tender and it puts out new leaves, you know that summer is coming. *29* In the same way, when you see people growing more tender and making attempts at a new life, you will know that they are incarnating the Good News into their lives.

35 "This will happen at different times for different people and different nations. *36* But the time will come when everyone will find their God in their own hearts and begin to live the Love that they are. *37* So be on the lookout for this and support it wherever you see it."

CHAPTER 14

1 The Passover and the Feast of Unleavened Bread were in two days. *2* The chief priests and the scribes were seeking a way to arrest Jesus and execute him, but didn't want to do it during the feast for fear of a riot among the people.

3 Jesus was in Bethany at supper when Mary Magdalene came in and anointed his head with rich perfume. *4* The apostles asked her why she was doing that. *6* Jesus said, "Can't you see how upset she is about me dying soon? *7* So why embarrass her? She has done me a very loving act. *8* She has anointed my body for burial. *9* And I want her love for me to be told wherever the Good News is preached throughout the whole world so that what she has done will be told as a memorial to her."

10 Then Judas Iscariot, one of the twelve, went to the chief priests to betray Jesus. *11* They were delighted and promised him money. So he was on the lookout for a way to do that.

12 On the first day of Unleavened Bread the apostles asked Jesus where he wanted them to prepare for the Passover. *13* So he sent off two apostles with the instructions, "Go into the city and follow the man you see with a water pitcher. *14* And wherever he enters say to the owner, 'The Teacher wants to know where the guest room is so he can eat the Passover with his friends there.' *15* He will show you a large upper room all ready for us." *16* The two went out and found everything exactly as he had said.

17 They prepared everything and were ready when Jesus arrived that evening with his other friends. *18* As they began eating Jesus said, "I assure you that one of you eating with me will betray me." *19* They were all very upset by this, and said to him, one after another, "It is not me, is it?" *20* He answered them, "It is one of those dipping with me in the bowl."

22 During the meal he took bread and gave thanks. Then he broke it and gave it to them saying, "This is my very body. Eat it so you will understand that I am in you." *23* Then he took a cup of wine and poured a little water into it, as was the custom. He then gave thanks. *24* He said to them, "This is my very blood, my new Covenant with you and in you. *25* The little water I put with the wine is a symbol of you. Now you and my blood are one. Drink this so you will know that you are me; and that we are indeed One and always will be."

26 After supper they sang a hymn as they walked to the Mount of Olives. *27* There he said to them, "You will all run away tonight, for it is written, 'I will strike the shepherd and the sheep will run away.' *28* But after my resurrection I will be with you when you return to Galilee."

29 Peter said to him, "Even if everyone else runs away, I never will!" *30* Jesus replied, "I assure you, Peter, this very night, before the cock crows the second time, you will have denied me three times." *31* But Peter insisted again that he would never disown him. They all said the same thing.

32 They came to a Garden called Gethsemane, and Jesus told them to sit down while he went and prayed. *33* But he took along with him Peter, James and John. *34* He began to get deeply distressed and said, "My heart is really burdened. Stay here and watch while I go on a little further to pray."

35 Going a little further he fell on his knees in tears. *36* He prayed, "Dad, I am anxious about tomorrow, but I know I have to leave them for them to really realize their own Divinity. I have told them that they are One with us, but they don't get it yet. Being freed from my body will make it easier for me to enter them and truly transform them into (union with) us."

37 He went back and found the three asleep. He asked them why they were sleeping, but it was already very late and they were tired. *38* He told them to pray and then went back to pray. *39* He opened his heart again to his Dad. *40* He knew he must go, but even though he loved his Dad so very much, he had also come to deeply love those who had walked with him. *41* He went back to talk with them a bit, but they were asleep again. So he went back and spent more time with his Dad. *42* Then he came back and woke them up and said, "Wake up; they have come for me."

43 Just then Judas arrived with a large mob with swords and clubs. They had been sent by the high priests. *44* Judas had told them, "The one I kiss is Jesus. Seize him and take him away." *45* So he went up to Jesus and kissed him. *46* Then they came up and arrested Jesus.

47 Peter was standing next to Jesus. He drew his sword and struck the high priest's servant and cut off his ear. *48* Jesus said, "Why have you come out with swords and clubs as though I were a criminal, *49* when every day I was right there in your temple preaching?"

50 But they just grabbed him and marched off. *51* A young boy was following Jesus, wanting to be a part of his friends. They tried to grab him, but all they could grab was his linen cloth. *52* He ran off naked.

53 They brought Jesus before the high priest and all the chief priests, elders and scribes that had assembled. *54* Peter kept following at a distance until they got into the high priest's courtyard. He sat down there with the servants and was warming himself by the fire.

55 The chief priests and all the Sanhedrin tried to find enough evidence to execute Jesus but were unable. *56* For even though they had gathered many false witnesses, their testimony did not agree.

60 Then the high priest stood up and asked Jesus, "Aren't you going to answer all these charges against you?" *61* But Jesus didn't say a word. Again the high priest questioned him saying, "Are you the Christ?" *62* Jesus said, "Yes, I Am Christ!" (*It should be noted that "I Am" is English for Yahweh, the Hebrew name for God. God was considered so distant and exalted that no one was permitted to even say his name. Jesus broke the law by stating the Truth.) *63* At this the high priest tore his garment and said, "We don't need any more witnesses. You have heard the blasphemy yourselves. *64* What is your decision?" And they all said he should die. *65* Some also started to spit on him. They blindfolded him and would hit him and challenge him to say who had hit him. And the attendants took him and slapped his face.

66 Peter was still below in the courtyard while this was going on. A high priest's servant girl came and saw Peter warming himself. *67* She accosted him and said, "You were with Jesus too!" *68* But he denied it and said he didn't know what she was talking about. Then he went out to the entrance and the cock crowed. *69* Later the servant girl saw him again and began to tell the people around that he had been with Jesus. *70* Again Peter denied it. A little while later a bystander said to Peter, "Surely you are one of them for you are a Galilean." *71* Then Peter swore an oath that he did not know the man. *72* At that very instant the cock crowed the second time. And Peter remembered that Jesus had prophesied this, and he went outside and wept bitterly.

CHAPTER 15

1 At dawn the chief priests gathered the elders, scribes and the entire Sanhedrin and handed Jesus bound over to Pilate. *2* Pilate asked Jesus, "Are you the King of the Jews?" He answered him, "If you say so." *3* Then the chief priests accused Jesus of many things. *4* Pilate asked Jesus, "Have you no answer to these charges?" *5* But Jesus said nothing. This confused Pilate.

6 At Passover Pilate used to release a prisoner that the Jews asked for. *7* There was one named Barabbas who was jailed for killing people during an uprising. *8* The mob shouted that they wanted the usual privilege of choosing a prisoner to be released. *9* So Pilate asked them, "Do you want me to release the King of the Jews?" *10* because he knew the chief priests had turned Jesus over simply out of envy. *11* However, the chief priests stirred up the crowd to ask that Barnabas be released for them. *12* Then Pilate asked them, "Then what shall I do to the one you call King of the Jews?" *13* They shouted, "Crucify him!" *14* Pilate asked them, "Why, what wrong has he done?" But they cried out even louder, "Crucify him!"

15 So Pilate released Barabbas to the crowd to calm them down. Then he had Jesus flogged and handed over to be crucified. *16* The soldiers lead him into the Pratorium in front of the entire cohort. *17* They dressed him in a purple robe and crowned him with a crown of thorns they had made. *18* Then they began to mock him by saluting him and saying, "Long live the King of the Jews." *19* Then they hit him over the head with a stick and spat at him. Finally they did him homage on bended knee. *20* When they finished their mocking, they took off the robe and put his own clothes back on him. Then they led him out to be crucified.

21 As they were walking along they forced a passerby, Simon, a Cyrenian, to carry his cross. *22* They led him to a place call Golgotha, the Place of the Skull, *23* and offered him a drink of wine flavored with myrrh to ease his pain, but he refused it. *24* They crucified him and cast lots for his clothes. *25* It was nine in the morning when they crucified him. *26* Over his head they put the inscription: The King of the Jews. *27* They crucified two thieves with him, one on each side.

29 The people walking by mocked him and said, "You were going to destroy the temple and rebuild it in three days. *30* If you have such power, come down from the cross." *31* In the same way, the chief priests mocked him saying, "He saved others, but can't even save himself. *32* If you really are the Christ, come down from the cross and we will believe in you." Even the thieves mocked him.

33 From noon until three o'clock darkness settled over the whole area. At three o'clock Jesus said, "Dad, I am coming home!" *37* Then he bowed his head and went home.

38 Just then the huge temple veil was torn from top to bottom, *39* and the centurion who saw all of this said, "Surely this man was God's Son!"

40 There were also women there looking on from a distance: his wife Mary Magdalene, his mother Mary, and the women who had been walking with him and helping him when he was in Galilee. *41* And many others who came up with him to Jerusalem.

42 When it was toward evening and the Sabbath was about to officially begin, *43* Joseph of Arimathea, an honored member of the Sanhedrin, and a person who had found the God within, went boldly to Pilate and asked for the body of Jesus. *44* Pilate summoned the centurion to find out if Jesus had indeed already died. *45* When he received word that he had, he released the body to Joseph.

46 Joseph had bought a fine linen sheet to wrap the body in after he had taken it down. Then he laid him in a tomb that had been carved out of rock and rolled a stone against the entrance. *47* Mary Magdalene and Mary his mother were there for this.

CHAPTER 16

1 Very early that Sunday morning, Mary Magdalene, his wife, and Mary, his mother, brought spices so they could anoint his body. *2* They arrived at the tomb at dawn *3* wondering who could help them remove the heavy stone from the entrance. *4* They were shocked to find the stone already off to the side of the entrance.

5 They went into the tomb and saw that it was empty. *6* They were struck with fear and total confusion seeing that the body was gone. *7* Jesus then appeared to them and said, "Do not be afraid! It is really me. I have risen! *8* Please go tell our friends that I am alive, that I have risen as I promised. *9* After they talked a bit, the two ran off still in shock to tell the others.

10 When the others heard that he was alive and that Mary Magdalene had seen him, they did not believe it. *11* So later he appeared to them himself, and chided them for not believing his wife.

12 He told them, "Go into the whole world and preach the Good News to everyone. *13* Baptize them with water to help them rethink their lives; *14* and baptize them with Spirit to help them begin to live their Divine Life. *15* And these signs will prove you believe in me, in God: you will be able to relieve people of negative energies; you will be able to preach in languages you don't know; *16* you will be able to lay hands on the sick and they will be healed.

17 So after Jesus had talked to them for a while, he disappeared from their eyes and entered their hearts. *18* The apostles went out to the whole world filled with the Spirit of Jesus, and manifesting the Gifts of Spirit to prove the Good News.

LUKE

CHAPTER 1

1 My dear friends, I have read and studied everything written by the eye-witnesses of Jesus' life and ministry, *2* and will present it here in an organized fashion, *3* so that you may know the validity of everything that has been presented to you.

5 When Herod was king of Judea, there was a priest named Zechariah and his wife Elizabeth who lived there. *6* Both walked daily with God. *7* They had no children because Elizabeth was barren, and both were now old. *8* One day Zechariah was serving his turn as priest, *9* and it fell to him by lot to enter the altar area for the incensing. *10* At the hour of the incense many people were outside the altar area praying.

11 An Angel of God appeared to him, standing to the right of the altar of incense. *12* When Zechariah saw him, he became very afraid. *13* But the Angel said to him, "Don't be afraid, Zechariah, because your prayers have been heard. Your wife Elizabeth will bear a son, and you are to name him John. *14* He will give you a lot of joy and happiness, and many will rejoice at his birth, *15* for he will be a great man in the eyes of God and the world. *16* He will be filled with the power and spirit of Elijah. *17* He will turn the hearts of parents to their children, the obstinate to the wisdom of truth, and prepare a people open to God."

18 Then Zechariah asked the Angel how he could be sure this was true. *19* The Angel answered him, "I am Gabriel, who stands in the very presence of God. I was sent to give you this Good News. *20* The sign that this is true will be that you will not be able to speak until it happens.

21 The people outside the altar area were wondering why Zechariah was taking so long. *22* When he finally came out, he could not speak, and they realized that he had seen a vision because of the radiance on his face. He tried to explain what had happened with signs. *23* As soon as his turn of service was over, he went home.

24 Then Elizabeth conceived and went into seclusion for five months, *25* to thank God for this huge blessing. *26* Then, in her sixth month, the Angel Gabriel was sent by God to the town of Nazareth in Galilee; *27* to a maiden named Mary. She was married to a man named Joseph, a descendant of David. *28* The Angel came to her and said, "Beloved of God, Greetings!"

29 Mary was overwhelmed by the Angel's presence and his greeting. *30* The Angel then said to her, "Don't be concerned, Mary, you are very beloved by God. *31* You are going to conceive a son and you are to name him Jesus. *32* He will be a Christ, *33* who is being sent to teach the Good News of the Divine Inheritance that all have."

36 "Also, your cousin Elizabeth is going to have a son in her old age. For she who was called barren is now in her sixth month, *37* for everything is possible with God." *38* Mary said simply, "I am here to do the will of God." The Angel bowed to her and left.

39 Mary got ready and hurried to the town in the hill country of Judea. *40* Elizabeth was so happy to see her. *41* When Mary greeted her the baby in her womb leaped for joy. *42* Then, filled with Spirit, she said, "How beloved are you among women, and how beloved is the child within you. *43* I feel so honored by your visit. *44* For when you arrived the baby in my womb jumped for joy. *45* How wonderful that you believed the marvels that God can do!"

46 And Mary said:

"I am so in love with God;

47 and God is so in love with me!

48 "He has chosen this humble servant

49 to help him spread his Message of Love.

50 "He is so wonderful!

51 "He is so wonderful!

52 "And he has chosen you

53 as the new Sarah,

54 to help bring everyone

55 into the New Covenant of Abraham!"

56 Mary stayed there until John was born and then went back home. *57* When John was born, the neighbors and all those around marveled at this miracle of God. *59* When they came to circumcise the baby, they were going to name him Zechariah. *60* But Elizabeth said, "No, his name is to be John." *61* They wondered at this, since none of their relatives had that name. *62* Then they asked Zachariah what he wanted the baby to be called. *63* He motioned for a writing tablet and wrote, "His name is John." This surprised them all. *64* And instantly his mouth was opened and he began to speak praising God.

65 A deep sense of awe came upon all the neighbors, and word of what had happened there spread throughout the entire hill country of Judea. All who heard of this took it to heart. *66* They said, "What kind of child will this be?" For it was obvious that God's hand was on him.

67 His father Zechariah was filled with Spirit and prophesized:

68 "Blessed be God, for he has looked with favor on his people and has brought us into his heart.

69 "He has raised up a powerful teacher after his own heart.

73 "He is reestablishing the Covenant of Love made with our father Abraham,

74 granting us a place in his heart forever,

75 and granting us his presence in our hearts forever.

76 "And you, little one, will be his Prophet, for you will open the hearts of people that he may manifest there,

77 to bring his people the knowledge of his immense love for them,

78 that his Divine Light might shine in our humble hearts,

79 and shine on those sitting in the darkness of fear, and direct us all into the path of Peace."

80 And the child grew and became a spiritual giant, praying in solitary places until the time of his Call arrived.

CHAPTER 2

1 In those days Caesar ordered a census of the whole world. 2 This was while Quirinius was governor of Syria.

3 They all went to their own city to be registered. 4 And so Joseph went down from Galilee to Bethlehem in Judea, the City of David; because he was of the house and family of David. 5 There he would be registered with his wife Mary who was close to giving birth.

6 While they were there, she gave birth to their firstborn son. 7 She wrapped him in swaddling clothes and laid him in a manger, since there had been no room for them in the inn.

8 There were shepherds in that area keeping night watch over their sheep. 9 An Angel of God appeared to them in great light, and they were very afraid. 10 The Angel said to them, "Don't be afraid. I have great news for you. 11 Today in the City of David a baby was born who is a Christ. 12 You will find him there wrapped in swaddling clothes and lying in a manger. 13 And suddenly there was with the Angel a choir singing, 14 "Glory to God in heaven; and peace to all his daughters and sons on earth."

15 When the Angels left, the shepherds said to one another, "Let us go to Bethlehem and see this which the Angel has told us." 16 And they went quickly and found Mary and Joseph, and the baby lying in the manger. 17 When they left there, they told all their friends what they had seen and what the Angel had said; 18 and all were very amazed at it. 19 Mary kept what the shepherds had said in her heart. 20 The shepherds went back to their flocks, thanking God for what they had seen, which was just like what they had been told.

21 The next week he was circumcised and given the name Jesus, as the Angel had told Mary before he was even conceived.

22 When the days for their purification were completed, they brought him to Jerusalem to present him to God. 25 There was an upright and devout man there named Simeon. 26 The Spirit was with him and had told him that he would not die before he had seen Christ. 27 Moved by Spirit, he came into the temple when Jesus' parents brought him there. 28 He took him in his arms and gave thanks to God and said, 29 "Now I can go in peace. You have kept your promise. 30 I have seen Christ, 31 who has come to bring the Good News to all nations, 32 a light for revelation to the Gentiles and to us Jews."

33 As his Dad and Mom were

wondering about the things Simeon had said, *34* Simeon blessed them and said to Mary, "Your son has been appointed to bring the Good News of God's inheritance to all his daughters and sons. *35* You both will suffer because of your great love for him, because he will be very persecuted, but God's love will see you through it all."

36 There also was a very old prophetess there. *37* She never left the temple, but prayed there all day and night. *38* She too came at that very hour and talked about how Jesus would bring Good News to all God's people.

39 When they had finished there, Joseph and Mary went back to Galilee to their hometown of Nazareth. *40* Jesus grew up filled with wisdom and the love for all.

41 Every year his parents went to Jerusalem for the Passover Feast. *42* When he was twelve they went there as usual. *43* After the Feast his parents started for home, but he stayed behind in the temple without his parents realizing it. *44* They thought he was in the caravan with friends and did not check on this till the next morning, *45* and when they did, they didn't find him, so they walked back to Jerusalem to look for him. *46* Two days later they found him in the temple, sitting among the teachers, listing to them and asking them questions. *47* All who heard him were astounded by what he asked and by what he said.

48 When his parents saw him, they were amazed, and his mother said to him, "Why have you done this? We have been worried sick looking for you." *49* He said to them, "Why were you looking for me? I was bound to be in Dad's house."

51 He went back home to Nazareth with them and continued to grow in wisdom and love. *52* Mary kept all these things in her heart.

CHAPTER 3

1 In the fifteenth year of Tiberius Caesar's reign, when Pontius Pilate was governor of Judea, Herod king of Galilee, *2* and Annas and Caiaphas high priests, the Call of God came to John, the son of Elizabeth and Zechariah, in the desert.

3 He went into all the areas on both sides of the Jordan River, preaching a baptism of rethinking one's life, *4* as Isaiah the prophet had said: "A voice of one crying in the desert. 'Prepare your hearts for the Coming of God. *5* Smooth out your hates and build up your love. *6* You will soon see the manifestations of God's love.'"

7 He said to the crowds that came to be baptized, "I baptize you with water to help you rethink and cleanse your lives." *10* They asked him, "Then what shall we do?" *11* He answered them, "Whoever has two tunics should share with one who has none, and those who have food should do likewise."

12 The tax collectors also came and asked what they should do. *13* He said to them, "Do not collect more than the appointed rate." *14* And when the soldiers asked the same thing, he said, "Do not extort by intimidating. But be content with your pay."

15 The people were beginning to wonder if perhaps John was a Christ. *16* John answered this by saying, "I baptize you with water, but there is one coming after me who will baptize with Spirit. He is a Christ."

18 The people were really impressed with what John was preaching; *19* but when he took King Herod to task for marrying Herodias, his brother Philip's wife, as well as about all the evils he had practiced, *20* he put John in prison.

21 As the people were being baptized, Jesus too was baptized. *22* Afterwards Spirit came down on him in the visible shape of a dove. A voice came from heaven, "This is my beloved son; I really love him!"

23 When Jesus began his ministry, he was about thirty years old.

CHAPTER 4

1 After this Spirit led Jesus into the desert for forty days. There he was to face his fears. *2* He did not eat anything for those forty days, so at the end he was hungry. *3* Then a negative voice said to him, "If you are God, turn this stone into bread." *4* Jesus answered him, "Does not scripture say that we do not live by bread alone, but by every word of God?" *5* Then in Vision he was led up a high mountain. *6* There the negative voice said, "Do you see all the kingdoms of the world? *7* I will make you king of all this if you will simply admit you are not God." *8* He replied, "How can I say I am not God when I am? How can I say I am not God when my Mission is to proclaim that everyone is God, that everyone is a daughter or son of God?"

9 Then in Vision he was taken to the top of the temple in Jerusalem. *10* There the negative voice said, "If you are really God, jump! Angels will catch you." *12* Jesus replied, "I know that will happen and so don't need to test it." *13* He never heard that voice again.

14 Jesus returned to Galilee and was filled with Divine Energy. His fame spread to all the surrounding regions. *15* He taught in their synagogues and was praised everywhere. *16* Then he went back to his hometown of Nazareth. That Saturday he went to the synagogue and stood up to read. *17* He was handed the book of the prophet Isaiah to read. He found the place where it is written, *18* "The Spirit of God is upon me. He has anointed me to preach the Good News to the poor. He has sent me to announce release of those in captivity, and restoration of sight to the blind, to set free the downtrodden, *19* and to proclaim God's Universal Love for all."

20 He rolled up the scroll and handed it back to the attendant and sat down. *21* He then said, "Today this scripture is fulfilled in your presence." *22* When he finished preaching, they all remarked on how wonderful his words were. They also said, "Isn't this Mary and Joseph's son?" *23* He said to them, "You will probably say to me, 'Do here in your hometown what we have heard you have been doing in Capernaum.' *24* But I assure you that no prophet is accepted in his own hometown."

28 When the people in the synagogue heard this, they were upset and thought he was a crackpot and blasphemer. *29* So they got up and threw him out of the synagogue and the city. *30* They even took him up to the brow of a hill to throw him off. But he escaped right through them and went away.

31 He went down to Capernaum and taught there the following Sabbath. *32* The people who heard him were overwhelmed at his teaching, since he taught with such great authority. *33* In that synagogue there was a man with a negative spirit. *34* It tried to bother Jesus, but he simply told it to leave the man. *35* So it did without hurting him.

36 A sense of awe came over all the people, and they said to one another, "This is amazing! He teaches with such authority and can even dismiss negative energies." *37* News of this went throughout all the surrounding country.

38 He went from the synagogue to Peter's home. Peter's mother-in-law was sick with a fever. *39* He went in and took her hand, and she was immediately cured. She felt so good she began to serve them.

40 At sunset all who had anyone who was sick brought them to him, and he healed them all. *41* Some of those there were possessed, and he removed all their negative energies.

42 At dawn he went out to a lonely place to pray, but the crowd found him and tried to keep him from leaving. *43* But he told them that he had to preach the Good News to the other towns around, for that was why he was sent. *44* And he went to Judea and preached there.

CHAPTER 5

1 Jesus went down by the Lake of Gennesaret. *2* There were two boats moored there, and the fishermen had gotten out and were washing their nets. *3* The people were crowding all around him to hear the Message of God. Then he stepped into Peter's boat and asked him to push out a little from shore. Then he sat down and began to teach the people.

4 When he finished teaching, he told Peter, "Push out into the deep and lower your nets for a catch." *5* Peter said, "Teacher, we have been working hard all night and have caught nothing, but if you want, we will try again." *6* And when they did they caught so many fish that their nets started to tear. *7* They signaled to their partners in the other boat to come and help them. When they did that, they filled both boats so full that they almost sank. *8* Peter was so overcome by what had happened that he said to Jesus, "Leave me, Teacher, for I am a sinful man." *9* His partners James and John were also totally amazed at what happened. *10* Jesus said to them, "Don't be afraid. From now on you will be catching people." *11* They rowed their boats back to shore, left everything and began to walk with him.

12 They walked to a neighboring town, and a man covered with leprosy saw Jesus and begged him to heal him. *13* Jesus reached out his hand and touched him and immediately the leprosy left him. *14* Jesus told him not to tell anyone. *15* But news of this spread everywhere, so large crowds gathered wherever he went to listen to him and be healed. *16* However, Jesus kept withdrawing to deserted places to pray.

17 One day as Jesus was healing, Pharisees and teachers of the law were there from Galilee, Judea and Jerusalem. *18* Some men came carrying a paralytic to have Jesus heal him. *19* They could not get in the door so they took him up to the roof and let him down on his couch.

20 Seeing their faith Jesus said to the man, "God loves you very much." *21* The scribes and Pharisees began to murmur among themselves, "Who does he think he is to know what God feels? He blasphemes since only God can know that." *22* Jesus was aware of this and so said to them, *23* "Which is harder to do, to know that God loves this person or to say to him, 'Get up and walk home?' *24* However, so that you may realize that I know the heart of God, I say to this man, 'Get up; pick up your cot and walk home.'" *25* At once the man got up, picked up his cot and walked home thanking God. *26* Awe fell on the crowd and they too began to give thanks to God. They went home saying, "We have indeed seen amazing things today."

27 After this Jesus went for a walk. He saw Levi collecting taxes at the revenue office. He said to him, "Come walk with me." *28* He got up and left everything, and began to walk always with Jesus. *29* Soon after this he gave Jesus a large banquet. There was a large group of tax collectors and others not-well-thought-of at the table. *30* The scribes and Pharisees grumbled at Jesus' friends saying, "Why do you eat with tax collectors and other trash?" *31* Jesus overheard this and said, "It is not the healthy who need a doctor, but those who are sick and hurting. *32* I have not come to call the people you consider wonderful, but the people God considers wonderful, which is everyone."

36 Then he told them this parable, "No one puts new wine into old wineskins. *37* If they do, the new wine will burst the old skins as it expands during fermentation. *38* New wine must be put into new wineskins which can still expand. *39* To understand the 'new wine' that I am teaching, your minds and hearts have to still be able and willing to expand."

CHAPTER 6

1 On a Sabbath they were walking through a wheat field, and they began to pick the wheat heads, and roll them in their hands and eat the grain. *2* The Pharisees saw this and asked Jesus why his friends were doing something that was not allowed on the Sabbath. *3* He responded, "Brothers, God gave us the Sabbath as a day of rest because he loves us. Let us continue that love."

6 On another Sabbath Jesus went into the synagogue to teach. *7* There was a man there whose right hand was withered. The Pharisees were watching to see if he would heal on the Sabbath, so they could accuse him of breaking the law. *8* Jesus knew this and so asked the man to stand in the center.

9 Then Jesus asked them, "Is it allowed to do good on the Sabbath?" *10* No one responded, so he said to the man, "Hold out your hand!" He did this and his hand was fully restored. *11* The Pharisees were very angry and talked about what they might do to Jesus.

12 Not long after that Jesus went up into the remote hills to pray. He spent the whole night there. *13* At daybreak he summoned his friends and chose twelve of them to be apostles. *14* Simon whom he called Peter and his brother Andrew; James and John, Philip and Bartholomew: *15* Matthew and Thomas, James the son of Alpheus and Simon called the Zealot; *16* Judas the son of James, and Judas Iscariot.

17 Then they all walked back down and found a huge crowd gathered there. They were from all over Judea and Jerusalem and even from up near Tyre and Sidon. They had come to hear him teach and to be healed of their illnesses. *18* Those troubled with negative energies were also healed. *19* They all tried to touch him because wonderful energy came out of him and healed everyone.

20 He looked intently at those gathered and said,

"Don't be concerned that you are poor; your life is actually easier than if you were rich, and you are probably closer to God.

21 "Don't be concerned that you are hungry, for the day is coming when you will have enough to eat.

"Don't be concerned that you are sad now, for the day is coming when you will rejoice.

22 "Don't be concerned when people hate you and speak ill of you because you believe what I say; they are simply jealous that you have found what they are looking for.

24 "You who have more than you need should be very careful. *25* Guarding what you don't need, rather than giving it to those who do, will end you up with a deep hunger in your heart, and a sadness in your soul. *26* And be careful when people praise you, for people like false prophets who don't care that they walk off the path of love.

27 "Now let me talk to you from my heart. Love your enemies; treat them with respect. *28* Bless those who curse you. Pray for those who abuse you, while trying to stop the abuse. *29* If someone hits you on one cheek, offer the person the other. If everyone did this, peace would come quickly to the whole world; since our hearts naturally manifest peace, and violence is a wound begging to be healed.

30 "If someone takes your coat, offer the person your shirt. That person may need it more than you do. Give to any anyone in real need who asks you. And if such a person takes your belongings, don't ask for them back. *31* Treat everyone exactly as you want them to treat you.

32 "If you love only those who love you, there is nothing Divine in that. For almost everyone does that. *33* The same is true with treating those with respect who treat you with respect. *34* And if you lend to only those you know will repay you, even the rich do that.

35 "So again, love your enemies. Treat them with respect even though they don't do that to you. In this way the love of God will manifest in you, for this is how he loves.

36 "Be merciful just as our Dad is merciful. *37* Don't judge because it always comes back onto you. Don't condemn because it too always ends up where it started. Pardon so you can feel the joy that it brings.

38 "Give generously and watch it come back to you in abundance. For how you give, opens the door to how you can receive."

39 And he told them this parable, "Can one blind person lead another? Will they not both run into something or fall into a hole? *40* A student is not above his teacher, but every well-trained student is like his teacher.

41 "And learn to realize that you notice things in others that you have first noticed in yourselves. When you notice a splinter in your neighbor's eye, look for the board in your own. *42* When you have taken the board out of your own eye, you can help you neighbor with the splinter in his.

43 "A healthy tree produces healthy fruit. An unhealthy tree produces unhealthy fruit. *44* Just as you can know what kind of a tree it is by looking at its fruit, you can tell what kind of a person you are dealing with by looking at their fruits. Mature people express mature thoughts and feelings, while the immature express immature ones. *45* For what people say comes from what is in their hearts."

CHAPTER 7

1 When he had finished these teachings, he went to Capernaum. *2* There a centurion's servant boy was ill to the point of death. The boy meant a lot to the centurion, *3* so hearing about Jesus, he sent Jewish elders to beg Jesus to come and heal the boy. *4* They told Jesus he had been very good to the Jewish people *5* and had even built their synagogue. Jesus decided to go back with them.

6 However, when they were not far from the centurion's home, they met a messenger from him saying he didn't feel worthy that Jesus should enter his house. *7* He had said, "I did not even feel worthy to approach you myself. Please simply say the word and my servant boy will be healed. *8* For I am a man also under orders. I do what I am told, and those under me do what I tell them."

9 Jesus marveled when he heard this and said, "I rarely find anyone with as much faith as this Roman." *10* He sent the messenger home to tell the centurion that his servant boy was healed. The messenger went back home and indeed found that the boy had been healed.

11 Shortly after that he went to Naim with his friends. *12* As he got near the city gate, a funeral procession was passing. It was of a boy, the only son of a widow. There was a large crowd from the city walking with her. *13* When Jesus saw her, his heart opened and he said to her, "Don't cry." *14* He walked over to the bier and the pallbearers stopped. He said, "Young man, I tell you to arise." *15* The dead boy sat up and began to speak, and Jesus gave him back to his mother. *16* Great awe came over everyone there. They thanked God and said, "A great prophet has arisen among us to show God's great love to us." *17* Word of this spread throughout Judea and all the surrounding country.

18 John heard about this *19* and sent two friends to ask Jesus if he was the Christ, *20* or if they should keep looking. *21* Jesus said, "Look around here and go tell John what you see. *22* The sick are being cured; the blind can now see; the lame can walk; lepers are cleansed; the dead are raised, and the poor are hearing that God loves them. *23* That will answer John's question."

24 After John's messengers left, Jesus began to talk to them about him. *25* He said, "John is the prophet many are seeking. *26* He does not live in a fancy house or wear elegant clothes, *27* and yet I tell you no human person is greater than he. *28* He is the one sent to help prepare the path to Divinity; *29* and yet anyone who has entered their Divinity is greater than he, greater than those who still believe they are only human." *30* But the Pharisees and the teachers of the law rejected this teaching and refused to be baptized by John.

CHAPTER 8

1 Later he went walking from one town to another, preaching the Good News of the presence of God in us. *2* The twelve also went with him, *3* as did Mary Magdalene and other women who helped support them out of their own means.

4 One day a large crowd gathered from the surrounding town, and Jesus told them this parable. *5* "A farmer went out to sow seed. Some seed fell along the road and was walked on or eaten by the birds. *6* Other seed fell in a rocky area and sprouted, but then withered because it could not put down roots. *7* Other seed fell among thorns and got choked out by them. *8* But most of the seed fell on good soil and grew and yielded a hundred-fold. Open your ears wide to hear what I am saying."

9 The twelve came up and asked him why he was teaching in parables and what this one meant. *10* Jesus replied, "Parables are stories of Truth. It is often easier to remember a story than to remember a Truth. And parables can carry a number of Truths at the same time.

11 "This is the meaning of the parable. The seed is the Good News. *12* Those along the road are the people who hear it, but negative energies or the cares of the world walk on it or even carry it away. *13* Those in the rocky area are those who responded with enthusiasm to the Good News, but don't continue when things get hard. *14* Those among the thorns are those who respond, but as time goes on, the Good News is choked off by worries, or wealth, or the pleasures of the world; and so never mature in their faith. *15* But the seed in the good soil are those who hear the Good News, believe it and always act from it."

16 Later he said, "No one lights a lamp and then puts a basket over it, but rather puts it on a stand so it can light the room for people. Let your light and love help illuminate and warm the world for those around you. *17* And remember that there is nothing hidden that will not be found out; nothing concealed that will not be brought into the light.

18 So always act as though the whole world knows what you are doing."

19 His mother, sisters, and brothers came to see him but could not get close because of the huge crowd. *20* So they told him, "Your family is here to see you." *21* He responded, "Tell them I will be there in a minute; but before I go, I want all of you to know that you too are my sisters and brothers. Together we all form the Family of God."

22 Later Jesus and his friends got into a boat to cross the lake. *23* As they were rowing, he fell asleep. A strong squall came up; and they were taking on water and were close to sinking. *24* They woke him and said, "Teacher, we are sinking!" He got up and calmed the wind and the sea. *25* Then he said to them, "Where is your faith?" Later they said among themselves, "Who is this who can even calm the wind and the sea?"

26 They landed at the country of the Gerasenes, which is across the lake from Galilee. *27* As Jesus stepped out of the boat, he was met by a man with a very negative spirit. *28* The man wore no clothes and had no home. *29* Jesus took pity on him and freed him from the negative spirit.

38 The man who had been healed begged Jesus to let him accompany him, but Jesus said, *39* "Go back to your family and neighborhood and tell them what God has done for you." So he went back home and told everyone what Jesus had done for him.

40 They crossed the lake again, and a large crowd was waiting for him, since everyone had been looking for him. 41 Jairus, a ruler of the synagogue, came and begged him to come to his home and heal his twelve-year-old daughter 42 who was dying.

43 Jesus started to go off with him, but could barely move because of the crowd. 44 A woman who had suffered from vaginal hemorrhages for twelve years was there. According to Jewish law this made her unclean and so not allowed to touch anyone. She had been to many doctors, but none could help her. She came up behind Jesus and touched the hem of his robe and was instantly cured. 45 Jesus said, "Who touched me?" Peter said, "Teacher, people are pressing in all around you and touching you." 46 But Jesus said again, "Someone touched me. I felt healing energy go out from me." When the woman realized he knew what she had done, even though it was against the law, 47 she fell before him and told him what she had done and how she had been instantly healed. He said to her, "Daughter, relax, your faith has healed you; go in peace." 48 Jesus made a point of finding out who touched him to teach the crowd that anyone can touch him, especially those who consider themselves unclean.

49 When she left someone came from Jairus' home and said, "Your daughter has died. There is no reason to trouble the Teacher anymore."

50 Jesus overheard this and said, "Don't be afraid; simply believe and she will be healed."

51 When he got to the home he allowed only Peter, James and John, and the girl's parents to go in with him. 52 Everyone there was really upset, but he told them to calm down, that the girl was only asleep. 53 But they knew she was dead and so laughed at him. 54 He went on in and took her hand and said, "Little girl, arise." 55 Her spirit returned to her and she got up. He told them to get her something to eat. 56 Her parents were dumbfounded, but he told them not to tell anyone what had happened.

CHAPTER 9

1 Calling the twelve together he gave them the ability to free people from negative energies and to heal all diseases. 2 He sent them out to preach that God is in their hearts and to heal the sick. 3 He said to them, "Take nothing with you for the journey, no staff, no money, or any extra tunic. 4 When you get to a town, follow your heart to a home you feel will be open to the Good News. Stay there and go out from there to preach and heal. 5 Wherever they won't accept you, bless them and leave." 6 So they went out from village to village preaching the Good News and healing everywhere.

7 When Herod heard of all this going on, he was confused because some were saying that John the Baptist had risen from the dead.

8 Others said that Elijah had returned and others said that one of the old prophets had returned. 9 So Herod wanted to meet whoever was doing all these things.

10 The apostles came back and reported to Jesus all they had done. He took them apart for a retreat near the town of Bethsaida. 11 But the crowds found out about it and followed them there. Jesus welcomed them and began teaching them that God was in their hearts and healing all their sick(nesses).

12 In the late afternoon the twelve came to him and said, "We believe you should dismiss the crowds so they can go and find food, for we are in a very isolated place." 13 But he said to them, "You give them something to eat." They replied, "We have only five loaves and two fish, unless we go and buy food for all these people." 14 For there were about ten thousand people there. But he told them to have the people sit down in groups of about fifty. 15 So they had them all sit down.

16 Then he took the five loaves and two fish and gave thanks, and gave them to the twelve to give to the crowd. 17 Everyone ate all they wanted, and the leftovers were picked up—twelve baskets full.

18 After the crowd left, Jesus went off by himself to pray. Later the twelve joined him. He asked them, "Who do the crowds say that I am?" 19 They answered, "Most say John the Baptist, though some say Elijah or one of the ancient prophets." 20 He then said, "But who do you say that I am?" Peter said, "The Christ of God." 22 He responded, "Yes I am, but realize that what you see in me, I see in you. You must also know that I will be rejected by the elders, chief priests and scribes and be executed. Then on the third day I will rise from the dead.

23 "This is an example of the fact that if you really want to walk with me into your Divinity, you must also pick up your daily human burdens and carry them. 24 For in this world you will need to be as I am; both human *and* Divine. 25 Divinity needs to be your goal; 26 but never forget that your humanity is your step up to your Divinity, until we can realize that both are the same ultimately. 27 I tell you honestly there are some standing here who will walk completely into their Divinity even before the death of their humanity."

28 A week later Jesus took Peter, John and James up the mountain to pray. 29 While he was praying his garments turned a dazzling white. 30 They saw two others with Jesus, Isaiah and Elijah. 31 They talked a bit about what was going to happen in Jerusalem.

32 Peter, John and James had then fallen asleep. When they woke up they saw Jesus in all his glory, and the other two still standing with him. 33 Peter said to Jesus, "It is really great to be here. Let us build three places where you can relax and sleep." 34 As he said this, a cloud overshadowed them. They were

completely awestruck. *35* Then a voice from the cloud said, "This is my beloved son. I really love him. Listen carefully to him." *36* At that time Jesus was the only one they saw. They told no one what they had seen and heard until after Jesus rose from the dead.

37 The next day when they came down from the mountain, a great crowd greeted them. *38* A man from the crowd shouted, "Teacher, I beg you to take a look at my son, for he is my only child. *39* He has convulsions and foams at the mouth. *40* I asked your friends to heal him but they couldn't." *41* Jesus replied, "Bring him to me." *42* He laid hands on him and healed him.

43 And all who saw this were overwhelmed at the love of God. *44* He called the three over who had been to the mountain the night before with him and said, "If you realize what you saw in me last night is also in you, you will be able to heal as I just did." *45* However, they did not understand what he said, but were afraid to question him about it.

46 Then a discussion came up among them as to who was the greatest. *47* Jesus was aware of this and invited a little girl to come sit next to him. *48* He said to them, "When your heart is as pure as hers, you will be the greatest. For the lowliest among you is the one who is truly great."

49 John said, "Teacher, we saw someone healing in your name and we told him not to. Jesus responded, "Don't tell him not to; but consider those who are not against you to be for you."

51 He knew his time was drawing near so he set out for Jerusalem. *57* As they were walking along the road, someone said to him, "I will follow you wherever you may go." *58* Jesus told him, "The foxes have dens and the birds have nests, but I have no place of my own in this world. To follow me you have to look way beyond this physical world."

CHAPTER 10

1 After that Jesus commissioned seventy-two to go ahead of him two by two into every community that he planned to visit. *3* He warned them that he was sending them out like lambs in the midst of wolves. *4* And he told them to take no money with them, *5* and to rely on the hospitality of those open to the Good News.

8 He said further, "When you enter a town, be happy to eat what is offered to you. *9* Heal those who are sick there and tell them the Good News that God is in their hearts."

17 Later the seventy-two came back to where he was with great joy saying, "Many were glad to hear the Good News and even more were healed." *20* But Jesus said, "Don't be as happy at what you were able to do as at the fact that you are beginning to really accept your own Divinity and act from it."

21 Jesus was deeply moved and said, "Dad, thank you for revealing these things to the little ones and not the learned ones. *22* For I know that is the way you like it."

23 Turning to the seventy-two he said, "You have been very blessed; *24* for many prophets and kings have longed to see what you have seen and didn't, and to hear what you have heard, but didn't."

25 Now a teacher of the law came up to put him to the test. He asked, "Teacher, what shall I do to enter Divine Life?" *26* Jesus asked him, "What is written in scripture about this?" *27* The teacher responded, "Love God with everything you are and everything you have, and your neighbor as you yourself." *28* Jesus said, "That's right. Do this and you will have Divine Life."

29 The teacher wanted to impress the crowd, so he asked, "And who is my neighbor?" *30* Jesus replied, "A man was going down from Jerusalem to Jericho when he was robbed, stripped, beaten, and left for dead. *31* A priest came down the road and saw him, and passed by on the other side. *32* Also a Levite saw him and passed on the other side. *33* Then a Samaritan traveling by saw him, and took pity on him. *34* He went over to him and bandaged his wounds and set him on his own donkey. He then took him to an inn and looked after him. *35* The next morning he took out extra money and handed it to the inn keeper and said, 'Please take care of him, and if there is any more owed, I will pay you when I come back through here.' *36* Which of these three was neighbor to the man who was robbed?" *37* He said, "The one who took pity on him." Jesus said, "Go and do the same."

38 During their travels Jesus went into a village where a woman named Martha welcomed him into her home. *39* She had a sister named Mary who sat down and listed to Jesus' teaching. *40* Martha continued to do housework, but finally she got upset at this and went to Jesus and said, "Teacher, tell Mary to help me." *41* He answered, "Dear Martha, you get anxious and worried about many things. I am telling Mary about God being in us, and us being God. *42* That is the only really important thing in this life. I am happy that Mary realizes this."

CHAPTER 11

1 Jesus was praying one day and when he finished, his friends came to him and asked him to teach them to pray. *2* He said to them, "When you pray, say something like this: 'Dad, Father of us all, we really love you. May we feel you in our hearts and see you in our actions. *3* Please give us what we need today, and help us share with others what we don't. *4* May we treat others with the same love and gentleness with which you treat us. And keep us always on the path to you."

27 Then a woman in the crowd said, "Blessed is the lady who bore you!" *28* He responded, "Yes, indeed. And blessed are those who listen to the God that is in their hearts."

33 Then he said, "No one lights a

lamp and then puts it under a box, but rather on top of a stand so that people might be able to see. *34* Your eyes are your body's lamp. When your eyes are open to the truth, your whole body is lit up; but if your eyes are closed to the truth, your whole body is dark. *35* So see that, you keep your eyes wide open. *36* If you do this there will be no reason to fear the dark."

CHAPTER 12

1 More people kept coming so they could barely move. He went on with his teachings and said, "Be very careful about falling into hypocrisy. *2* Nothing is hidden that will not be seen; or secret that will not become known. *3* So whatever you say in the dark will be heard in the light, and whatever you whisper in private will be proclaimed on the rooftops.

11 "When you are arrested and brought to trial, don't worry about how to defend yourselves, *12* for Spirit will inspire you as to what to say."

13 A person in the crowd said to him, "Teacher tell my brother to share the inheritance with me." *14* But he said to him, "Who made me judge over your things?" *15* He then said to the people, "Be careful about greed, for what is important in life is not the abundance of one's possessions, but the abundance in one's heart."

16 Then he told them another parable, "A rich man had a great harvest. *17* He tried to figure out what to do, since his barns couldn't hold the harvest. *18* So he decided to tear down the barns and build bigger ones so he could store all the harvest. *19* He thought by doing this he could relax and enjoy himself for a year. *20* But that night he died, *21* and God asked him why he hadn't shared the abundance he gave him with his sisters and brothers in need."

22 Jesus then said to those around him, "So don't worry about what you will eat or about what you will wear; *23* for life is about much more than food and clothes. *24* Look at the birds, they don't sow or build barns to keep their seeds in, but Dad takes care of them.

25 "Who among you can add a moment to your life by worrying? *26* So if you can't change even that little bit, why be anxious about the rest? *27* Look at how the lilies do things. They don't go looking for food or spin their clothes, but Solomon in all his glory was never dressed as wondrously as they are. *28* And if Dad clothes them so well, won't he clothe you, if you just believe?

29 "Do not worry about what you are to eat or what you are to drink, or about anything. *30* For the non-believers worry about all these things. Dad knows you need them even before you do. *31* So look for him in your heart, and when you find his reflection there, you will know all these things will be taken care of. *32* Don't be afraid of anything for

Dad longs to show you his presence and his love.

33 "So feel free to sell everything you own, or give it to those who need it. Crawl into God's heart, and he will do the same to you. *34* This is the greatest and only real treasure. And know that where you believe your treasure is, that is where your heart will be. *48* When you do open your heart, all you need will be given to you, and you will be expected to treat those around you with the same generosity.

49 "Dad has sent me to bring peace to all the world. *50* But his Message is so far from where many hearts are that it will cause great discord until people accept it—accept his total love for them.

57 "Try to settle things among yourselves. *58* Courts are only for those unwilling or unable to see the truth, to see justice."

CHAPTER 13

10 On a Sabbath Jesus was teaching in the synagogue. *11* A woman who had had a bad back was there. She had had this for eighteen years and was now bent double and could not straighten up. *12* Jesus said to her, "Sister, you are healed of your ailment." *13* He laid hands on her and she instantly stood up straight, and thanked God.

14 But the ruler of the synagogue was very indignant that Jesus had healed on the Sabbath. He said to the congregation, "There are six days when work can be done, so come

on one of those days to be healed." *15* Jesus said to him, "Doesn't everyone here lead his ox or donkey to water on the Sabbath? *16* Shouldn't this woman, a daughter of Abraham, who has suffered for eighteen years be healed on the Sabbath?" *17* At these words those against him were ashamed and sat back down, while the rest rejoiced for the wonderful healing.

18 Then he said, "What does the Divine Life in us resemble? *19* It is like a mustard seed that a man took and planted in his garden. *20* Though starting out so very small, it grew into a tree large enough that even the birds could make their nest in it. *21* Or it is like yeast which a woman took and mixed into three batches of flour until they were all raised."

22 He continued on his way to Jerusalem passing through towns and villages, teaching and healing. *34* He had a great love for Jerusalem and said, "Oh Jerusalem, how often I have wanted to gather your children as a hen gathers her brood under her wings."

CHAPTER 14

7 At a supper he noticed many guests trying to get the best places, so he told them this parable. *8* "When you are invited to a wedding banquet, do not sit in a place of honor. Someone more esteemed by your host may come, *9* and you would be asked to move down. *10* Rather take one of the humble places so when you host arrives, he may ask you to move up higher. *11* For whoever tries to be important will be humbled, and the humble will be honored."

12 He also told them, "When you give a dinner or supper don't invite your relatives or friends or well-to-do neighbors, for they will surely invite you in their turn. *13* Instead invite the poor and downtrodden, for they have no way to repay you. *14* Your payment will be the joy of sharing.

33 "Unless you learn the joy of sharing, you will have great trouble walking with me. *34* And unless you are willing to lay everything else aside, you won't be able to. *35* Listen well to what I am saying."

CHAPTER 15

1 Many tax collectors and others not-well-thought-of were crowding around to hear Jesus. *2* The Pharisees and scribes objected to this and said, "He welcomes everyone and even eats with them." *3* So he told them this parable: *4* "Would not a shepherd who has a hundred sheep and loses one, not leave the ninety-nine and go and search for the one that is lost? *5* And when he finds it, he lays it on his shoulders and carries it home rejoicing. *6* Then he asks his friends and neighbors to come and celebrate that he has found the one which was lost. *7* This is the way God is. He often rejoices more over one who was lost and comes home, than over ninety-nine who have never been lost.

8 "The same can be said for a woman who has ten silver coins and loses one. Does she not light a lamp and sweep the whole house until she finds it? *9* And when she has found it, does she not call her friends and neighbors to come and celebrate with her that she has found the lost one? *10* I tell you there is often more joy in God's heart over finding a lost one than over those who have never been lost."

11 And he told a third parable: "A man had two sons. *12* The younger said to his father, 'Dad, please give me my portion of the inheritance now.' So the father split the property in two and gave the younger son his half. *13* After a few days the younger son took all that he had and traveled to a distant country. There he squandered all his money on reckless living. *14* When he was totally broke, a famine hit that country and he became desperate. *15* So he went and hired himself out to a man who sent him to take care of his pigs. [Remember pigs were very dirty animals under Jewish law.] *16* He was so hungry that he even wanted to eat the bean pods that the pigs were eating, but no one gave him any. *17* Then he came to his senses and realized that even his father's hired hands had something to eat. *18* So he decided to go back home and humble himself before his father, *19* and ask to become one of his hired hands.

20 "So he got up and went home. But while he was still a long way off his father saw him coming and was deeply moved. He ran out and hugged his son and gave him a kiss. 21 The son said, 'Dad I have betrayed you and God. I no longer deserve to be called your son.' 22 But the father called the servants and said, 'Run and get the best robe and put it on him. Put a ring on his finger and sandals on his feet. 23 Get the fatted calf and butcher it. Let's have a feast and celebrate. 24 For my son was dead and has come to life again. He was lost and is now found.' So they began to celebrate.

25 "Now the older son was in the field working, and as he was coming home he heard music and dancing. 26 He called one of the servants aside and asked what was going on. 27 He said, 'Your brother has come home safe and sound, and your father has butchered the fatted calf to celebrate. 28 The son got really angry at this, and would not even go in to the celebration. His father came out and pleaded with him to come in. 29 But he replied, 'No, I have worked for you all these years, and you have never given me so much as a young goat to celebrate with my friends. 30 But when this son of yours comes home after squandering all his inheritance on prostitutes, you have the fatted calf killed for him.' 31 But he replied, 'Son, you have indeed always been with me and everything I own is yours. 32 But we just have to have a great celebration, for your brother was dead and has come to life; he was lost and is found.'"

CHAPTER 16

13 Jesus told his friends, "It is extremely important that you realize a servant cannot serve two masters. He will listen to one or the other, but never both. You cannot serve both God and money. 14 The Pharisees were listening to all this and were making fun of his teaching because they loved money. 15 So he told them, "You claim to be righteous, but God knows your hearts. 16 You have learned to follow the law, but you have not learned how to love. 17 You have learned how to spend money, but you have not learned how to share it."

CHAPTER 17

5 The apostles said to Jesus, "Please give us more faith." 6 Jesus responded, "If you have faith the size of a mustard seed, you could say to this mulberry tree, 'Be uprooted and planted in the sea,' and it will happen. Your faith will grow as your Love grows. Faith is the exercise of Divinity, and Love is God."

11 As he continued on toward Jerusalem, he crossed from Galilee into Samaria. 12 As he entered a village there, he was met by ten lepers. 13 They cried out to him, "Jesus, Teacher, take pity on us!" 14 He told them, "Go and show yourselves to the priests." For that was what they were to do after being healed. And on their way there they were healed.

20 Some Pharisees asked him, "When will the kingdom of God come?" 21 He answered them, "The

real kingdom of God is not something outside that will come; it is something inside that is already there. *23* So if you want to find the real kingdom of God, look into your heart and listen quietly. *24* There you will find the God you have been seeking. *33* And when you really find God, you will realize that nothing else is as important as this. Not even your own life."

CHAPTER 18

1 He then told them a parable to encourage them to pray always. *2* "There was a judge with no reverence for God, and no regard for people. *3* There was a widow in that city who kept coming to him asking for justice. *4* He didn't care about her or about justice. *5* But he finally gave her justice just to get her off his back."

6 Then he said, "Look at what this crooked judge did, he gave the widow what she asked for. *7* If a person like that can respond to requests, *8* imagine what your Dad in heaven can do when you ask *him*!"

15 Some parents were bringing their children to Jesus to have him bless them, but his friends tried to stop them. *16* So Jesus said to them, "Let the little children come to me and don't stand in their way, *17* for they already know that the God of Love dwells in their hearts."

18 A ruler of a synagogue asked him, "Teacher, what shall I do to have Divine Life?" *19* Jesus said to him, "You know the commandments.

20 Follow them." *21* He replied, "I have kept them all my life." *22* Jesus could see his heart and knew that he had put wealth where God should be so he said, "You still lack one thing. Go and sell everything you have and give the money to the poor, then come back and walk with me." *23* When he heard this, he was very sad, for he was extremely rich. *24* So Jesus said, "How hard it is for the wealthy to really find God. It is easier for a camel to crawl through the low openings in the city wall than for a rich man to truly find God."

26 His listeners said, "Then what about us?" *27* Jesus said, "It is impossible to find God where you are looking. But if you look in your hearts and listen very carefully, God will do the impossible in you." *28* Peter said, "What about us; we have left everything to walk with you?" *29* Jesus said, "I assure you that anyone who has left anything to walk with me, has already found God, and the road to happiness. *30* The things of this world are important on the human level, but I am walking with you to the Divine Level. There you will understand what is truly important and what the true life really is."

31 Taking the twelve off by themselves he told them, "We are going up to Jerusalem now and all the prophesies about me will be fulfilled. *32* I will be handed over to the Gentiles and be ridiculed and spat upon. *33* They will flog me and execute me, but on the third day I will rise again." *34* But they did not understand this at all.

35 As they were approaching Jericho, a blind man was sitting along the road begging. *36* Hearing the crowd coming, he asked what was going on. *37* They told him that Jesus was about to go by. *38* So he shouted, "Jesus, son of David, have pity on me." *39* Those around told him to be quiet, but he shouted even louder, "Jesus, have pity on me!" *40* So Jesus stopped and asked that he be brought over. *41* Jesus asked him what he wanted. He said, "I want to see!" *42* Jesus said to him, "Receive your sight, your faith has healed you." Instantly he regained his sight and began to walk along with Jesus, thanking God. And all who saw it thanked God.

CHAPTER 19

1 As he was passing through Jericho, *2* a man named Zacchaeus, a wealthy tax collector, tried to see who Jesus was, *3* but he was too short to see over the crowd. *4* So he ran up ahead and climbed a sycamore tree that Jesus was about to pass.

5 When Jesus looked up and saw him, he said, "Zacchaeus, come down, I want to visit with you." *6* He scrambled down from the tree and gave him a hearty welcome. *7* Those around complained that Jesus was going with a wealthy tax collector. *8* So Zacchaeus paused and said to Jesus, "Teacher, I will give half of everything I own to the poor, and if I have wronged anyone I will pay it back fourfold." *9* Jesus told the crowd, "Today this man has seen that God dwells in a loving heart, and not in material possessions. *10* I have come to seek the lost, and today one of these is found."

28 After this he continued on toward Jerusalem. As they got near Bethany, at what is called the Mount of Olives, *29* he was very tired so he sent two apostles into the town telling them, "Go into the village and you will see a colt tied up; *30* untie it and bring it here. *31* And if anyone asks you about his, say 'The Teacher needs it.'"

32 They went and found everything just as he had said they would. *33* As they were untying the colt, the owner asked them what they were doing. *34* They told him the teacher needed it. *35* Then they brought it to Jesus and put their coats on it and helped him mount.

36 As he rode down from the Mount of Olives, a jubilation began, since he had returned to Jerusalem. *37* They gave him a prophet's welcome.

45 He went right into the temple and began to drive out those selling animals for sacrifice, saying, "This is a house of prayer, not a business. *46* Do you not know that God wants you to love rather than to offer sacrifices?"

47 And every day he went there to teach while the chief priests and scribes tried to figure out how to destroy him. *48* But they couldn't since all the people considered him a prophet.

CHAPTER 20

1 One day when Jesus was teaching in the temple the chief priests and scribes came up to him, *2* and asked him by what authority he was doing the things he did. *3* He replied, "I will ask you a question too. *4* Was John's baptism from God or from us humans?"

5 They said among themselves, "If we say 'From God,' he will ask us why we didn't believe in him. *6* But if we say 'From us humans,' all the people will stone us because they believe John is a prophet. *7* So they answered that they did not know. *8* Jesus said to them, "Then neither will I respond to your question about who gave me the authority to do these things."

19 They wanted to grab him right then but couldn't because of the people. *20* They decided instead to send spies to try to trick him so they could have reason to turn him over to the governor, since they did not have the authority to condemn anyone to death.

21 But before they left they asked him, *22* "Is it lawful for us Jews to pay tribute to Caesar by paying taxes to him?" *23* Jesus saw their trick and said, *24* "Show me a coin," since it was unlawful for Jews to carry coins with images on them. But they had one anyway and showed it to him. He then said, "Whose image is this?" They said, "Caesar's."

25 He said to them, "Then give to Caesar what is Caesar's but to God what belongs to God." *26* They were astounded that he got out of their trap and went away quietly.

CHAPTER 21

1 Looking up he saw the wealthy putting their donations into the treasury. *2* He saw a poor widow put in two copper pennies. *3* He said to those around, "I tell you that poor widow has put in more than all the rich together. *4* For they gave from their surplus, while she gave everything she had to live on."

5 Some began to talk about how beautiful the temple was, how many beautiful stones were in it. *6* He said, "The time is coming when not one stone there will be left upon another; all of this beauty will be completely torn down." *7* They asked him when this would happen, or what sign would indicate it was about to happen. *8* He said, "Be careful not to be misled. Many will say 'The time is near.' Do not believe it. *9* For the transition will not come all at once.

10 "Many external things will happen. *11* There will be wars between nations, *12* and wars within families. *13* You will be arrested and persecuted because you have walked with me and continue to preach the Good News. *14* Don't worry about what to say when these things happen. *15* I will always be walking with you, even though you may not be able to see me with your eyes.

20 "But when you see Jerusalem

surrounded by armies, be assured that her downfall is near. *21* This beautiful temple must fall and disappear to help people realize the real temple of God is inside them, in their hearts. *22* When people ask you when I will return, tell them to look in their hearts. *23* I will return when they see me there. *24* My return will be known by internal things like peace of mind and love of heart, *25* like people caring and sharing. *26* And giving to the needy what they don't need, and even at times what they do need."

37 Jesus continued to teach in the temple every day, and to pray on the Mount of Olives at night. *38* Each morning all the people would come back to the temple to hear his Message.

CHAPTER 22

1 The Passover Feast was coming up, *2* and the chief priests and scribes were looking for a way to kill him, but they were very afraid of the reaction of the people. *3* Judas Iscariot, who was one of the Twelve, was considering betraying Jesus. *4* So he went to talk to the chief priests and temple officers about this. *5* They were delighted and told him they would pay him for doing it. *6* He agreed to do it and looked for a chance to do it when there was no crowd around.

7 Then came the day when the Passover Meal was to be eaten. *8* So Jesus sent Peter and John to get things ready. *9* They asked him where he wanted them to prepare it. *10* He replied, "Go into the city and you will see a man carrying a pitcher of water. Follow him and go into the house he goes in. *11* Tell him, 'The Teacher wants to know where he can eat the Passover with his friends.' *12* He will show you a large upper room all furnished. Prepare it there." *13* So they went and found everything just as Jesus had said, and they prepared the Passover Supper.

14 When the time for the supper came, they all sat down at the table. *15* Jesus said to them, "I have been longing to eat this Passover with you before I die. *16* I want you to know that this is my last supper." *17* And taking a large cup of wine he said, "This is my last toast. *18* Drink this to celebrate the end of my mission on earth and the beginning of your mission; your mission to spread the Good News that the God of Love dwells in the hearts of all, especially those who love. My Message of Love is how my presence of Love will go out to all the world."

19 He then took bread, gave thanks and broke it. Then he gave it to them saying, "This is my body, this is my very being. I give this to you, and all who will receive this, so that you will know we are one. Do this to remember we are the same thing." *20* After supper he took a cup of wine and poured in a bit of water, as was the custom. He said, "This is the new Covenant in my blood, poured out of me and into you. I put a bit of water in it to represent you, to show that now you are part of my blood, part of me. As you drink this remember that my blood is your blood; my life is your life from now and forever." Everyone there sat in amazement at what he had said and what he had done.

21 After this stunned silence, Jesus said, "Tonight I am going to be betrayed by one of you sitting here." *22* Again they were totally stunned by what he said. *23* And they started talking among themselves about who it might be.

24 As the reality that Jesus was no longer going to be with them set in, they began to talk about who would become the new leader. *25* But he told them, "The kings of this world lord it over others. *26* You are not to act that way. The most prominent among you must be as the youngest, and the leader as one who serves. *27* I have been your Teacher, but have come among you as one who serves.

31 "Peter, I have prayed for you so that even after you fall, *32* you may come back to me and strengthen your brothers." *33* Peter said, "Teacher, I am ready to go to prison and even die for you." *34* But Jesus said to him, "I tell you, Peter, that before the cock crows tomorrow you will have denied three times that you even know me."

39 Then they went out to the Mount of Olives as usual. *40* When they got there, he said to them, "Pray for help tonight and tomorrow." *41* He then went on another stone's throw and knelt down and prayed,

42 "Dad, I am ready to come home, but I don't look forward to tomorrow. Help me!"

45 He got up from praying and walked back to the others. They were all asleep. *46* He woke them and said, "Why are you sleeping? You should be praying for help."

47 As he was saying this, the mob coming with Judas Iscariot arrived. He went up to Jesus and kissed him. *48* Jesus said, "Judas, are you betraying me with a kiss?" *49* When those with him realized what was happening, they said, "Teacher, shall we use the sword?" *50* But before Jesus could respond, one of them struck the servant of the high priest and cut off his ear. *51* Jesus said, "Stop this!" And touching the ear, healed the servant.

52 Then Jesus said to the temple officers who had come to arrest him, "Why have you come out here with swords and clubs as though I were a criminal, *53* when every day I taught in the temple and you never raised a hand against me?"

54 They arrested him and took him to the house of the high priest. Meanwhile Peter followed back at a distance. *55* In the courtyard the servants had built a fire to warm themselves. Peter sat there for a while. *56* Then a maid noticed him and said, "This fellow was with Jesus too." *57* But he denied even knowing him. *58* A little later another servant recognized him and said, "Yes, you are indeed one of them." But Peter said, "I am not!" *59* About an hour later another servant said, "I am sure I saw you with him." *60* But Peter said, "I don't know what you are talking about!" Just then the cock crowed. *61* Jesus turned around and looked at Peter, and he remembered what Jesus had said would happen. *62* And he went out and wept bitterly.

63 The men guarding Jesus ridiculed him and flogged him. *64* Then they blindfolded him, struck him and said, "You claim to be a prophet; tell us who hit you?"

66 When dawn came the chief priests and scribes had Jesus brought into their Sanhedrin, their governing body. *67* They said to him, "If you are the Christ, tell us." He said to them, "But you will not believe me if I tell you." *70* Then they all shouted at him, "Are you the Christ or not?" He responded, "Yes, I Am." *71* They shouted, "We don't need any more testimony. We have personally heard him blaspheme."

CHAPTER 23

1 They then rose as a body and took him to Pilate. *2* And there they started to accuse him, "We found this man breaking our laws and telling our people not to pay taxes to Caesar. He said that he himself is the Christ, the king."

3 Pilate asked him, "Are you the King of the Jews?" He answered, "If you say so." *4* After examining him further he said to the chief priests and the crowd, "I find nothing at all criminal in this man." *5* But they strongly insisted, "He stirs up the people all over Judea, and from Galilee to Jerusalem."

6 Pilate asked if he was a Galilean, *7* and learning that he was under Herod's jurisdiction, he sent him to Herod who was in town that week.

8 Herod was very pleased to see him. He had been hearing a lot about him and was hoping to see him perform a miracle. *9* But though he questioned him at length, Jesus never answered him. *10* Meanwhile the chief priests and scribes were standing there accusing him with all their might. *11* Then Herod and his soldiers mocked him, and put a splendid robe on him and sent him back to Pilate. *12* From that day on Herod and Pilate became friends, even though before they had been enemies.

13 Pilate then summoned the chief priests and scribes and said, *14* "You brought me this man and accused him of inciting the people to rebellion. I have examined him in your presence and have found him not guilty of any of your accusations. *15* Neither, in fact, has Herod, for he sent him back to me, saying he had done nothing deserving death. *16* So after a scourging, I am going to let him go."

17 During the feast it was customary for the governor to release a prisoner for the people. Pilate asked them if they wanted him to release Jesus. *18* But they all shouted, "Away with him! Release Barabbas for us!" *19* Barabbas had been arrested for causing a riot in the city and for murder. 20 Pilate wanted to release Jesus so he tried again, 21 but they continued to shout, "Crucify him, crucify him!" 22 For the third time he said to them, "What wrong has he done? I find that he has done nothing deserving death. So after a scourging I will let him go." 23 But they continued to shout their demand that he be crucified. 24 Finally Pilate gave in and released Barabbas, 25 and ordered Jesus to be crucified.

26 As they lead him away, they forced Simon, a Cyrenian, to carry the cross for Jesus. 27 A large crowd followed Jesus, many of them women. They were beating their breasts and crying for him. 28 He turned to them and said, "Don't cry for me for I am going home. 29 Weep for those who have not heard or accepted my Message of God's love. 30 Now it is your turn to teach this and to live this."

32 Two criminals were also led away with him to be crucified. 33 And when they reached the place called The Skull, they crucified him and the two criminals, one on his right and one on his left. 34 And Jesus said, "Dad, I know you will continue to love those who crucify me. They don't really know what they are doing." And they divided his clothes among themselves by casting lots.

35 Many people stood by quietly, remembering what he had done for them. However, the elders sneered, "He saved other, let him save himself if he really is the Christ!" 36 The soldiers too ridiculed him saying, "If you really are the King of the Jews, save yourself!" 38 For there was an inscription above him: "This is the King of the Jews."

39 One of the criminals beside him said, "If you are the Christ, save yourself and us too." 40 But the other reproved him and said, "Do you not fear God? 41 We are paying for what we did, but this man has done nothing wrong." 42 Then he said, "Jesus, please take me home with you!" 43 Jesus said to him, "I assure you, today you will be with me in the home of our Dad."

44 It was then about noon, and darkness came over the whole land, and this lasted till three in the afternoon. 45 At that time the veil in the temple was torn in two. 46 Jesus cried out, "Dad, I'm coming!" And with these words he went home.

47 When the centurion saw what had happened, he praised God and said, "Truly this man was innocent." 48 And when the crowd there saw all this, they went home beating their breasts. 49 All his friends there, and the women who had come along with him from Galilee, were at a distance watching and praying.

50 Now Joseph of Arimathea, 51 one of the few members of the Sanhedrin who had not voted for the plot against Jesus, 52 went to Pilate and asked for the body of Jesus. 53 He took it down and wrapped it in linen, and laid it in a tomb carved

out of rock, in which no one had yet been laid.

54 It was getting toward evening and so the Sabbath rest was about to begin. *55* The women who had accompanied Jesus from Galilee followed and watched where his body was laid. *56* Then they went back to prepare spices and perfumes for when they could return and anoint the body after the Sabbath rest.

CHAPTER 24

1 At dawn on the first day of the week, his family went to the tomb with spices they had prepared for the anointing. These were Mary Magdalene, his wife, Mary his mother, and Mary and Joanna, his sisters. *2* They found the entrance stone rolled back, *3* and when they stooped down and went inside, the body of Jesus was not there. *4* They were shocked by this and wondered what had happened. *5* Then they saw Jesus in dazzling clothes standing there. *6* They were very afraid and bowed down, but Jesus said to them, *7* "Don't be afraid. It is really me! I have risen! *8* Don't you remember that I told you about all this while we were still in Galilee?"

9 His family was filled with amazement, their hearts overflowing with joy and peace. *10* After they had hugged and talked a bit, they hurried off to tell the eleven and the rest that Jesus was risen. *11* But no one would believe them. *12* Some of them did, however, run to the tomb. They looked into the tomb but saw only the linen burial clothes lying there, and were very confused.

13 That same day two of Jesus' friends were walking to Emmaus, about seven miles from Jerusalem. *14* They were talking about all that had happened. *15* As they were talking, Jesus came up and started walking with them, *16* but they did not recognize him. *17* He said to them, "What are you talking about?" *18* They stopped in amazement and one of them, Cleopas, said to him: "Are you the only person in Jerusalem that does not know what has just happened here?" *19* He asked, "What things?" *20* They said to him, "About Jesus of Galilee, a mighty prophet, whom the chief priests had crucified. *21* We had hoped that he was the one who was going to deliver Israel.

22 "This is the third day since he died and today his family went to the tomb. *23* They say they saw him, that he is alive. *24* Some of his apostles went there and verified that his body is not in the tomb."

25 Then Jesus said, "Let me help you understand." *27* He then opened the scriptures to them about the Christ.

28 When they got to Emmaus, Jesus was going to go on, *29* but they talked him into staying there since it was so late. So he went in with them. *30* And when they sat down to eat, Jesus took the bread and gave thanks. Then he broke it and gave it to them. *31* At that moment they realized who he was, and he vanished.

32 They talked about how moved they were when Jesus was opening the scriptures for them as they walked along. 33 So they got up and ran back to Jerusalem and found the eleven and the others gathered there in prayer. 34 The Community told them that Jesus' family had seen him. 35 Then those from Emmaus told the Community what had happened to them and how they had recognized Jesus in the breaking of the bread.

36 While they were talking about all this, Jesus came and stood in their midst and said, "Peace to you." 37 They were terrified, thinking they were seeing a ghost. 38 He then said to them, "Why are you so shocked and disbelieving? 39 Look closely at my hands and my feet. It's really me. Touch me and see for yourself. 40 A ghost does not have flesh and bone as you can see that I have."

41 Since they still were having trouble believing it was really Jesus, he asked them, "Do you have anything to eat?" They gave him a piece of broiled fish. 42 He sat down and ate it to prove he was not a ghost. 43 They were beside themselves with joy that it was really Jesus.

44 Then he began to remind them of all that he had taught them before. 45 He opened their minds to the scriptures 46 that talked about his suffering, death and resurrection. 47 He told them to begin in Jerusalem and then go and teach the Good News to the whole world.

48 "You will be witnesses to all of this. And I will send the blessing upon you which Dad has promised. 49 But wait here till you receive this very special blessing."

50 Then he took them out to Bethany and blessed them. 51 As he did that he disappeared from their eyes and entered their hearts. 52 They knew then that he would truly be with them, and in them forever. They walked back to Jerusalem rejoicing and praising God, for the Jesus they had walked with, and for the Jesus who was now in their hearts.

ACTS

CHAPTER 1

1 In my former book, I taught about all that Jesus did and taught during his life here. *2* After his resurrection he gave instructions through his Spirit to his apostles. *3* He appeared to them for forty days after his resurrection and taught them more about the Divine Life.

4 When he met with them, he told them not to leave Jerusalem until they had received the Spirit Dad had promised them through him. *5* And he told them that just as John had baptized with water, after a few days they would be baptized by Spirit.

6 The apostles asked if he was going to restore the Kingdom of Israel. *7* He said to them, "My Mission was never about an external kingdom, but about an internal Love. It was and is about the Good News of being the daughters and sons of Dad, about being God as he is. *8* You will understand this more fully as you receive spiritual Gifts when Spirit comes upon you. These will help you be my witnesses here in Jerusalem, in all of Judea and Samaria, and even to the ends of the earth."

9 After he had said these things he began to disappear from their eyes and entered their hearts. They could no longer see him, but they could definitely feel him now being in their hearts.

12 Then they went back to Jerusalem, which is about a Sabbath-day's walk from the Mount of Olives, where they had been. *13* And when they got there they went to the upper room where they were staying—Peter and John, James and Andrew, Philip and Thomas, Bartholomew and Matthew, James the son of Alpheus and Simon the Zealot, and Judas the son of James. *14* All these gathered together constantly for prayer and fellowship, together with their wives, and Mary the mother of Jesus, Mary Magdalene, his wife, and his sisters and brothers.

15 Then one day Peter got up among those gathered, some hundred and twenty, and said, *21* "Sisters and brothers, you all know that Judas, who lead those who arrested Jesus, has left and we must replace him. *22* We need to select someone who has been with us from the baptism of John through the resurrection.

23 The Community nominated two men: Joseph called Barsabbas, who was surnamed Justus, and Matthias. *24* Then they prayed asking brother Jesus to let them know which one he wanted to take Judas' place. *25* Then they cast lots and the lot fell on Matthias, and he was added to the eleven apostles.

CHAPTER 2

1 When the day of Pentecost finally came, the Community was together praying *2* when suddenly it sounded like a mighty wind had started. *3* Then they saw tongues of fire that descended on each of them. *4* And they were filled with Spirit and began speaking in strange languages as Spirit moved their hearts.

5 That day there were devout Jews in Jerusalem from every known nation, *6* and when they heard the wind they came to see what was happening. *7* They were amazed to hear each of them speaking in their own native language. In their amazement they asked, "Are all these speaking not Galileans? *8* So how can each of us hear them in our native language? *11* We are from all over the world and yet we hear them talking about the wonders of God in our own language!" *12* They were all at a loss as to how to understand this. Some said, "What does all this mean?" *13* Others simply sneered and said, "They are just drunk."

14 So Peter got up with the other apostles and addressed them, "People of Judea, and all you visiting Jerusalem, please listen to us. *15* These people are not drunk; after all it is only nine o'clock in the morning. *16* But this is what God foretold through the prophet Joel: *17* "In the new days I will pour forth my Spirit over all people. Your daughters and sons will prophesy; your young people will see visions and your elders will dream dreams. *18* Even those considered lowly will receive my Spirit and prophesy. *19* And I will show my love in wonders in the heavens and on the earth.

22 "People of God, listen closely. Jesus of Nazareth was sent by God, as has been shown though his mighty words and wonders, as you already know. *23* Yet you killed him by hanging him on a cross. *24* But God raised him from the dead. *32* We who stand here before you are witnesses to this Truth.

33 "Jesus was born of Spirit and raised from the dead by Spirit. Today he has poured out his Spirit on us, as manifested by what you see and hear around you. *36* So without a shadow of a doubt all of you should know that this Jesus, whom you have crucified, is indeed a Christ!"

37 As they were listening, they were moved to the depths of their hearts, and said to Peter and the other apostles, "Brothers, what shall we do?" *38* Peter responded, "Open your hearts to Jesus and his Spirit and be baptized with water and Spirit, and you will receive his Gifts. *39* For the Promise of Covenant with God is to you, your children and to everyone without exception.

40 Peter talked to them at length about what it meant to open their hearts to Jesus and live their lives in him, as he will live his life in them. *41* Then those who welcomed his Message were baptized, some three thousand that day.

42 And they grew with the apostles' teaching, in fellowship, in the breaking of the bread, and in prayer. *43* Awe surrounded everyone as they saw the wonders and signs that took place in Jerusalem through the apostles.

44 The believers met together and had everything in common. *45* They sold their property and their belongings, and gave everything to the needy. *46* They went every day to the temple and had all their meals together. *47* So they received spiritual and physical nourishment, and praised God with happy and peaceful hearts. They were admired for the way they lived, and every day more people joined them through Spirit.

CHAPTER 3

1 One day Peter and John went up to temple for the three o'clock prayer. *2* There was a man there who had been lame all his life. Friends would bring him there so he could beg from those who came to pray.

3 When he saw Peter and John coming toward the door he asked for alms. *4* They looked at him intently and said, "Look at us." He looked at them, hoping to get something. *5* But Peter said, "We don't have any money to give you, but we will give you what we do have. *6* In the name of Jesus of Nazareth, get up and walk." *7* And taking him by the hand they helped him up. *8* Instantly his feet and ankles were healed. He jumped up and began to walk around. Then he went into the temple with them, walking and jumping and praising God.

9 When the people around saw him walking around and praising God, *10* they recognized him as the beggar that used to be at the temple gate. They were completely amazed at what they saw. *11* And as he kept clinging to Peter and John, everyone crowded around them at Solomon's Door.

12 When Peter noticed this, he said to the crowd, "People of God, why are you amazed at this? And why are you looking at us as though we had healed this man with our own power or prayer? *13* God himself, through his son Jesus, whom you disowned before Pilate, has healed this man. *16* By faith in this Jesus, this man here, whom you know, has been healed and restored to perfect health as you can clearly see."

CHAPTER 4

1 As they were speaking to the people, the priests, the captain of the temple guards, and some Jewish leaders came up. *3* They arrested them and put them in jail overnight. *4* But many of those who had seen the miracle and heard the Message believed, and the number of believers grew to five thousand that day.

5 The next day the Jewish leaders *6* and the high priests had Peter and John brought before them. *7* They asked them, "By whose power or in what name have you done this?" *8* Then Peter filled with Spirit replied, "Priests and rulers of the people, *9* if today we are being called to account for a good deed done to a crippled person, *10* then you and all the people of God should know that it was by the name of Jesus of Nazareth, whom you crucified, that this man was healed."

13 The leaders were amazed that Peter and John could talk so boldly since they had no education. Then they realized that they had been with Jesus. *14* And seeing the man who had been healed standing with them there was nothing they could say, *15* so they had them sent out.

16 They then consulted together and said, "What can we do with these men? It is obvious that they have performed a mighty healing, and all Jerusalem knows it. *17* However, we have to stop news of this from spreading, so we will strongly warn them not to speak of this again."

18 Then they summoned them again and warned them not to talk about the miracle or preach in the name of Jesus. *19* But Peter and John replied to them, "Whether it is right for us, in God's eye, to listen to you rather than to him, is easy to decide. *20* We cannot stop telling what we have seen and heard about Jesus."

21 They threatened them again and let them go, for they saw no way to punish them because of the people, who were all praising God for what had happened. *22* For the man who had been cured had been crippled for forty years.

23 After they had been released, they went back to the Community and told them all what had happened and what the priests and leaders had said. *24* Then those who heard this said, "Dad, we know these things were coming because your Spirit speaking through David foretold them. *29* So now, in the face of these threats, we ask you to give your servants here, special strength to preach fearlessly the Message of your son and our brother, *30* as you reach out through your son Jesus to heal and to work wonders. *31* And as they prayed, the place shook, and they were filled with Spirit and they rejoiced in the Message of Jesus.

32 The Community of believers was of one mind and heart. No one claimed anything for himself, but everything was held in common. *33* With great power the apostles gave witness to the resurrection of brother Jesus, and a special anointing was over them all.

34 No one among them was in need, *35* for those who owned property sold it and gave the money to the Community, who gave it to all who were in need. *36* Joseph, called Barnabas by the Apostles, sold his place and gave all the money to the Community.

CHAPTER 5

12 Many signs and wonders continued to be performed among the people by the apostles and others. The Communities continued to meet regularly in Solomon's Portico. *13* Many of those who did not belong to the Communities were afraid to join them because of the persecution, but they held them in high esteem. *14* While every day women and men who believed in Jesus kept entering the Communities.

15 Some went so far as to bring their sick out into the street and lay them on rugs and mats so that when Peter or James or John would pass by they would be healed. *16* The sick and troubled, even from outside of Jerusalem, were brought and all were cured.

17 Now the priests and Jewish leaders were filled with jealousy at this, *18* and so had the apostles arrested and put in jail again. *19* But an Angel of God came that night and let them out and said, *20* "Go back into the temple and tell everyone about Divine Life."

21 So they went into the temple at daybreak and began to teach this. The high priests summoned the Jewish leaders and even the senators and sent word to the jail to bring the men. *22* But when the attendants got to the jail they could not find them, so they went back and reported, *23* "We found the jail securely locked with sentinels at all the doors, but when they opened the doors there was no one inside."

24 When the captain of the temple guard and the chief priests heard this, they couldn't understand what had happened. *25* Then someone came and said, "The men you arrested yesterday are in the temple teaching the people." *26* Then the captain and his officers went to the temple and brought them in, but not forcibly because they were afraid the people would stone them.

27 They brought them before the leaders gathered there and the high priests said, "Didn't we strictly forbid you to teach in this name? And yet you even continue teaching in the temple and blame us for his death."

28 Then Peter, James and John replied, "Are we not to obey God, rather than humans? *29* God raised up Jesus whom you killed by hanging him on a cross. *32* And not only are we witnesses to this truth, but so is Spirit whom God bestows on those open to him."

33 As they listened they got furious and decided to have them killed. *34* Then Gamaliel, a teacher of people, arose and ordered the apostles to be put outside for a bit. *35* Then he said, "Men of God, be careful what you do to these people. *36* We know from what we have already seen that movements that are not from God die off of their own accord. *38* So I advise you to leave these men alone, for if their movement is not from God it will die by itself; *39* but if it is from God, we may find ourselves fighting against God." *40* They accepted his counsel and had the apostles brought back in, then had them flogged, and sent away.

41 The apostles went out and rejoiced that they had been treated as Jesus was, and kept right on teaching about his resurrection and his Message. *42* They did this both in the temple and in the homes of believers.

CHAPTER 6

1 In those days, as the number of believers kept growing, the Greek Jews complained that their widows were being overlooked in the daily distribution of food. *2* So the twelve apostles called a council of the Communities and said, "We should not stop preaching Jesus' Message to wait on tables. *3* Therefore, sisters and brothers, look for seven people of good reputation from the Communities and full of Spirit, *4* and we will appoint them for this task so we can continue dedicating our lives to prayer and teaching the Message of Jesus."

5 This suggestion was accepted by all the Communities and they selected Stephen, a man full of faith and Spirit; also Philip, Prochorus, Nicanor, Timon, Parmenas and Nicolas. *6* They presented these to the apostles who prayed over them and laid hands on them.

7 So the Message of Jesus kept on spreading. The number of believers in Jerusalem increased rapidly with even a large number of priests joining the Communities.

8 And Stephen, full of Spirit and his Gifts, performed many signs and wonders among the people, *9* but some of the different non-believers would debate with him. *10* However, the wisdom given him by Spirit always prevailed.

11 So they decided the only way to deal with him was to kill him. They stirred up the people by lying and saying, "He is speaking against Moses and God." *12* As a result he was taken before the high court. *13* There they produced false witnesses who said, "This man talks against the temple and the law. *14* We have heard him say that this Jesus of Nazareth will tear down our temple and destroy the law handed down to us by Moses." *15* The judges looked at him and saw that he had the face of an Angel.

CHAPTER 7

1 The high priest asked him, "Are these charges true?" *2* Then Stephen said, "Brothers, our father Abraham was given the land we live in and promised it would go to his heirs, even though at the time he had no children.

"God came and made a Covenant of Love with Abraham, but that has not been honored. Now he has sent his son to bring his people back to him, and you have killed him."

54 At this the judges charged at him and threw him out of the city and had him stoned to death. *55* The witnesses laid their coats at the feet of a young man named Saul. *56* As they were stoning him, he said, "I see the heavens open and Jesus at the side of God beckoning me." *57* Then he said, "Brother Jesus, bring me home!" *60* Falling on his knees he said, "Brother, don't hold this against them." And with these words he went home.

CHAPTER 8

1 A young man named Saul had been in charge of the stoning of Stephen, and then led a severe persecution against the Communities in Jerusalem, so that all but the apostles fled the city. *2* Saul had been causing havoc with the Community members, *3* breaking into their homes and putting them in prison.

4 Those who had to flee Jerusalem went everywhere preaching the Good News of Jesus. *5* So Philip came down to a city of Samaria and preached Jesus there. *6* The people were happy to attend his meetings and see the miracles he performed. *7* The possessed were cleansed; the lame were healed; *8* there was rejoicing all around.

14 When the apostles in Jerusalem learned that Samaria had accepted the Message of Jesus, they sent Peter and John to them. *15* When they arrived they prayed for the new believers to receive the Spirit. *16* For so far they had only been baptized with water, and had not received Spirit. *17* Then Peter and John laid hands on them and they received Spirit. *25* After they had witnessed and shared more of Jesus' Message to many Samaritan Communities, they went on their way.

26 Then an Angel of God told Philip, "Get up and at noon go down the road that runs between Jerusalem and Gaza. *27* So he got up and went there. He ran into an Ethiopian eunuch of Queen Candace who was returning from a visit to Jerusalem to pray. *28* He was riding along reading the Book of Isaiah.

29 The Spirit told Philip, "Go up and greet him." So Philip ran up to his chariot and heard him reading Isaiah. *30* He asked him if he understood what he was reading. *31* He responded, "How can I, unless someone explains it to me?" And he invited Philip to climb in and ride with him.

32 Now the scripture passage he had just read was this: "As a lamb he was led to slaughter, but he did not open his mouth." *34* The Ethiopian turned to Philip and asked him who the prophet was referring to. *35* Then Philip began to explain the passage, and go on to explain to him about the Good News of Jesus.

36 They came to some water and the Ethiopian asked if he could be baptized. *37* Philip told him if he really believed what he had been hearing, he could be baptized. And he replied, "I believe that Jesus is a Christ, a Son of God." *38* So he ordered the chariot to stop, and they both went down to the water and Philip baptized him.

39 And when they came out of the water, Spirit took Philip away, and the Ethiopian went happily on his way rejoicing in his new life. *40* Philip, however, was found in Azotus, and as he went through the cities, he preached the Good News all the way to Caesarea.

CHAPTER 9

1 Now Saul was still persecuting the believers. *2* He went to the high priests and asked them for letters to the synagogues in Damascus, so that he might arrest any believers there and bring them back to Jerusalem and put them in jail.

3 As he approached Damascus a bright light from heaven suddenly shone all around him. *4* He fell to the ground and heard a voice say to him, "Saul, Saul, why are you persecuting me?" *5* He said, "Who are you?" The voice answered, "I am Jesus, whom you are persecuting." *6* Flabbergasted and very frightened, he asked, "What do you want me to do?" Jesus said to him, "Get up and go into the city, and I will tell you there what to do."

7 The men who were traveling with him were speechless. They had heard the voice clearly but had not seen anyone. *8* Saul got up but when he opened his eyes he could not see anything. So they led him by the hand into Damascus. *9* And for three days he remained blind and did not eat or drink anything.

10 Now there was in Damascus a believer by the name of Ananias. *11* Jesus said to him, "Get up and go to Straight Street and ask at the home of Judas for a man called Saul from Tarsus for he is there praying. *12* And he has had a vision of you coming and laying hands on him that he might see."

13 Ananias replied, "But Brother, I have heard about him and how much he has hurt your saints in Jerusalem. *14* And now he has authority to put anyone in chains who believes in you." *15* But Jesus said to him, "Just go. For I have chosen him to bring my Good News to the Gentiles, and all the people of God. And I will show him ahead of time how he will suffer for doing this."

16 So Ananias went to where Saul was. *17* Then, laying his hands on him said, "Brother Saul, Jesus, the one who appeared to you on your way here, has sent me to you so that you might recover your sight and be filled with his Spirit." *18* Instantly something like scales fell from his eyes and he could see again. He got up and was baptized. *19* Then he ate and regained his strength.

20 Saul stayed in Damascus for some time in prayer and fellowship with the believers. He even began preaching in the synagogues that Jesus was a Son of God. *21* All who heard him were amazed and said, "Isn't this the man who was causing such havoc in Jerusalem, and then came here to take all believers back to Jerusalem in chains?" *22* But Saul was growing every day in Spirit and the Gifts of the Spirit so he could prove his sincerity and Message by the wonders he performed.

23 After a while the Jewish leaders decided he had to be killed, *24* but news of this got to Saul, *25* and so he was let down over the wall at night in a basket by the believers.

31 Then the Communities all over Judea, Galilee and Samaria began to enjoy peace, and the members increased in Spirit and in numbers.

³² As Peter was traveling around proclaiming the Good News he visited the saints in Lydda. ³³ A man there named Aeneas had been bedridden for eight years. ³⁴ Peter said to him, "Aeneas, Jesus heals you. Get up and make your bed." ³⁵ Instantly he got up, and all the people in Lydda saw this and became believers.

³⁶ At Joppa there was a saintly believer named Tabitha. ³⁷ About this time she got sick and died and was laid out in an upper room. ³⁸ Now since Joppa was near Lydda, her family sent a message to Peter begging him to come. ³⁹ So Peter came to Joppa and went to the upper room where people were gathered in mourning. They showed him the wonderful things she had sewn when she was with them.

⁴⁰ Peter asked everyone to leave, and then knelt down and prayed. And then turning to the body he said, "Tabitha, wake up." She opened her eyes and sat up. ⁴¹ Peter gave her a hand and helped her up and then called the people back in to see her alive.

⁴² As news of this spread, the number of believers increased. Peter stayed there for some time in the home of Simon the tanner.

Chapter 10

¹ Now there was a man living in Caesarea, a captain of what was called the Italian Cohort. ² He was a very generous and prayerful person. ³ At three in the afternoon he had a vision of an Angel of God coming to him and saying, ⁴ "Cornelius, your prayers and your charity have touched God. ⁵ Send men to Joppa and have them find Peter, ⁶ who is staying with Simon the tanner who lives by the sea.

⁷ As soon as the Angel left, he called two of his servants and a devout soldier and sent them to Joppa, ⁸ with the instructions from the Angel.

⁹ The next day while they were on their way to Joppa, Peter went up on the balcony at about noon to pray. ¹⁰ During prayer he got hungry and wanted something to eat. But while dinner was still being prepared, a trance came over him. ¹¹ He saw heaven open and a white sheet descending to earth. ¹² On it were all sorts of animals, reptiles and birds. ¹³ Then he heard a voice say, "Get up, Peter, kill and eat." ¹⁴ But Peter said, "No way. I don't eat unclean things." ¹⁵ Again the voice said, "Anything God has made you must not consider unclean." ¹⁶ This happened three times, and then the sheet was taken back up to heaven.

¹⁷ While Peter was trying to figure out the message of the vision, ¹⁸ the messengers from Cornelius were at the gate calling to ask if Peter was there. ¹⁹ Peter was still trying to better understand the vision, so Spirit said, "There are three men at the gate looking for you. ²⁰ Go down and greet them and go with them for

I have sent them." *21* So Peter went down and said, "I am Peter, what can I do for you?" *22* They said, "Captain Cornelius, a holy man, was told by an Angel to invite you to his house and listen to your Message."

23 So he invited them in to have dinner with him. *24* The next day he started off with them together with some of the sisters and brothers from Joppa. *25* The following day they arrived at Caesarea. Cornelius had invited his family and close friends to his home, and as Peter entered, he fell at his feet to reverence him. *26* But Peter raised him up and said, "Get up, I am your brother!"

27 Peter went into his home and found the large gathering there. *28* He said, "You know that Jews have not been allowed to visit Gentiles, but God has now told me that everyone is his daughter and son. *29* That is why I came without hesitation to your home. May I ask why you have invited me here?"

30 So Cornelius told him about the Angel's visit and what he had been told to do. *33* Then he said, "So here we are before God to listen to what he has taught you. *34* Now I understand that God loves everyone, *35* and the things our brother Jesus has made known to us, *36* the Good News of peace and love."

37 Then Peter said, "You probably know what has happened all over Judea, beginning from Galilee after the baptism that John preached. *38* How God anointed Jesus of Nazareth, and how he went through the land preaching and healing, for God was truly with him. *39* And we are witnesses to all he did, especially in Jerusalem where they finally crucified him.

40 "But God raised him from the dead, and he appeared to many of us whom he had chosen to be his witnesses. *41* He even ate and drank with us after his resurrection. *42* Then he told us to preach God's Love and to show it through healing."

44 While Peter was still preaching Spirit descended upon all those gathered. *45* The believers with Peter were amazed that the Spirit was poured out on the Gentiles too, *46* for they heard them praying in chant praising Jesus.

47 Then Peter said, "How can we refuse them the baptism of water since they have already received the baptism of Spirit?" *48* So he directed that they be baptized in the name of Jesus. *49* Then they begged him to stay with them a few days.

CHAPTER 11

1 Now the apostles and the sisters and brothers who live in Judea heard about the Gentiles welcoming the Good News. *2* So when Peter came to Jerusalem, those who still believed in the law confronted Peter about the need for circumcision. *4* Peter responded by giving the history of what had happened in Joppa with his vision from heaven, *5* and his instruction not to consider unclean what God had made clean. *6* And also what had happened in Caesarea with the vision given to Cornelius to invite Peter and listen to him. *7* Then Peter shared about the miracle of Spirit coming on the Gentiles in Caesaria, *8* and concluded by saying, *9* "Now since God had given them the same gift of the Spirit as he has given us, who was I to stand in God's way?" *18* When they heard this, they were amazed at the actions of God and praised him for his amazing love.

19 Those who had fled Jerusalem because of the persecution surrounding Stephen, made their way as far as Phoenicia, but preaching the Word to no one but the Jews. *20* And there were Greek speakers who went to Antioch and spoke to the Greeks there, as well as preaching the Good News about our brother Jesus. *21* Jesus' hand was with them, and a great number began to believe in him.

22 When news of this reached Jerusalem the Communities there sent Barnabas to Antioch. *23* When he arrived he was amazed at what Jesus had done there and encouraged all to walk closely with him. *24* Barnabas was a good and holy man and helped many to give their lives to Jesus.

25 Then he went to Tarsus looking for Paul, *26* and brought him to Antioch where they stayed an entire year preaching the Good News and healing the sick. It was at Antioch where the believers were first called Christians.

27 About this time a number of prophets came down to Antioch from Jerusalem. *28* One of them, named Agamas, stood up and revealed, through Spirit, that a terrible famine was coming. *29* So the believers there sent a contribution for those who lived in Judea, *30* and sent it back with Barnabas and Paul.

CHAPTER 12

1 About that time Herod started his attack against the Communities. *2* He killed James, the brother of John, *3* and since this made him popular with the Jewish leaders, he arrested and imprisoned Peter. This took place during the Feast of Unleavened Bread. *4* Peter was put under heavy guard.

5 While Peter was in prison, the Community was in constant prayer. *6* Peter was double chained to keep him from escaping. *7* One night an Angel suddenly stood beside him and a great light shone from heaven. He woke Peter and told him to get up. *8* His chains fell off and the Angel told him to get dressed, put on his coat and follow him. *9* Peter followed him not realizing what was actually happening; he thought it was a vision. *10* They passed one guard and then another and reached the prison door. It opened by itself. They walked out and then the Angel left him. *11* When he realized he was actually out of prison, he thanked God for releasing him and saving him from Herod's plot.

12 When he realized where he was, he went to Mary's house, the mother of John Mark, where he knew there would be a large number praying. *13* When he knocked on the door, Rhoda came to answer it. *14* She recognized Peter's voice and ran to tell the Community, forgetting to open the door in her excitement.

15 They told her she was crazy, but she insisted he was there. *16* Meanwhile, Peter kept on knocking, and when they finally opened the door they were amazed to see him. *17* He told them how the Angel of God had led him out of prison and asked them to tell James and the brothers about his release. Then he left.

18 When morning came the soldiers were at a loss as to how Peter had escaped. *19* Herod sent for Peter and was told he had escaped. Herod had the guards executed and then went to his home in Caesarea.

CHAPTER 13

1 Now there were many prophets in the Community at Antioch like Barnabas, and Simon, known as Niger, and Lucius from Cyrene, and Manaen, a childhood friend of Herod the king, and Paul. *2* When they were in prayer, Spirit said "I have called Barnabas and Paul for a special Mission." *3* So after fasting and praying, they laid hands on them and sent them out.

4 They were lead by Spirit down to Seleucia, and from there they sailed to Lupus. *5* Arriving at Salamis, they preached the Good News in the synagogues.

6 They crossed the island as far as Paphos. *7* And there the proconsul Sergius Paulus sent for them in order to hear the word of God. *12* When he saw the wonders Paul worked in the Spirit, he became a believer. He was astonished at the teachings about Jesus.

13 From Paphos Paul and his company sailed away to Pamphylia, *14* and then on to Antioch. *15* Entering the synagogue there on the Sabbath, they were invited to share with the congregation. *16* So Paul got up and began to speak. *17* He first of all gave an overview of the history of the Jewish people beginning in their time in Egypt. *18* Later, he talked about how God appointed David as their King and how Jesus was his offspring.

He talked about Jesus and his teachings, and how the Jewish leaders had had him crucified, even though there was no proof he had committed a crime. Then God raised him from the dead, and he appeared to his friends who then became his witnesses. These began to preach the Good News of Jesus.

42 As Paul and Barnabas were leaving the synagogue, the people asked them to come back the next week. *43* They continued to spend time with Paul and Barnabas, to hear more about the Good News.

44 The next Sabbath nearly the whole town came to hear them. *45* The Jewish leaders got very jealous and angry about this. They rejected the teachings and plotted to get rid of them. *46* But Paul and Barnabas continued to preach in great strength and wisdom. *47* Finally, because of the opposition of the leaders, they announced that they had been sent first to the Jews, but because they would not accept the Good News of Jesus, they were now going to the Gentiles.

48 When the Gentiles heard this, they rejoiced and many became believers in Jesus. *49* And so the Good News was carried all over the country. *50* The Jewish leaders stirred up a persecution against Paul and Barnabas and drove them out of the territory. *51* So Paul and Barnabas went on to Iconium. *52* And the believers were filled with joy and Spirit.

CHAPTER 14

1 The same thing happened in Iconium. They went into the Jewish synagogue and preached from so deep in Spirit that many Jews and Greeks became believers that day. *2* But the non-believing Jews stirred up lies against the brothers. *3* Even so, the brothers stayed there quite a while speaking from the heart of Jesus, who gave witness to their Message by granting signs and wonders at their hands.

4 The town became divided, some siding with the Jewish leaders and some with the apostles. *5* But when both the Jewish and Gentile leaders started a plot to kill them, *6* and they found out about it, *7* they fled to the Lycaonian towns of Lystra and Derbe and the surrounding areas where they went on preaching the Good News.

8 In Lystra there was a man crippled since birth who had never walked. *9* He was there when Paul was speaking. Paul looked straight at his heart, and saw that he had the faith to be healed. So he said in a loud voice "Stand up, you can walk." So the man jumped up and began to walk.

10 When the crowd there saw what Paul had done, they said in Lycaonian, *11* "The Gods have come down to us in human form!" *12* They called Barnabas Zeus and Paul Hermes, since he was the main speaker. *13* The priest of Zeus even brought oxen to the gates of the city to join the people in offering sacrifice.

14 But when Barnabas and Paul heard of this, they ran out to the crowd and shouted. *15* "What are you doing, people? We are just like you! We are bringing you the Good News that you don't need sacrifices because we have a God of Love. *16* In the days of old he seemed distant from us, *17* but with the coming of brother Jesus we know he is in our very midst. He gives us rain for our fields and joy for our hearts."

18 Yet even having said this, they had trouble stopping the people from sacrificing to them. *19* But Jews came from Antioch and Iconium, and convinced the people to stone them. So they stoned Paul and dragged him out of the city thinking he was dead.

20 However, the believers circled him and began to pray. He then got up and walked back into the city. And the next day went to Derbe with Barnabas.

21 They brought the Good News to that city, and after a large Community was established there, they went back to Lystra, Iconium and Antioch. 22 There they assured all the believers in Spirit to stand firm in the faith and said, "Sometimes walking with Jesus brings us the same sufferings that he endured." 23 In prayer with the Communities, they appointed elders to help people continue in the Good News.

24 After going through Epicedia, they went to Pamphylia, 25 and after preaching the Good News in Pergo, they went on down to Attala. 26 From there they sailed to Antioch where God had manifested his great love.

27 When they got to Antioch, they called the Communities together and told them how God had opened the door of faith to the Gentiles. 28 They spent a long time there in the Communities of believers.

CHAPTER 15

1 Some of the former Jews who came down from Jordan were preaching the old belief that if you were not circumcised you could not be saved. 2 Paul and Barnabas had to explain how this was contrary to the Good News of Jesus. They explained that the law of circumcision was superseded by the Good News that we are *already* the daughters and sons of a God of Love, and so there was no longer a need to be saved, only a need to realize what the Good News taught.

Then the Community listened intently as Paul and Barnabas told of the many signs and wonders that God had already done among the Gentiles through them. Paul said, "By this time it is obvious that Spirit is being poured out on Jew and Gentile alike, and he is now cleansing our hearts as previously we believed the law would do. Let us reopen our hearts to the Good News of our brother Jesus who taught us that God is Love. God is Love and so Love is everything (necessary).

"Jesus' Good News of our being literally daughters and sons of God redeems us from the law of Moses, and re-establishes our original Divine inheritance. We can now see that the law of Moses had nothing to do with the Covenant of our Father Abraham. The love-relationship that God tried to establish got sidetracked back into fear, based on the need to keep the law. I believe it is time to walk out of the synagogues and into the Good News of Jesus. We commit to walk with you out of the fear of the law and into the Love of God. Any other message is not from us and is not from our brother Jesus." 35 Paul and Barnabas stayed on in Antioch teaching and preaching with many others the Message of Jesus.

36 Sometime later, Paul said to Barnabas, "Let's go back and visit

the sisters and brothers in every city in which we have preached the Good News of Jesus, to see how they are all doing." *37* Barnabas wanted to take along John Mark, *38* but Paul didn't want to since he had left them before in Pamphylia. *39* Since they couldn't agree, they decided to separate. Barnabas sailed to Cyprus with John Mark, *40* and Paul took Silas *41* and went through Syria and Cilicia strengthening the Communities there.

CHAPTER 16

1 Paul came down to Derbe, where a believer by the name of Timothy lived. *2* He had been highly recommended by the sisters and brothers in Lystra and Iconium. *3* Paul invited him to come along with him.

4 As they traveled from one city to another *5* the Communities were strengthened in the faith and continued to grow. *6* They then crossed Phrygia and the Galatian country and then came down to Troas.

9 During the night Paul had a vision of a man from Macedonia begging him to come there and help them. *10* He got up at once and made plans to go there, sure that Spirit had called them to take the Good News there.

11 So we sailed from Troas straight to Samothrace, then to Neapolis, and finally to Philippi, a colony and major city of Macedonia. *12* We stayed there for a few days. *13* On the Sabbath we went outside the city by a river where we had heard there would be a service. *14* A group of ladies was gathered there, one by the name of Lydia from Thyatira. She was a devoted person, and Jesus opened her heart as Paul was preaching. *15* She asked to have her family baptized and then invited us to stay at her place.

19 But on the way there we were grabbed by men who dragged us to the local authorities and said, *20* "These men are Jews and are creating a disturbance by advocating things that are against our Roman law. *22* A crowd gathered around and joined in denouncing them. *23* The authorities had them stripped and flogged, *24* and then had them put in jail under high security.

25 About midnight Paul and Silas were praying, and singing hymns while the other prisoners listened to them. *26* Then suddenly a tremendous earthquake hit, which rocked the prison to its foundations, and all the doors flew open and everyone's chains fell off. *27* When the jailer saw all the doors open, he drew his sword to kill himself, thinking all the prisoners had escaped. *28* But Paul called out to him, "Don't kill yourself; we are all still here."

29 Getting a lantern, he rushed in and fell at the feet of Paul and Silas saying, *30* "What must I do to be saved?" *31* They replied, "Believe in our brother Jesus, together with your family." *32* Then they taught him and his whole family the Good News of Jesus.

33 At that very hour of the night,

the jailer took them home and attended to their wounds. *34* Then he and his whole family were baptized. Next they had a meal together and all were rejoicing in brother Jesus.

35 At daybreak the magistrates sent word to have them released. *36* The jailer told this to Paul. *37* Paul replied, "After flogging us without a trial and throwing us into prison, even though we are Romans, he wants to send us away in secret? No way! Let them come here themselves and take us out."

38 The orderlies reported this to the magistrates who were alarmed to find out they were Roman citizens. *39* They came and apologized to them, and begged them to leave the city. *40* So they left the prison and went to Lydia's home and fellowshipped with them and then left the city.

CHAPTER 17

1 Going through Amphipolis and Apollonia, they arrived at Thessalonica. *2* As usual Paul went to the synagogue on the Sabbath to preach. *3* For three Saturdays he explained things from the scriptures about the Christ. Then he told them, "The Jesus that I preach to you is Christ."

4 Some of them became believers and associated themselves with Paul and Silas. A large number of them were devout Greeks, and some were prominent women.

5 But the Jewish leaders grew jealous and gathered together a group of the very poor to start an uproar in the city. *6* They went to Jason's house, since many believers used to gather there to pray, but they did not find them. So they dragged Jason from his home and took him to the city fathers shouting, *7* "Jason has taken in those who have turned the world upside down. They talk against Caesar and say there is a different king by the name of Jesus." *8* The magistrates and the crowd were stirred up when they heard this. *9* and had them roughed up and then let them go.

10 That night the sisters and brothers took Paul and Silas away to Berea. The next day they went to the synagogue and got a much better reception than they had in Thessalonica. *11* For the people there were open to the Good News and daily studied scripture to understand it better. *12* Many of them became believers.

13 But when the Jewish leaders got wind that Paul was preaching in Berea, they went there to stir up trouble for him. *14* So the sisters and brothers sent Paul all the way to the sea, while Silas and Timothy stayed there. *15* Those escorting Paul took him all the way to Athens, and then went back with instructions that Silas and Timothy should join him as soon as possible.

16 While Paul was awaiting them in Athens, he was deeply troubled in seeing all the idols there. *17* He talked in the synagogue about this problem and to anyone who would listen to him on his walks about the town. *18* Some of the philosophers there said, "What is he babbling about?" Others said, "He seems to be talking about some strange God," since he was talking about the Good News of Jesus and his resurrection. *19* They took him to the Areopagus and said, *20* "We want to know more about these strange things you are saying." *21* They loved nothing better than to discuss new ideas.

22 So standing in the middle of the Areopagus, Paul began to speak: *23* "People of Athens, as I walk through your town I notice how religious you are, since I find altars everywhere. One of them is even dedicated to 'The Unknown God.' It is this unknown God about which I want to speak to you now.

24 "The God your heart seeks is not found in temples built by human hands. *25* Neither is he served by human hands as though he lacked something. *26* The creator of all remains in all. We have failed to find him because we have been looking for him outside. All these many millennia he has been hiding in us waiting to be found by us. Recently his love could wait no longer, and he came and walked among us, as us. And he even told us that we *too* are God. Those who could not open their hearts to this Truth decided to kill him. After they had killed him to try to disprove his Truth, he rose from the dead and thus proved his Truth.

27 "He is our life; he is our actions; he is our self. Philosophy tries to separate things to understand them. He taught us that true wisdom comes only from seeing the unity of All. Thus, true wisdom comes not from the mind but from the heart, or better, from the union of these two into one.

28 We are the daughters and sons of God, and the ultimate reality is the Family of God as some of your own poets have expressed so well. *29* And since we ourselves are God, we will never find God looking for him in things made of silver, or gold, or stone.

30 So now that we know that God is in our hearts, *31* he invites us to find him and become him. This will be our own resurrection."

32 Hearing about this resurrection some scoffed, but others said, "We would like to hear more about this." *33* With this Paul left. *34* However, some followed him and became believers. Among them were Dionysius, a member of the court of the Areopagus, and a woman named Damaris and many others.

CHAPTER 18

1 After this he left Athens and went to Corinth *2* where he met a Jew named Aquila, from Pontus, and his wife Priscilla, who had recently come from Italy because emperor Claudius had ordered all Jews to leave Rome. *3* He went to visit them, and since they were tentmakers too, he stayed with them and worked with them. *4* And every Sabbath he went to the synagogue and won over many Jews and Greeks.

5 When Silas and Timothy finally arrived from Macedonia, Paul was completely absorbed in teaching the Message of Jesus, and the fact that he was and is a Christ. 6 But since the Jews there kept opposing him and defaming him, he left saying, "From now on I am going to the Gentiles."

7 Then he left there and went to the house of a good man called Titus Justus, whose house was right next to the synagogue. 8 Crispus, the leader of the synagogue began to believe Jesus together with his whole family. And many of the Corinthians believed and were baptized.

9 In a dream Jesus said to Paul, "Don't be afraid to speak out here, 10 for no one will attack you because I have many friends here." 11 So he settled down there for a year and a half teaching the Message of Jesus.

12 However, when Gallio was appointed proconsul of Achaia, the Jewish leaders united and brought Paul before the court. 13 They accused him of worshipping God in an unlawful way. 14 But before Paul could respond, Gallio told the Jewish leaders, 15 "This is not a serious crime and I have no interest in dealing with your laws." 16 And had them all removed from his court.

17 After more problems with the Jewish leaders there, 18 Paul left and went to Ephesus with Priscilla and Aquila. 19 Paul decided to go on his own to visit a number of cities.

24 Now there was a Jew in Ephesus, from Alexandria. 25 He had a burning spirit for Jesus, but only knew about the baptism of John. 26 He began speaking in the synagogue and when he finished Priscilla and Aquila explained to him the rest of the Good News of Jesus.

27 And as he planned to cross over to Achaia, the sisters and brothers wrote a note to the believers there asking them to welcome him. 28 He proved to be a passionate preacher and showed how Jesus is a Christ.

CHAPTER 19

1 When Paul returned to Ephesus he asked some of the believers if they had received the baptism of Spirit. 2 They responded that they had never even heard of the Spirit, 3 that they were baptized with water as John had done. 4 So Paul explained that John had pointed to Jesus, and that the risen Jesus is the Spirit.

5 When they heard this they asked to be baptized in Spirit. 6 And as Paul laid his hands on them Spirit came on them and they began to chant prayers and to prophesy. 7 All together about twelve were baptized.

8 Paul also went to the synagogue for some three months talking in the Spirit, and explaining how the Spirit of the risen Jesus fuses with our Spirit to give us Divine Life. 9 However, some did not believe this new way, and so Paul and the believers began to meet in the

school of Tyrannus. *10* He stayed there preaching for two years so that everyone in the province of Asia had an opportunity to hear the Good News.

11 God also performed many amazing miracles at the hands of Paul there, *12* to such an extent that people would take handkerchiefs and other things touched by Paul to the sick and they would be healed.

21 Then Paul decided under the inspiration of Spirit to go to Rome by way of Macedonia and Achaia. *22* So he sent Timothy and Erastus ahead of him to prepare the way, while he stayed on for a while in Asia.

CHAPTER 20

1 About that time there was a tumult caused by the worshippers of Artemis, and those who made their living from making images of Artemis. *2* So Paul decided to start out for Macedonia. But before leaving he called all the believers together and encouraged them to follow Jesus, and to *be* Jesus through the indwelling of his Spirit.

3 Then he encouraged the believers he met as he traveled along until he came to Greece, where he spent three months.

4 When he reached Macedonia, we were accompanied by Sopater, Aristarchus and Secundus, Gaius, Timothy, and Tychicus and Trophimus; *5* and they went on ahead of us to Traos. After the Feast of Unleavened Bread, *6* we sailed out from Philippi and in five days reached Troas where we stayed a week.

7 We gathered that Sunday for the Breaking of the Bread. Since Paul knew he was leaving the next day he preached until midnight. *8* There were numerous lamps in the upper room where we were gathered. *9* A young man there named Eutychus fell asleep and fell out the third floor window, where he was sitting, and was killed. *10* So Paul went down and prayed over him and said, "Don't worry; he is alive." *11* Going back up we Broke Bread, and Paul preached till dawn and left without sleeping. *12* They took the young man who had been raised from the dead with them and became believers.

13 Paul had decided to walk to Assos, but told us to take the ship. *14* So when he met us there, he came aboard and we sailed on to Mitylene. *15* We had continued traveling on the same ship, *16* since Paul wanted to be in Jerusalem for the Feast of Pentecost.

17 While we were in Mitylene, Paul sent messengers to Ephesus asking the elders to come there. *18* When they arrived, he said to them, *19* "You are well aware of all that I have done since I first set foot in Asia. You know of the persecutions I have suffered from the leaders of the Jews. *20* Yet I never wavered in my preaching of the Good News either publicly or in your homes.

22 "And now Spirit is sending me to Jerusalem, and I don't know what is going to happen to me, *23* except that he keeps telling me that bonds and affliction await me. *24* However, I am not concerned about anything; even my life is only important to me for finishing the Mission that Jesus gave me of spreading his Good News.

25 And even though you have seen me many times on my visits to you, I know that the reason that you invited me here *26* was so that I could remind you of all I have taught you. *27* And also that I would urge you now to continue teaching that to those you have been called to serve. *28* Shepherd the Communities of God whom Jesus has filled with Divine Life.

29 "For I know that after I leave, wolves will try to enter your flocks and destroy your teachings. *30* And even among those of you here, some may arise to lead others astray. *31* So be on guard and keep in mind that for three years, I never stopped teaching you about Jesus, even when things were rough.

32 "And now I commit you to God and to his Love. He is able to build you up and give you your inheritance as his daughters and sons.

33 "You know that I never asked for money, *34* but that these very hands supplied my needs and the needs of my companions. *35* I did this to give you an example of how we are to help take care of ourselves and others and to remind you that Jesus said: 'It is more blessed to give, than to receive.'"

36 Having said this he knelt down with all of them and prayed. *37* They were all crying and hugged and kissed him. *38* They were terribly upset to know they would never see him again. Then they escorted him to the ship.

CHAPTER 21

1 It was very hard for Paul to get away because of the people's great love for him. *2* But when we did manage to leave, we sailed straight to Cos. *3* Then we sailed on and finally came to Syria and docked at Tyre.

4 We looked up the believers and stayed with them for a week. They saw in Spirit what was going to happen to Paul in Jerusalem and advised him not to go there. *5* But when the week was up, the believers and their families escorted us to the beach. *6* We knelt there and prayed together; then embraced one another and embarked and the people went back to their homes.

7 We arrived at Ptolemais and greeted the sisters and brothers, and stayed with them for a day. *8* Then we went on to Caesarea where we called at the home of Philip the evangelist, who gave us hospitality.

10 We had been there for several days when a prophet named Agabus came down from Judea to visit us. *11* He took Paul's belt and wrapped it around his hands and feet. Then he said, "Spirit tells me that the Jewish leaders in Jerusalem will do this to you and deliver you to the civil authorities."

12 When we heard this, we and our hosts urged Paul not to go to Jerusalem. 13 But Paul replied, "What are you trying to do by weeping and telling me not to do what Spirit has asked me? I am willing not only to be bound, but even to die in Jerusalem for our brother Jesus." 14 And since we could not dissuade him, we stopped trying and said, "May God's will be done."

15 So when our time there was finished, we got ready and went to Jerusalem. 16 Some of the Caesarian believers who went with us, took us to the home of Mnason, a Cypriot and early believer, who gave us hospitality.

17 When we arrived in Jerusalem, the sisters and brothers welcomed us joyfully. 18 And the next day we all went with Paul to visit James. 19 All the elders were gathered there. After Paul had greeted them, he recounted all that had happened in his ministry with the Gentiles.

20 As they listened to him, they thanked God and then said to him, "Brother, you see how many thousand Jews have become believers, and yet they remain zealous of the law. 21 But they have been told that you are teaching all the Jews who live among the Gentiles to turn away from the law of Moses, from circumcision and ancient Jewish customs. 22 Is this true? For if it is, they will learn that you are here and be upset."

26 The following day Paul went to the temple anyway. 27 About a week later some Jews from Asia saw him in the temple and stirred up the crowd and grabbed him shouting, 28 "This is the man who teaches everyone everywhere against our nation, the law, and this place."

30 So all the Jewish leaders got upset and dragged Paul outside the temple. 31 They were trying to kill him when the commander of the cohort heard about the riot. 32 So he went there at once with soldiers. Those who were pummeling Paul stopped when they saw the commander and the soldiers. 33 The commander took charge of Paul and ordered him bound with two chains. 34 Then he asked who he was and what he had done.

35 But the entire mob was shouting at once so he ordered Paul to be taken to the barracks so he could question him. 36 But when Paul got to the steps of the barracks, he had to be carried by the soldiers because the mob was there still trying to kill him.

37 At the barracks door Paul said to the commander in Greek, "May I have a word with you?" 38 So the commander thought he was the Greek who recently stirred up a rebellion with a band of four thousand cutthroats. 39 But Paul told him he was a Jew from Tarsus in Cilicia, and begged him to allow him to speak to the people. 40 He gave his permission, and Paul stood on the steps and motioned to the people for silence. And when they had quieted

down, he addressed them in Hebrew with these words:

CHAPTER 22

1 "Sisters and brothers, mothers and fathers, please listen to my defense." *2* As soon as they realized he was speaking Hebrew, they quieted down even more. So he proceeded, *3* "I am a Jew, born in Tarsus in Cilicia, but raised here in Jerusalem. I received a very thorough education in the law from Gamaliel himself and was as full of zeal for God as you are today.

4 "As such I persecuted, imprisoned and killed Christians, *5* as even the high priests and the council of elders can verify. For I even received letters from them to the Jewish leaders in Damascus, where I was going, to bring back prisoners to Jerusalem for punishment.

6 "But as I was getting near Damascus at about midday a huge light shone down from heaven, *7* and as I fell to the ground I heard a voice say, 'Saul, Saul, why are you persecuting me?' *8* I responded, 'Who are you?' And he said, 'I am Jesus of Nazareth, whom you are persecuting.' *9* My companions only saw the light, but did not hear the voice of the one who spoke to me.

10 "I then said, 'What do you want me to do?' Then Jesus said, "Get up and go into Damascus. There you will be told about all the things I have called you to do.' *11* However, because of the brilliance of that light I could not see; so my companions took me by the hand and led me into Damascus.

12 "Then a man called Ananias, a man devoted to the law and well thought of by the Jews who lived there, *13* called on me and said, 'Brother Saul, recover your sight,' and instantly I could see. *14* He then said, 'Our fathers' God has chosen you to see Jesus and hear a Message from him. *15* And you are to be a witness to everything you have seen and heard. *16* Now get up; it is time you are baptized.'

17 "Then later in prayer, I had another Vision of him and heard him say, *18* 'Hurry and get away from here, because they will not welcome your testimony about me.' *19* I replied, 'Jesus, you know very well that I went from synagogue to synagogue arresting and beating up those who believed in your Message. *20* And when your martyr Stephen was killed, I was standing by and watching over the clothes of those who killed him.' *21* And he said to me, 'Go now for I will send you far away to the Gentiles.'"

22 The Jewish leaders had listened to him up to that moment, then they shouted, "Kill him, for he is not fit to live." *23* They continued yelling and started throwing things at him, *24* so the commander ordered him to be brought into the barracks. Then he ordered Paul to be flogged so they could find out why the people shouted as they did. *25* But when they had tied him up to be flogged, Paul asked the captain if it was legal to flog a Roman citizen without a trial. 26 On hearing that the captain went to the commander and told him what Paul had said and asked him what to do.

27 The commander then went to Paul and asked him if indeed he was a Roman citizen. He said "Yes, I am." 28 The commander then said, "My Roman citizenship cost me a lot of money." Paul replied, "But I was actually born a Roman citizen." 29 Then those who were to examine him kept their hands off him, and the commander was afraid because he had had him bound without a trial.

30 In order to find out why the crowd had shouted so much, the next day the commander had him unbound and called a meeting with the high priests and the Jewish elders and brought Paul out to face them.

CHAPTER 23

6 Paul was very aware that there were two strong factions in the court, so he made a statement siding with one side. 7 A dispute then arose between those two factions, 8 since the Pharisees believed in an after-life, but the Sadducees considered this heresy. 9 The Pharisees took Paul's side since he said he was a Pharisee, while the Sadducees were beside themselves because of Paul's statements about Jesus' resurrection.

10 The discord grew so deafening and bitter that the commander was afraid that they might tear Paul to bits. So he sent a detachment down to bring him back to the barracks.

11 That night Jesus appeared to him and said, "Take heart, brother. For just as you have given witness to me here, you must do it in Rome."

12 The next morning a group of more than forty Sadducees took an oath that they would not eat or drink until they had killed Paul. 14 They hatched a plot with the chief priests 15 to trick the commander into releasing Paul to them so they could kill him.

16 However, Paul's nephew got wind of the ambush and went and told the commander. 23 So he made preparations to send Paul to Governor Felix. 25 He sent along a letter explaining what had happened and why he had sent Paul to him. 31 The soldiers took Paul that very night to Antipatris. 32 The next day the cavalry took Paul on to Caesarea 33 and presented him and the letter to the governor. 34 After reading the letter, the governor had Paul kept in Herod's palace, 35 saying he would hear Paul's case when his accusers arrived.

CHAPTER 24

1 Five days later Ananias, the high priest, arrived with a group of elders and Tertullus, an orator. 2 They came to present their case against Paul. 3 And so after Paul had been called in, 4 Tertullus began to present their charges. 5 "We have found this man to be like a plague, stirring up all the Jews on earth. He is a ringleader for the sect of Jesus of Nazareth." 6 And then went on to explain the whole

history that had brought them to this point. *10* And when he finished, the governor asked Paul to respond.

11 Paul presented an eloquent defense, explaining how he had simply been in the temple praying when he was attacked. *12* He refuted all their charges, *13* and said they had no proof of any of them. *14* He admitted he was a Christian, *15* but said that was simply a way of believing in God that was consistent with his heritage. *16* And he aligned himself with the belief of his accusers. *17* He went on to explain that the real reason he was being charged was that he believed in the resurrection, in life after death.

22 Felix understood the teachings of Christianity quite well and so told them that he would decide the case when the commander came and testified. *23* Then he gave orders that Paul be guarded, but in a respectful manner.

24 A few days later Felix and his wife Drusilla, who was Jewish, asked Paul to come and talk to them concerning faith in Jesus. *25* At this point Paul still believed in a coming judgment and this frightened Felix, so he sent him away. *26* He was really hoping to get a bribe from Paul and so later called him back a number of times to talk. *27* But after two years he was replaced with Porcius Festus, who also left Paul in prison to gain favor with the Jewish leaders.

CHAPTER 25

1 Three days after he arrived in the Province, Festus went up from Caesarea to Jerusalem. *2* The chief priests and prominent Jews there begged him to send Paul to Jerusalem. *3* They had a plan to ambush and kill him. *4* Festus replied that Paul was under guard in Caesarea and that he was returning there, *5* so that if they wanted to join him they could make their charges there.

6 After spending a week there, he returned to Caesarea. The next day he took his seat on the tribunal and ordered Paul to be brought in. *7* When Paul was brought in, the Jewish delegation from Jerusalem presented their charges against him and even though they were very serious, they had no evidence to support them. *8* Then Paul said simply, "I have committed no wrong against these men, the temple, nor Caesar."

9 But Festus wanted to win the support of the Jewish leaders, and so asked Paul, "Are you willing to go to Jerusalem to be tried on these charges?" *10* But Paul said, "I am standing at Caesar's tribunal, where I should be tried. I have in no way wronged the Jews, as you well know. *11* If you believe me guilty of anything deserving death, I am willing to die. But if there is nothing to their charges, no one can surrender me to them. I make my appeal to Caesar." *12* So after conferring with his council, Festus said, "You have appealed to Caesar, so you shall be sent to Caesar."

13 A few days later King Agrippa and his wife Bernice came to Caesarea to welcome Festus. *22* They were interested to know more about Paul and so Festus arranged for them to question him. *26* Festus said he was doing this to help formulate a letter to Caesar summarizing the charges against Paul.

CHAPTER 26

1 Then Agrippa said to Paul, "Feel free to speak in your own defense." Then Paul made his defense:

2 "Concerning all the charges against me by the Jewish leaders, I am completely innocent." *5* He went on to explain his actions from being raised a Pharisee, to his severe persecutions of Christians. *12* Then he told about his experience on the way to Damascus, when he was authorized by the chief priests to imprison the Christians there.

13 He shared his vision of Jesus, *18* and how Jesus had appointed him a minister and witness of what he had seen and heard there. He promised to continue to guide him through his Spirit. *23* He talked about Jesus being raised from the dead after his crucifixion and how his belief in this is the real reason for the charges being brought against him.

30 After all this testimony Agrippa held council with the governor and Bernice, *32* and they concluded he had done no wrong and could have been released had he not appealed to Caesar.

CHAPTER 27

1 When it was decided that we should sail to Italy, they turned Paul and some other prisoners over to Julius, a captain of the Augustan Court. *2* Once we were on our way many difficulties came up. *3* However, Julius was very kind to Paul and would allow him to fellowship with the believers we met in the various ports.

9 As winter approached, Paul warned that if they continued on, *10* they would lose not only the cargo and ship but even the passengers. *11* However, Julius decided to trust the captain rather than believe Paul so we sailed on.

14 Things went well for a few days and then we were hit with a huge storm, known as a northeaster. *18* As the storm continued on, they threw the cargo overboard, *19* and then finally the ship's tackle. *21* After many more days of storms and hunger, Paul reminded them of his prophesy in Crete, *22* and then went on to say, "Cheer up. You will lose only the boat and not your lives. *23* For last night an Angel of God appeared to me and said, 'Don't be afraid, Paul. You have to appear before Caesar, *24* and God has granted your prayer for the lives of those on board.' *25* So relax, my friends, for I believe the Angel, *26* even though we will be stranded on an island."

33 Two weeks later, as the storm continue to rage on, Paul urged them to eat saying, "You haven't eaten in two weeks *34* but you must now because you will need your energy for what is about to happen. *35* Having said this, he took bread and gave thanks to God in the presence of all. *36* Then they were all encouraged and began to eat too. *37* All together there were two hundred seventy six of us on board. *38* When they had all eaten their fill, they threw the wheat overboard too.

39 Then as they tried to make their way into an inlet on the island, *41* the waves crushed the ship. *42* The soldiers wanted to kill the prisoners to keep them from escaping, *43* but since Julius wanted to save Paul he didn't allow them to do this. He ordered those who could swim to jump over board and swim to shore, *44* and those who could not, to wait and float in on what would be left of the ship. And so they all reached the shore safely.

CHAPTER 28

1 When we got to shore we learned that the island was Malta. *2* The people there showed us remarkable kindness. They lit a huge fire for us because of the rain and cold. *3* A viper crawled out of some wood that Paul brought to the fire and fastened to his hand. *4* When the people saw this they said, "This man is surely a murderer for this to happen to him." *5* But he simply shook the viper off his hand. *6* They kept waiting for him to keel over dead; and when he didn't they said, "This man must be a god."

7 The chief lived in that part of the island, a man called Publius. He took us all in and took care of us for three days. *8* His father was sick and so Paul went to visit him and, laying hands on him in prayer, healed him. *9* When word of this got around, all the other islanders who were sick came and were healed. *10* Everyone was very kind to us, and when we left they gave us everything we needed for the journey.

11 After three months we sailed out on an Alexandrian ship that had wintered on the island. *13* When we landed at Puteoli, *14* we found some believers who invited us to stay with them for a week.

15 Then we went on toward Rome. When the sisters and brothers there heard of us, they came from as far away as the Forum of Appius and the Three Taverns. As soon as Paul saw them he thanked God and rejoiced.

16 When we arrived in Rome, Julius handed over the prisoners to the captain of the guard, but Paul was allowed to live by himself with a soldier to guard him.

17 After three days he invited all the Jewish leaders to visit him. *18* He didn't get very far with them, *19* since they had heard that Christianity was a heresy. *22* But they did agree to come back with a larger delegation and listen to what Paul had to say.

30 Paul lived for two more years in Rome and welcomed everyone who came to his place. *31* He taught about Jesus living within us and all the Good News quite openly.

PAUL'S INTRODUCTION

Paul's Introduction to this new edition of his Letters:

My dear sisters and brothers, I write to you anew to move my teaching from my Jewish roots to my Christian Faith. When Jesus came to me so powerfully on the road to Damascus, I was very much a Jew. A Jew by blood, a Pharisee by choice. As he worked with me in the desert, I opened to his new teaching, but my Jewish bones interfered with my hearing completely his radically new teachings. And even though God said so clearly through my beloved prophet Hosea, "It is Love that I want and not sacrifice," at that time I *still* believed in the need for sacrifice. Our bones often impede our hearing! I have watched my brother who is rewriting this for me struggling with my old Jewish bones; and now want to free both of us to proclaim Jesus' real Message.

Jesus does not want sacrifice; he wants Love, because he *is* Love. He has reincarnated in all of you, so that you could become completely one with him. So please open to the Jesus that you are. Once you walk in Love, forget about the law. It tried to point us to the Truth, but couldn't because Jesus is the Truth! And he is Truth, not law.

Forget what I told you before about the need for salvation. You are already God's Children. You do not need to be saved from anything other than your belief that you are only human. You were already saved when you were born. You were saved from nothingness. That is the only salvation you ever need, except perhaps from the fear that is still in you, instead of faith.

You were born into the Light, into God, into Love. The God that you are does not need to be saved, only recognized. You do not need to be saved; you only need to recognize you are indeed already the Daughters and Sons of God. You are God, as my brother John relates [10, 34]. John's eagle perspective of Jesus' real Message is the basis of this, but my more practical perspective is also needed.

I did not reincarnate for a long time after my life as Paul since I wanted to soak up all of Jesus in me. I was very surprised to learn that Jesus wanted to soak up all of me too. It is so very hard to walk in the reality of our Divinity. Realizing our Divinity needs to be our first priority.

Loving our Divinity is our second.

I have a totally different concept of Spirituality than I had on the road to Damascus. Jesus coming to me that day obviously changed my whole life, but it took a number of years to change my whole self. But I have done it, and I want to help you do it too. Together we can present Jesus' Message to the world.

I realized all this as I walked toward death, but my writings were already out there with my old beliefs. How I have longed through these two millennia to remold my writing with the hands of God!

Please don't be scandalized and believe this is a new scripture. It is not. It is simply the Scripture that had not made it from my head to my heart when I originally wrote these letters. Open your hearts and you will know this comes from me. You now have the real Truth from the very Heart of Paul, which is now also the Heart of Jesus. And please don't be surprised if parts of my previous letters are not here. We have included only what was divinely inspired.

Please don't let this shock you, since God's Love and Wisdom is way beyond anything written.

ROMANS

CHAPTER 1

1 I, Paul, a servant of our brother Jesus, called to be an apostle to spread the Good News to the Gentiles, now to my sisters and brothers in Rome. *2* God had promised through his prophets in the scriptures all that I preach. *3* His son Jesus was a descendant of David in his humanity and of God in his divinity. *4* His divinity was shown most clearly in his resurrection from the dead. *5* It was by this same Jesus that I was called to be an apostle, and sent to the Gentiles to proclaim and live his Message. *6* All of you, God's loved ones in Rome, are also called to live according to his Teachings. *7* Grace and peace to you from our Dad God and our brother Jesus.

8 I would like first to thank God for all of you through Jesus Christ, because your faith is talked about all over the world. *9* God knows how often you are in my daily prayers, *10* that I may someday be able to visit you. *11* For I long to bestow on you some spiritual gifts. *12* I mean that we may be mutually strengthened by your faith and mine.

13 I want you to know, dear sisters and brothers, that I have often planned to visit you so that I might reap a spiritual harvest among you as I have among the other Gentiles, but so far I have been prevented from doing this. *14* I have been very blessed by my ministry to both the learned and unlearned. *15* So I am very eager to present the Gospel to you in Rome as well. *16* For God's Love is revealed as we ourselves grow in our love-connection with him through faith. *17* This is what really gives us life.

18 God has such deep compassion for those who have not yet made this love-connection with him, because they have not yet seen and experienced the truth of the immense love he has for them. *19* He longs for the day when they will see this truth. *20* Through the awe of a starry night to the warmth of the rising sun, his power and love have been manifested since the beginning of time. *21* But many have failed to open their minds and hearts to this glory. *22* Their fear had hid this truth from them. *23* So instead of seeing the Glory of God, they settled for the dust of this world. *24* God waited patiently for them to mature through their acts of dishonor to him and themselves.

CHAPTER 2

1 Be aware that whatever you judge in your neighbor is what you have already judged in yourself. *2* Be gentle with your neighbor, just as God is gentle and loving with you. *3* God's judgments are always true, and his final judgment over us is that we are his beloved daughters and sons. *11* For there is love for all in God. *13* But this does not give anyone license to walk in darkness, for those who try will stumble or fall. *14* Even though we are always loved, it is extremely important that we walk the path to God our Dad. *15* Even those who do not know our God can walk the path to God. *16* When Jesus came and called us sisters and brothers, the final judgment was made. *17* We are and always will be in the Family of God, and even though we can try to walk out of the family, we cannot walk out of the heart of God; it is just too big for that to be possible.

18 Work hard to help those who are blind to their union with Jesus and walk in the darkness where God can only be seen in the distance; so that they may be aware of the invitation of their brother Jesus and the welcome of their Dad God. *19* By helping them, you help yourselves since they are indeed your other selves.

CHAPTER 4

17 As is written of Abraham: 'I have made you the father of many nations.' God spoke thus of Abraham because he was a man of great Faith. *18* Abraham lived in God long before Jesus came and told us we could too. *19* He believed God would make him a father even when neither his nor his wife Sarah's body was capable of procreation. *21* He did not waver in his belief that God could and would do what he had promised. *24* And we have the same invitation to faith as Abraham had, as we are called

to believe in him who raised Jesus from the dead.

CHAPTER 5

1 Faith is living God, and when we do this, we are at total peace with God through Jesus. *2* Through Jesus we have learned not only that we (can) live in the family of God; but also that we (can) live in God himself. *3* And knowing this we can endure struggles, knowing that this gives us perseverance, *4* and perseverance character, and character hope. *5* And we are not disappointed in hope, because the love of God has been poured out in our hearts by Spirit who has been given to us. *6* For when we were weak, Jesus came into us to make us strong. *11* And we rejoice in God through our brother Jesus, through whom we have been ushered into the Life of God. *21* For it is through Jesus that (the awareness of) our Divine life has come to us.

CHAPTER 6

4 We have been buried with our brother Jesus, and just as he was raised from the dead by Dad, even so we also can walk in our new life with and in him. *5* For if we have been united with Jesus in his death, we shall also be united with him in his resurrection. *6* Knowing that our old self has died with him; we can rejoice in our new (Divine) Life with him. *8* Since we have died with Jesus, we believe we shall also rise and live with Jesus. *9* Knowing that

Jesus was raised from the dead and can die no more, we also know that we can die no more even when our mortal bodies pass away. *10* For his resurrection pointed to our way back into realizing our own Divine Life. *11* And all of us have been raised to this same Divine Life. *12* So don't fall back into the belief that you are only human, but walk always in your Divinity, *23* in your Divine Life in Dad God.

CHAPTER 7

6 We should always serve in the newness of the Spirit and never in the oldness of the law. *15* I don't understand what I am doing sometimes, *16* for I do what I don't want to, and don't do what I want to. *17* It is the fear in me that drives me to this craziness. *18* I know I can always decide to live out (of) my Divinity, but sometimes I don't do it. *19* I want to do the right thing, but I sometimes end up doing the wrong thing. *20* It seems at times I am a slave of my fear rather than of my God.

CHAPTER 8

1 We are as though hidden in Jesus where there is no judgment or condemnation. *2* For the new law of the Spirit of Life in God has set us free from the old law and death. *14* For we who are lead by the Spirit of God, realize we are daughters and sons of God. *15* For we did not receive the spirit of bondage to fear, but rather the Spirit of Adoption by which we cry out, "Abba, Dad!"

16 The Spirit bears witness with our own spirit that we are indeed Children of God. *17* And if children, then heirs—heirs of God and joint heirs with brother Jesus.

18 I consider the sufferings I am going through to be nothing, compared to the honor of sharing with you what has been revealed to me. *19* For all of creation is waiting for the day you will all realize that you are the daughters and sons of God.

20 When that happens all the creation will be delivered into the same glorious realization of being the Children of God. *22* Creation is already groaning with the labor pains of this new birth. *23* As are we who have already received the first fruits of Spirit, and experience our adoption into the Family of God as his daughters and sons. When that happens, not only we, but also our very bodies, will be transformed. *24* This is exactly what we have been hoping for, and now it is so close we can almost taste it. *25* We will keep our hope strong as we patiently wait for this.

26 Spirit will help us in this, even when we are weak. *27* For sometimes we don't know what to pray or how to pray. But Spirit himself prays in us with supplications beyond words. For God looks at our hearts and sees Spirit there praying for all of us. *28* But we who love God and try to follow his will, understand better than many how God makes everything work together for the good of all.

29 We also know that he has chosen all of us to share the likeness of his son so that he may be the first born of many, many sisters and brothers; *30* and that he has predestined all of us to be his daughters and sons, having been born of his own image and sanctified through his immense love.

31 From all of this it is obvious that "If God is for us who can be against us?" *32* He even gave us his very own son as our brother, model and mirror; and he will shower us with the same Love he has for his son, our true brother. *33* Who can possibly come against God's daughters and sons? If God has set us free, who can condemn us? *34* Jesus died in his life and rose in our life, so we are now God's right hand. *35* So what possibly can separate us from God's love, from Jesus' love? Affliction? Anxiety? Hunger? *36* And even if we suffer all these things, *37* we will overcome them all through him who loves us.

38 For I know that neither death nor life, neither Angels nor Archangels, neither present nor future problems, neither powers on high nor of the depths, nor anything at all created *39* can possibly separate us from the Love of God that is now in us as the Spirit of brother Jesus.

CHAPTER 9

1 Jesus is the Truth, and through him I speak, strengthened by Spirit as I say: *2* I have such deep sadness and constant distress for my Jewish sisters and brothers. *3* that I would go so far as to say I would allow myself to be banished from my beloved Jesus for their sakes. *4* They have everything. *5* They were called to be the Ark of the Covenant of God's presence. Theirs are the patriarchs from whom Jesus himself was descended.

6 I want to be very clear that I am not saying that God's plan has failed, but simply that all the children of Israel have not followed his path; *7* and the same is true of Abraham's children. *8* This means it is not simply Abraham's biological descendants who are the true Children of God, but *everyone* born is a child of God, with absolutely no exceptions. *9* We must believe this as firmly as Abraham believed his wife would bear him a son even though she was sterile and very old. We may feel old and sterile, but that does not limit God's life-giving ability.

16 God calls all to be his daughters and sons; but all do not hear his invitation or accept it. *17* Scripture is full of stories of this.

21 If we open our hearts to be molded by our loving God, he can mold us into his daughters and sons just as a potter molds clay with loving hands. *25* The Jews may have believed that only they are the chosen people, even though the quiet prophet Hosea pointed out so very clearly that God's love is totally universal. *26* God calls everyone "My Beloved," and all peoples "My People." *27* And the great prophet

Isaiah points out that while it is very hard for humanity to accept its Divinity, after feeling so distant from God for so very long, *28* it is still true that God's Love can overcome this human resistance.

30 Then what are we really saying? Simply that the Gentiles as well as all peoples, are God's People. All who live in God are God's People, and we all live in his heart whether we know it or not. Faith is simply walking in(to) God's Life. Faith is the path out of the darkness of believing we are simply human, into the reality of our Divinity. *31* And sometimes the Gentiles have found this path first. For just as action flows from being, so Love flows from Divinity and draws all into God's love.

CHAPTER 10

1 Sisters and brothers, when I believed in the need for salvation, *2* I was extremely concerned for my Jewish sisters and brothers who had lost their way on their journey to God. *3* They believe in the law of God rather than the Love of God. *4* Jesus brought the law to an end and revealed that God's loving arms are open to all. *5* We need to live from our Identity, which is Love. But humankind's eyes had not yet been opened to this Truth and so got stuck on the law. *6* Love transcends the law. Love ends the need for law by substituting a higher Truth. *7* Those who truly Love have no need for law,

because their natural actions fulfill it without the need for it.

8 It is Faith which we preach, but not simply the faith of believing in the Message of Jesus, but the faith of living the Life of Jesus, as Jesus, as God, as Love. Faith is the living in God. And when we live in God, we Love in God; we act out of Love.

10 Faith in God is the door to Life. Living without faith is like a baby trying to run a marathon. He does not yet have the maturity to do that. As faith matures, love expands, so that we can live not by human effort, but by Divine Energy. We are all predestined to be God simply because we have always been God.

Creation did not leave the creator, rather creation was *birthed* from God in and with the same Divine Life that is God's. The Birth Trauma of our creation simply blocked our remembrance of our Divine Identity. Jesus came to us to unblock us, to save us from this memory loss. He did not change reality, he simply reminded us of it. *11* So he is our Reminder rather than our Redeemer. Gods don't need to be redeemed, but simply reminded of their Reality, of their Identity, of their birthright. This Word of Truth is what we preach. It is this journey from the law of the Mind to the Love of the Heart that we proclaim. *12* When this journey is complete, we will see that we humans are all the same; *13* that we are all equal in the eyes and the heart of God.

14 I want this Message to be

preached from the housetops. God sent Jesus to bring us this Message, and has asked us to take it to the entire world. *15* Not to save the world, but to remind it of the glorious birthright of everyone, of the glorious reality that we are all literally daughters and sons of God, as proclaimed by the Life and Teachings of our dear brother Jesus!

16 We are all sent, whether to the Mission fields or to the cities. We are all sent whether to our own families or to distant peoples. *17* There is absolutely nothing else as important as this. And we need to do it even if it means losing everything else. *18* The world longs for prophets. *19* Become one and open the world to Jesus' Message of universal Love, Love from all, Love for all!

20 Isaiah helps complement all this by pointing out so lovingly and with such wisdom, that God himself will find us when we are lost, will show himself even to those not even looking for him, *21* that God's most beloved children are his most rebellious ones!

CHAPTER 11

1 I want to make it clear that I am a Jew by blood, a descendant of Abraham by birth; and a follower of Jesus by choice. *2* God has not repudiated his people; he has simply taught us that *all* are his people. *3* The past betrayals of his people have not lessened his Love. *4* He always responds, "I love you," even when people forget to say that in words or in actions. *5* There have always been a few who have been able to hear this. *6* There have always been a few whose hearts have stayed open. *7* God gave all of us hearts to direct us back to him when we fail or fall. *8* So those who fall are not to be judged, but simply helped to get back up.

9 Some who have the greatest Call, also have the greatest fall. *10* But God never judges even if we believe he does. *11* Those who say differently have never seen the heart of our Dad. *12* We who have seen God's heart feel compelled to live God's life and bring others to this same Glory.

13 I am writing to you Gentiles, because Jesus has asked me to be an Apostle to the Gentiles. I feel deeply humbled and honored by this Call. *14* I also feel a Call to bring the Message of Jesus to my Jewish sisters and brothers.

17 But don't be arrogant about now being part of what has been called the Chosen People. *18* Arrogance always blinds the heart and hinders the mind. Rather, be simply grateful that Jesus' Message of Love is for all. *19* And also be aware that you too can lose your way. *20* Do not let the fact that God can always bring you back, tempt you to try to wander out of his heart. *21* Stay where you have Life. *22* God's Love-call to you cannot be broken since nothing is stronger than Love. *23* Keep this Truth in the back of your mind and heart in case you may need it in the future.

³³ Remember the immensity of our Dad's Love and Wisdom. How wonderful are his judgments of Love, and the guidance of his wisdom. ³⁴ And also remember that we are not only made in his image, but we are indeed made into him, by the rebirthing into him that Jesus has called us to. ³⁵ The awesomeness of our reality should dispel all fear and instill all love. ³⁶ We are called to be God and to proclaim to all that they too are God; that we have not only come from God, but also are God. This indeed is the Good News Jesus came to teach to all of us.

CHAPTER 12

I beg you, sisters and brothers, with all my heart, to give yourselves to our brother Jesus and our Dad God with all your heart. Not as a sacrifice, but as a first step into true happiness. To unite with Jesus is to unite with yourself; and uniting always brings peace. ² And don't live by worldly values for that will only bring you misery, but be transformed into Jesus, into you! Slide into the perfect will of God and slide out as the perfect you. ³ Be humble as Jesus was humble, and truthful about the Gift of God you have received.

⁴ For just as our body is one thing, but has many different parts with many different functions, ⁵ so we all together form the body of Jesus, because each of us is related to all the other members. ⁶ But each of us has different Gifts depending on what God has given us, and what we have opened to. If our Gift is prophecy, let us use it as God intends. ⁷ If it is service to our sisters and brothers, let us exercise it with love. ⁸ The same for all Gifts; they are from Spirit and should be used as Spirit wills.

⁹ Let your Love be sincere, connected with service and not with arrogance. ¹⁰ Be joined together in a union of mutual Love, trying to outdo each other in showing respect, serving our brother Jesus in all our sisters and brothers. ¹¹ Be on fire with God's Love flowing into service through you, ¹² keeping the faith in affliction, praying always, ¹³ and taking care of one another.

¹⁴ Bless those who persecute you; don't curse them. ¹⁵ Share the joy of those who are happy, and the grief of those who grieve. ¹⁶ Love is harmony with all. Don't try to be important, but walk with the humble.

¹⁷ Don't ever pay back a wrong with a wrong. Always try to do what is right and noble. ¹⁸ If possible, in so far as you can, live in peace with everyone. ¹⁹ Do not avenge yourselves, dear friends, but realize that you *are* your sisters and brothers.

²⁰ Instead, "If your enemy is hungry, give them something to eat; if they are thirsty, give them something to drink." ²¹ Don't let the meanness of others get you down, but respond from the Love of Jesus and Dad flowing through you.

CHAPTER 13

1 Let everyone be obedient to just governments for they come from God; *2* to rebel against them is to rebel against God.

3 Those walking in the light have no fear of authority; only those do who walk in darkness. *4* God tries with our help to establish a just world, so we should cooperate in this. *5* We should always work for peace, not because of fear, but because of Love.

6 Pay all your just taxes, *7* and all your just obligations. *8* Don't owe anyone anything except Love, for whoever loves has done all that is required. *9* Remember the commandments: "Do not commit adultery; do not kill; do not steal; do not covet." All the other Commandments are contained in this one: "Love your neighbor as yourself." *10* Jesus' Commandment to Love goes beyond all laws for it includes them.

11 Let us wake up and see Jesus coming toward us, bringing us the light. *12* Let us follow him out of our darkness, *13* and learn what it means to walk always in the Light, to walk always in Jesus. *14* Let us strive to clothe ourselves only with our brother Jesus and our Dad God and also respond to their invitation to be them.

CHAPTER 14

1 Be very kind to the weak believers, and do not make fun of them. *2* We all have different levels of faith that allow us to do different things. *3* Be very open to this diversity, *4* so that it can be brought into unity.

5 One person believes this and another person believes that. *6* This does not matter as long as we live what we believe, *7* and believe in what we live. *8* For while alive we must be alive in brother Jesus. When we die we must die in brother Jesus and Dad God. So whether alive or dead we must be in God. *9* For Jesus died to show us his Divine Life; so that alive or dead we would have this Life.

10 So why do you criticize your sisters and brothers and find fault with them? *11* For we together form the Family of God. And what our Dad God wants most is that we become one. *12* That is the most important thing.

13 So let's decide to get along together and love one another. *14* Let us do this in union with Dad who birthed the whole world in his image. *15* Be sensitive to those who do not yet know this. *16* Don't walk on others' beliefs simply because they are not yours. *17* The most important thing in all of this is to follow one's conscience, the voice of God within our hearts. *18* When we don't follow this inner voice, we don't follow God; *19* but when we do follow this inner voice, we contribute to everyone's growth and peace. *20* Be sensitive to those who are less mature in faith and still walk under the law. *21* Help them walk out of the path of law and into the path of Love by simply loving and respecting them.

22 Let your faith be your guide to live in and with God. *23* If you follow the path of God, you will be happy. If you don't, you won't.

CHAPTER 15

1 We who are strong *2* ought to support those who are weak. *3* For even Jesus did not live simply for himself, but always opened his heart to support others. *4* It is through listening to the voice of God in scripture that we have hope in following Jesus. *5* But many use scripture to justify their erroneous beliefs, rather than to form beliefs based on the Revelations of God. *6* May God, who bestows such great Love and Wisdom, grant you understanding of Jesus' real Message, that together with one voice you may praise the God who is Dad not only of Jesus but also of yourselves.

7 So accept and love one another just as Jesus accepted and loves you. *8* Jesus became a servant to the Jews on behalf of the Love of God to fulfill the promises made to our own forefathers, *9* and to show his immense love for everyone. *10* Therefore we should all be glad *11* and praise God together in mutual love.

13 So may God, the fountain of all hope, fill your hearts with deep joy and peace, so that you may enjoy hope in abundance from the power and love of Spirit. *14* For you, my dear sisters and brothers, are so filled with this Love and Wisdom, that you can be of immense help to one another.

17 In union with Jesus, I take pride in my service to God, *18* for I will not speak of anything but what Jesus has done through me to bring the Gentiles to the path of God, by the power of signs and miracles worked through the power of Spirit. *19* For I have preached the Good News of Jesus from Jerusalem to Illyricum. *20* I have tried very hard to preach only where the name of Jesus was not known; so as not to build on the foundation of someone else. *21* But as it is written: Those who have never been told of him will hear, and those who have never heard of him will see.

22 It is for this reason that I have written to you before. *23* But now my work is done where I am, and I have been wanting to visit you for many years. *24* When I have a chance to go to Spain, I hope to visit with you also, and enjoy your fellowship for a while.

25 Now I am on my way to Jerusalem to give the saints there a collection taken up in Macedonia and Achaia for their poor. *28* When I have handed over the collection I shall visit you on my way to Spain. *29* And I know I shall be very blessed by my visit to you and pray that I also may be a blessing to you.

30 I beg you, sisters and brothers, by our brother Jesus and the Love of Spirit, *31* that I may minister well in Judea and Jerusalem *32* and that after that I may come to you with a happy heart and enjoy a spiritually refreshing visit with you. *33* And may the God of peace be in you all. Amen.

CHAPTER 16

1 May I present to you, Phoebe, a deaconess of the Cenchreae Church who will accompany this letter. *2* Please help her in any way you can since she has helped so many, including me.

3 Please give my greeting to Priscilla and Aquila, my fellow workers in Jesus, *5* and the members of the Community that meets in their home. *16* Give my special greetings to everyone there, and greet one another with a holy kiss. All the Communities of Jesus send you their greetings. *19* The report of your faithfulness to Jesus has been heard by everyone here, and it makes us so happy for you. *20* May the grace of our brother Jesus be with you.

21 Timothy, my fellow worker, sends you greetings. *22* I, Tertius, who have scribed this letter, send you my greetings in our brother Jesus. *24* The love of our brother Jesus and our Dad God be with you all.

FIRST CORINTHIANS

CHAPTER 1

1 Paul, called by God to be an apostle of Jesus, and our brother Sosthenes, *2* to all the saints of the Communities of God in Corinth. *3* Love and peace to you from our brother Jesus and our Dad God.

4 I thank Dad every time I think of you and the Divine Life you have with Jesus. *5* For with Jesus you have indeed found Divine Life and Wisdom. *6* In this you are witnessing what I taught you *7* and displaying all the Gifts of Spirit *8* that come from your being with the Resurrected Jesus. *9* Dad is so very wonderful, calling you his daughters and sons.

10 But in the name of our brother Jesus I beg you to live out this oneness in him by being of one mind and one heart. *11* For I have heard all kinds of reports that some of you are not doing this; *16* that you are arguing over who baptized you. *17* For Jesus didn't send me to baptize but to preach the Good News not with wisdom, but with the power to make you one with your Brother.

18 The Message of Jesus doesn't make any sense to those determined to live by worldly wisdom; *19* but for us determined to follow Jesus in heart and mind, his Message is as important as breathing air. *20* Without this radical commitment to Jesus, his wisdom seems stupid. *21* The path of human wisdom never leads to Dad; only divine wisdom does. *22* Seeing signs and having human wisdom may help a little, *23* but only the courage to be thought stupid will truly get us to Dad. *24* For even Dad's stupidity would surpass human wisdom, *25* and Dad's weakness surpasses human strength.

26 Just look at yourselves, sisters and brothers, and your Call. *27* Humanly speaking, not many of you were wise; not many of you were great, yet Dad chose the world's foolish to outshine the wise, and the weak to outshine the strong. *28* Dad has also chosen the world's insignificant and despised people to bring down those considered special. *29* So that all may be equally loved daughters and sons of Dad.

30 Jesus himself became Divine Wisdom and strength to show us we all are his sisters and brothers, all One with him. *31* So if we want to brag, we can brag about that.

CHAPTER 2

1 So when I came to you, dear sisters and brothers, I came with no great elegance or wisdom, even when I told you about Jesus' Message. *2* All I wanted to do was share with you about Jesus and how he had risen in me, and how he could rise in you. *3* And as I did this I felt very weak and afraid.

4 You know that my message was never persuasive or learned, but that it was the energy of Spirit flowing through me that touched your hearts; 5 so that your faith might be based on the Divine Life now in you rather than on any human wisdom. 6 I did indeed share wisdom with you, but it was not the wisdom of this world or of any leader of this world, since all of that will pass away. 7 Instead I fed you Divine Wisdom straight from Jesus' heart. 8 None of the leaders of the world have understood this, or they would not have crucified him. 9 For he tried to tell us: "No eye has ever seen; no ear has ever heard, and no heart has ever conceived, what Dad has prepared for those who open to his Love."

10 But Spirit has let me see and hear and conceive all of this, for he fathoms even the depths of Dad's Love for us. 11 For in humankind it is our inner Spirit that understands us, and it is the same Spirit who understands the thoughts and loves of Dad. 12 And we have received this Spirit, Spirit of the Risen Jesus, so that we may realize the Divine Life and the Divine Love that Dad has for us.

13 The words I use come not from human wisdom, but from Spirit Wisdom; that I may interpret spiritual truth to spiritual people. 14 But unspiritual people think these things are stupid and do not understand them because they do not live on the spiritual plane. 15 On the other hand, spiritual people are able to understand and honor all those things, 16 for they think with Jesus' mind and love with Jesus' heart.

CHAPTER 3

1 Now I hope you can see why I had to go so slowly with you. You were not yet mature spiritual people, but rather baby sisters and brothers of Jesus. 2 That is why I fed you milk rather than solid spiritual food. 3 Even now many of you are still unspiritual, 4 as when you argue about who is your spiritual father and who is your spiritual minister. 5 Both Apollo and I are ministers of the Gospel who brought Jesus to you and helped you believe. 6 I planted the faith: Apollo watered it; but Dad made it grow. 7 So neither the one who planted nor the one who watered is really important, since it was Dad who caused your faith to grow. 8 However, the one who plants and the one who waters have to work together, for we are Dad's fellow workers.

9 You are Dad's field in which this is done, and you are the building Dad is constructing. 10 Because of the immensity of the blessing of my Call, I knew enough to build a strong foundation upon which others could then build. 11 And the foundation I laid is the only foundation there is, since it is Jesus himself.

12 Those who build on this foundation may use different material, 13 but each one's work will become evident in the daylight and will be proven by fire, for fire is always the ultimate test. 14 Those whose work survives the fire will be blessed; 15 those whose work does not survive will have to build again with

better material until they are purified in the fire.

16 Do you not also realize that you are God's Temple and as such God dwells in you, as you? *17* Thus you yourselves are God, and therefore whatever you do to yourself, you do to God! So live as the holy God that you are!

18 Don't let anyone fool you. Those among you who believe they are already wise must become foolish in order to become truly wise. *19* For worldly wisdom is foolishness in Dad's eyes. *20* This fact is repeated often in the scriptures.

21 Therefore don't boast about trivial things since *everything* is yours, *22* your life, the universe, all you can see, all you can imagine. *23* It is already all yours since you belong to Jesus and Jesus belongs to God.

Chapter 4

1 People should consider we who are Apostles as servants of Jesus and stewards of his Message. *2* To be a steward you must be trustworthy. *3* I don't really care much about what you think of me, or what the judges think of me; I don't even judge myself. *4* The only important judge for me is Jesus. *5* He sees our hearts and reads our minds, and in spite of what is there, he always loves us. *6* And don't let anyone tell you anything different.

9 I really believe that God has appointed us Apostles from the least of humankind. *10* For we face death regularly and are often put on exhibition to the universe, to Angels as well as to people. *11* Even today we are hungry and thirsty, roughly treated and homeless. *12* We have to work until we are exhausted. *13* Being slandered, we bless; being persecuted, we patiently endure; being ridiculed, we try to bring comfort. We are often considered the scum of the earth.

14 I don't write these things to embarrass you, but to warn you as my dear children. *15* For although you have many teachers, you have only one father, because in Jesus I became your father by sharing with you his Good News. *16* So I urge you to live as I live. *17* For this reason I am sending Timothy to you. *18* He is my beloved and faithful son in Jesus, and he will remind you of what I have taught, the same things I teach to all the Communities.

19 I hope to come to you shortly, and then I will be able to see how you are living Spirit, exercising his Gifts; *20* for they are the signs of the presence of God and not simply nice words.

Chapter 5

1 I write to you again, my dearest sisters and brothers, with tears in my eyes, and regret in my heart, for all the pain I have caused you by the previous letter. *5* I want to write an entirely new one with my expanded wisdom. I now see so clearly how difficult it is to change, and how lovingly Jesus waits for us to do this.

I was a dyed-in-the-wool Pharisee when Jesus came to me. He opened my heart to such new realities that I cried many days as my belief in sacrifice and law started to melt away. And then when I returned to ministry, all those things came back to me. Not as strong as before, but enough to cause havoc to the weaker sisters and brothers.

I now know that sexual deviance generally comes from being violated, and that I should have opened my arms in love to those afflicted with these wounds, and helped them grow out of them. Please forgive me!

My prayer now is that we return sexuality to its rightful place next to spirituality. I now see that sexuality is the marvelous expression of spirituality on the physical level. As matter is to energy, so sexuality is to spirituality. Sexuality is the Divine Gift to augment our Spirituality. Its primary purpose is spiritual growth, not human birth. Human birth happens only very rarely whereas spiritual growth is needed constantly!

If we can direct sexual energy into spiritual growth, as was originally intended, we could solve most of the problems of the world, since they all arise out of a lack of Spiritual Growth.

Stop sexual abuse. Start redirecting sexual energy toward Spiritual Growth. This will get us out of the mud of materialism. Love the deviant into wholeness. Help the healthy into further growth.

As I have said (sometimes wrongly) in my previous writings: Don't let anyone convince you otherwise.

Enter the heart of Dad's Love and you will feel this Truth.

CHAPTER 6

15 Be aware that your bodies are members of Jesus. They too are made in the image of God. *19* Be aware also that your bodies are Temples of Spirit, the Risen Jesus, given to you by Dad to help you live as the Spirit, as the Risen Jesus. Making love is making God, since God is Love. Move your sexuality totally into your Temple and act out from that sacred place. Move your Sexual energy, your creative energy, into the world and shower it with Love.

CHAPTER 7

1 Now turning to the question you asked in your letters to me. Marriage and celibacy are both wonderful callings from Jesus. Equally valid, but very different. As we have already written, sexual energy is for spiritual growth, and whether this energy is directed internally in celibacy or externally as in marriage, it is always to be used for spiritual growth. Looking into our hearts and bodies helps us determine our Call from God.

Divorce is to be always seen as the last resort and done only when a marriage has died and serious attempts have been made to bring it back to life. Jesus is always gentle in his dealings with us.

12 Mixed marriages are always a challenge and must be entered into after deep prayer and very open communication. *15* If after a very serious attempt it does not work, separate in peace.

20 Let each one stay in the calling received from Jesus, unless Jesus himself changes the Call. *24* Following the will of God is the only path to happiness. *31* Following worldly values will only bring you pain.

CHAPTER 8

1 Knowledge can puff us up, but Love always builds us up. *2* It is fine to know things, *3* but it is more important to love. *6* Always be centered first on God. He is our Dad, the maker of all, and his son is our brother who taught us we are Dad incarnate. *7* Not all realize this. Many still worship idols, such as money and power. *13* Try to gently move your sisters and brothers from worshipping these, to loving our true God incarnated in us.

CHAPTER 9

1 Let me speak to you now from my heart. I have been so very blessed to have seen Jesus. He asked me to be an apostle, and taught me how to do it. *2* Some say I am not an Apostle, but you know that I am. You living the Good News proves I preached the Good News. *13* My Jewish roots led me to feel a right to live from my preaching, but somehow I knew in my heart that I could never do that. *16* For preaching the Good News flows naturally from my heart. And when I don't preach, I don't feel like me.

17 When Jesus called me, he changed my heart, so I can no more stop preaching than I can stop loving him. His love has made me a captive of his Word. *18* So what do I get out of this? The pure joy of preaching my beloved Jesus' Message without charging anyone. *19* Jesus has made me free, but I have made my heart captive to all, in order to bring them to Jesus. *20* I walk by the side of everyone to lead them into the Family of God. *22* To the weak, I have become weak to bring them into Dad's Family. I have become everything to everybody to do this. *23* I do this to share the Good News so I may become the Good News.

24 You know when there are races in the stadium, only one is the winner. With Jesus, we are all winners, for he has finished the race for us. *25* All those wanting to run to Jesus keep in shape. This race is much more important than the one in the stadium. *26* This is why I run straight ahead, keeping always in shape; so that as I urge others to run with me, I will not stumble.

CHAPTER 10

13 Dad is always faithful to us and will not allow us to be tempted beyond our strength; and even in the midst of temptation, will help us find a way out. *14* So dear sisters and brothers, let us always keep our minds and hearts centered on him.

16 Is not the sacred cup that we consecrate, a fellowship in the blood of Jesus? Is not the bread we break together, a fellowship in the body of Jesus? *17* Though we are many, we become one bread, one body, since we really are already One.

31 Even when we are simply eating or drinking, or anything else, we should do it all in a sacred manner. *33* I try to do this. Not seeking my own advantage, but that of others that I may lead them to Jesus.

CHAPTER 11

1 Imitate me as I imitate Jesus. *2* Thank you for praying for me and keeping the traditions I have taught you. *23* And this is by far the most important tradition, for I have received it directly from God: That Jesus, the night before he transitioned out of his humanity and into our Divinity, *24* took bread and gave thanks. Then he broke the bread and gave it to his friends and said, "This is my Body, broken in two so that we may become one. Let me come into you; that you may come into me. Do this to remember that you are me." *25* And after supper he took the cup and said, "This is my Blood. This is my Life. Let it flow into you so that you may become me. Do this to keep this Truth always in your hearts. *26* For every time you eat this Bread and drink this Wine, I become a little more you, and you become a little more me, until we become totally One! So always do this in a very sacred way."

CHAPTER 12

1 Now I want to share with you, my dear brothers and sisters, about the spiritual gifts, the Gifts of Spirit. *4* There are a number of different Gifts, but they all come from the same Spirit. *5* There are also different ministries, but they all come from the same Jesus. *6* There are also different kinds of miracles, but they all come from the same Divine Energy.

7 The spiritual gifts are always given for the benefit of the Community. *8* The Spirit gives one person the Gift of Wisdom, to another the Gift of Knowledge, *9* to a third the Gift of Faith, to yet another the Gift of Healing, *10* to another the Gift of Miracles, to this one the Gift of Prophecy, to that one the Gift of Discerning Spirits, to a third the Gift of Prayerful Chant, and to yet another the Gift of Interpreting Prayerful Chant. *11* All these many Gifts come from the One Spirit, who grants them to all who are open to them.

12 For just as the body is One, and yet has many different members, so it is with the Family of God. *13* For by one Spirit we have all been baptized into one body, and have many manifestations of the same one Spirit.

14 The body consists of not simply one, but many members. *15* If, for example, the foot should say, "Because I am not a hand I do not belong to the body," it would nevertheless still be part of the body. *16* Or if the ear should say, "Because I am not an eye I do not belong to the body," it would still belong to the body. *17* And if the entire body were an eye, how would we hear? Or if all were an ear, how could we smell? *18* But God has placed different members into one body each with a different, but equally important, Gift.

26 Each member is so interconnected that when one suffers, we all share in the suffering. And when one member is honored, all share in the glory.

27 You are all Jesus' body, each and every one of you. *28* And God has appointed in the Communities apostles, prophets, teachers, miracle workers, healers, social workers, administrators, and chanters. *29* Not all can be apostles, prophets, teachers, chanters, or interpreters of this chant. *31* But I want you each to seek the more valuable Spiritual Gifts. And I am now going to explain what they are.

CHAPTER 13

1 Even though I can speak eloquently, even as the Angels, but if I do not Love, I am simply a noisy bell or a clashing cymbal. *2* Even if I have the Gift of Prophecy and can see through every mystery, and through all that may be known, and have enough Faith to move mountains; but

if I don't love, I am really nothing at all. *3* And even if I give away all that I own to feed the hungry, but do it without Love, it serves me no good.

4 Love is patient and kind. Love is not jealous. Love does not try to impress. *5* It is not conceited or rude. It is neither self-seeking nor irritable. Nor does it keep track of wrongs done to it. *6* It does not try to cheat, but simply to be honest. *7* It accepts everything with patience, has unquenchable faith and enduring hope that knows no bounds.

8 Love lasts forever, whereas Prophecy will pass away. Prayer Chant will stop, and Knowledge will lose its meaning. *9* For Knowledge is sometimes fragmentary, and also may come out of Prophecy. *10* But when perfect Love comes into our hearts, it will last forever.

11 When I was a child I talked like a child and I acted like a child, but when I became an adult I put aside these childish ways. *12* For now we see indistinctly as in a mirror, but when perfect Love comes, we will see Dad face to face, since he *is* Love. And we will see that we too are the same Love. Now we only understand partially, but then we shall understand Love as we are understood by Love.

13 So there are these three main things: Faith, Hope and Love, but the greatest of these is Love.

CHAPTER 14

1 Seek first after Love, and then the Spiritual Gifts, especially Prophecy.

2 For the one who prays in chant does not speak to us, but to God. And no one understands what is being said, since it is the mysteries of Spirit. *3* But the one who prophesies connects God's mind and heart to our own.

4 The one who prays in chant grows in Spirit; but the one who prophesies helps the entire Community grow. *5* I wish all of you might pray in chant, but I would rather have you all prophesy. The one who prophesies is more important to the Community than the one who prays in chant, unless he can interpret the prayer so the Community can understand it.

6 If, for example, I came to you and prayed in chant, what good would it do you, unless I also gave you some revelation or information or prophecy or teaching? *7* Unless musical instruments, like the flute or harp, produced distinct tones, how will anyone know what is being played? *8* If the trumpet sounds an indistinct call, who will get ready for battle? *9* In the same way, unless your tongue gives an intelligent message, who will understand you? You will be talking in the air.

10 Who knows how many different languages there are in the world? *11* So if someone speaks to me in a language I do not understand, we will seem like foreigners to each other, *12* which is similar to what happens when someone prays in chant in a Community gathering. So since you are eager for Spiritual Gifts, I urge you to seek those that help build up the Community.

13 It is nice when one who is chanting prayer can also translate or interpret them, but it is not necessary because those who hear this type of prayer know there is an intimacy of heart going on that is often beyond normal words.

18 I give thanks to Dad that I have this Gift, and give thanks for the intimacy with him that it brings me, *19* although sometimes I wish people could understand the beauty that I feel. *24* And in prophecy this beauty shines out clearly in Truth. People understand prophecy and can also easily understand that its Truth comes directly from God. *25* Many have been converted in this way.

26 So, sisters and brothers, when you pray together, let everyone contribute a part—a song, a teaching, a revelation, a prayer-chant, an interpretation of it. All these can be very helpful. *27* It is better to have the prayer-chants translated, *28* but if there is no one to do this, simply have it increase the prayer-energy of the Community.

29 And be sure to have prophets speak, for their Messages from God are very important. *33* Keep this all in order, for God always brings peace with his Message to Communities and our people. *34* And have everyone listen closely as all of this is going on. *35* The time to talk about it is later at home.

37 Let the community discern who has the Gift of Prophecy to insure its validity. *39* In conclusion let me say, seek after prophecy to let God lead the Community; let the prayer chants increase the energy that supports this, and do everything in a sacred manner.

CHAPTER 15

1 Here again I would like to clarify what I had written before. As a Pharisee, living my whole life under the law, I saw Jesus initially as the one who saved us from it. Later I realized that in Jesus we are only under Love. For those who believe they are still under the law, Jesus died to save us from our sins. For those who believe they are under Love, Jesus died in his humanity to be resurrected as our Divinity.

Wherever you are, my dear sisters and brothers, Jesus will help you, Jesus will save you. If you feel under the law, he will save you from sin; if you feel under Love, he will save you from your fear. Please, please accept everyone where they are, so that you can all grow in Love together; so that you can grow in God together. In this way we can all rejoice in the Good News of Jesus. For what we believe, is less important than how we live, and how we love.

5 I told you before that after his resurrection he was seen first by Mary Magdalene, and then by the apostles and other friends when they were together. *6* Later he appeared to more than five hundred sisters and brothers together at the same time, and most of these are still alive.

Afterward he appeared to me. *9* For I am the least of the apostles since I had persecuted Jesus in his friends.

10 But through Jesus' grace and love, I am now his apostle. I have worked very hard to be this, or I should say, Jesus' Love has manifested so profoundly in me that I can be this. *11* So that through me or any of the other Apostles, the Message of Jesus that you have come to believe, has been preached.

35 Now some of you have asked about the Risen Body. We can look to nature to help us understand this. *36* The seed that is sown in the ground does not come to life unless it first dies. *37* The same is true of our bodies. *38* Our resurrected body comes to life only after our human body dies, and is completely different from it.

39 All flesh is not the same. One kind is human, another animal, another fowl, and another fish. *40* There are heavenly bodies and also earthly bodies, and the radiance of the heavenly is one kind, and that of the earthly another kind. *41* The sun is radiant in one way and the moon in another way; the stars are still a different way. So also does one star differ in radiance from another. *42* So too the resurrected bodies. The human body is sown in mortality and resurrected in immortality. *43* It is sown in weakness and raised in power. *44* It is sown in a natural body and raised in a supernatural body. There is a spiritual as well as a physical body. *45* So it is written,

"The first man, Adam, became a living soul; the last Adam became a life giving Spirit."

46 Remember that the first man was from the earth; the second Man is from Heaven. *49* And just as we have borne the likeness of the earthly ones, we shall bear the likeness of the heavenly ones. And we should note that these seeming polarities melt into oneness when seen by the eyes of God who is beyond all division.

51 Please listen closely because I am going to tell you a secret. The whole universe is going to go through a radical transformation as God washes over it; Jesus' prayer for unity extends through humanity to the entire universe. The deification, that is now beginning in humanity, will extend out until All has been reborn back into the One God. In the meantime, we shall not all die before we have been reborn into God.

52 The Angels are already preparing to trumpet this rebirth. Jesus rose to begin the resurrection of the universe. *53* Some of the Universe was stillborn and needs to be reborn out from this lack of Love. Lack of Love means lack of God, since God is Love. *54* Being reborn into Love, is being reborn into God. *55* When that happens, death will die. *57* When that happens, we will follow Jesus back into the womb of God to be reborn as truly God's daughters and sons.

58 So let us begin to act as such by serving and loving All.

CHAPTER 16

19 All the home Communities of Asia send you their greetings in the Love of Jesus. *20* All the sisters and brothers send you greetings. Greet one another with a holy embrace. *21* Here is my greeting in my own handwriting. Paul. *23* The Love of Jesus be with you. My love to you all in brother Jesus.

SECOND CORINTHIANS

CHAPTER 1

1 I, Paul, by the will of God an apostle of our brother Jesus; and our brother Timothy; to the Communities of God in Corinth, and to all the saints in Achaia. *2* Love and peace to you from God our Dad, and from Jesus our Brother.

3 We are so happy that our God is our Dad, and that he is also the Dad of our brother Jesus. He is so caring of us, especially when things are really tough. *4* He consoles us in our every trouble, so that we may be able to console others in theirs with the same Divine Love. *5* Being with our brother Jesus is a two-sided blessing; we suffer with those who suffer and yet are always so deeply consoled by his immense love for us all.

6 When we are troubled, it is because we love you so much. When we feel consoled, it is because we see you loving one another. *7* Our love for you is unshaken since we see you walking with those who are suffering, and with those who are rejoicing.

8 And so, sisters and brothers, I want you to know that things got so bad in Asia that I was afraid they would take my life. *9* I finally just gave my life totally to our brother Jesus, *10* knowing he could either receive it, or give me enough faith to go on living. *11* This surrender, and your prayers, brought me through this valley of death.

12 I am so happy that with our brother Jesus' help I have learned to live in his energy and not by worldly wisdom. *13* Counting on this Divine Energy that lives in both you and me, we can easily communicate. *14* So that when we appear before him, he will recognize his resurrection in us all. *15* It was in this assurance that I planned to visit you on my way to Macedonia and on my way back; *16* and with this double blessing you would then send me on to Judea. *17* I planned all of this listening closely to our brother Jesus, so I would not be confused by worldly wisdom. *18* So I could take each step of the journey following his guidance. *19* Since brother Jesus, who Silvanus, Timothy and I preached to you, could help keep us all on the right path. *20* He is Truth, so all we have to do is say, "Amen" to his guidance for his glory to shine through us. *21* But he who has made us one in God, *22* has also stamped us with our own Divinity as the first deposit in our hearts of Spirit. *23* May this deposit become our true identity, *24* so that we may be totally Divine as is our brother Jesus.

CHAPTER 2

1 Please know that I love you, and that the only reason I write this is to help you grow in your Divine Life.

4 And please remember this even if at times I am critical. *8* We must always open our hearts even to those who have not yet found their way to this new Life. *10* For when you open your heart, my heart is opened, because of the Oneness that we are.

12 When I arrived in Troas to preach the Good News of Jesus' Message, I did not find my dear brother Titus, so I went on to Macedonia. *14* But thanks be to God who always helps me in my weakness and distress, I was able to dispense the fragrance of his Love. *15* For to God we are the fragrance of our brother Jesus, for those who come close enough to smell his Love. *17* For my only interest is to bring everyone close enough to our brother Jesus that the fragrance of his Love may guide them in following him.

CHAPTER 3

1 Your loving our brother Jesus and following his Message are validation of my Ministry. *2* You are our letter of recommendation, written in our heart, read and acknowledged by everyone. *3* This makes it obvious that you are Jesus' letter delivered by us, not on tablets of stone, but on tablets of the heart.

4 As I stand in our brother Jesus' presence I am filled with confidence. *5* It is not the confidence that comes from the ego, but the confidence that comes from God. *6* And he has called us and approved us to be ministers of a New Covenant, not of the old law, but of the new Spirit. For law tends to stifle, whereas Spirit is always life-giving. *10* The glory that once was the old law, now has no glory at all.

12 I am filled with such great hope, as I open to the New Covenant with Spirit. *13* The Old Testament has been replaced by the New Message of Jesus. *15* Up until now when Moses' law was read, a veil covered the heart of God. *16* Jesus' Message has taken this veil away, and we can now see the loving heart of God. *17* For Jesus is the Spirit and where the Spirit of Jesus is, there is freedom and love. *18* Now that this veil has been lifted, we can look as in a mirror and see the glory of Jesus, as his resurrection reaches its fullness in us. For Jesus has saved and restored our old identity by becoming Spirit in us.

CHAPTER 4

1 Therefore being engaged in this ministry though a divine call, we are filled with profound hope. *2* We continue in this hope through purity of heart and action. *3* Some have tried to obscure the radiance of Jesus' Message; *4* but this does not alter the fact that Jesus is God, and that he taught us that we are also God.

5 For we do not proclaim our ego selves, but rather Jesus as God; and ourselves as parts of God. *6* Because God can bring light out of darkness, as he had brought divinity to light in our human hearts. So now when we look closely at our own hearts we see the face of Jesus there, God there.

7 However, we are keenly aware that this amazing treasure comes from God's divinity and not our humanity. 8 We are closed in on every side, but do not give up; 9 we are persecuted, but do not feel deserted. 10 Because all the while we carry Jesus within us, so we can act in a Godly manner.

11 Almost every day we face death for Jesus' sake, and he lets his life shine forth in us. 12 So the death of this world cannot touch the life of Jesus.

13 Furthermore, we have the same faith of the prophets who spoke out of their belief. We know our God raised Jesus from the dead and that he will raise us up too. 14 He will raise us from our humanity into his divinity. 15 The more we believe this, the more the gates are opened for it to happen in us.

16 Knowing these things gives us immense hope, for even though in the human dimension we may be dying every day, 17 in the Divine Dimension we are already beginning to rise into Jesus, 18 until that glorious day when these two dimensions become one, and Jesus' prayer for unity will be completely realized.

CHAPTER 5

1 For we know that if our human dimension body that we are living in should pass away, we would still have our Divine Dimension place in our Dad's Heart forever. 2 So it is that while we live in this human body, our heart longs to be clothed with the love of God, 3 so that with this clothing we may no longer feel naked or afraid. 4 For we groan deeply while in this human body, not so much to be out of it, as to be in God's heart which is where True Life lives.

5 For when we were baptized in Spirit, our mind and heart were cleansed so we could see this Truth. 6 This Truth gives us hope and draws us deeper into the heart of God, 7 where we walk solely by faith into Love. 8 So our heart has locked onto this Love which draws us home. 9 Therefore, we surrender totally to Love, our real home. 10 For the more fully we open to Love, the deeper we can burrow into the heart of God.

11 Knowing all of this, is what motivates us to long to bring all of our sisters and brothers with us as we return home. 12 Look into our heart and into yours, and you will know that this is True. 13 This longing in my heart, is the same longing as is in the heart of our Dad God, opening to all his daughters and sons. 14 For the Love of our brother Jesus lives in our hearts, and points us toward home. 15 Because he died so that we might die to all fear of returning home to Love, for when we die to fear we can rise in love.

16 So we no longer think in terms simply of the human dimension, for Jesus has opened our eyes to the Divine Dimension. 17 As we open to Life in the Divine Dimension,

our life in the human dimension is absorbed into this new Life. *18* We are so deeply grateful that our brother Jesus has led us through the sea of fear, so we can now see God's heart of Love. *19* We feel so extremely blessed to have been asked to bring this Light of Love to all of you. As we walk out of the age of fear into the Age of Love, the heart of God opens to all with no exceptions. Love knows no boundaries; Love knows no limits.

20 On behalf of Jesus, we are ambassadors of God who uses our Voice to express his Love. We beg you in his name to walk into the arms of our Dad God. *21* For when Dad God looks at us he sees only daughters and sons, nothing else.

CHAPTER 6

1 As God's fellow lovers, we beg you not simply to walk into Love, but to walk through Love to our other sisters and brothers, who long for this Good News, even though they may not realize it. *2* For this is a very special time. A time of at-one-ment, a time of Universal Reconciliation. A time of the reconciliation of all people and peoples to one another; and all people to the rest of creation. *3* Universal Oneness is God's deepest desire.

4 And we have made this our ministry. Even though things are often rough for us, the Oneness we feel with our brother Jesus, our Dad and their Spirit, always brings us through to joy and peace.

11 And so, our sisters and brothers in Corinth, open your hearts wide to this same ministry, the ministry of God's Love. Nothing else matters. *16* Remember God has said, "I will live in them and walk with them. I will be their God and they will be my people." *18* And, "I will be your Dad, and your will be my daughters and sons."

CHAPTER 7

1 We walk in these promises and have invited you to walk with us. *2* Open your hearts to us and to all, *3* as we have to all of you. *4* Knowing of your love has filled us with joy even when things were rough, *5* as they were when we reached Macedonia. *6* But Dad God took pity on us and sent Titus, and warm greetings from you. *7* He told us of your great love for one another and for us.

8 I know that my last letter was tough, but it came from Love. *9* I am so glad that you responded so well to it. *10* For when we respond in love it always leads to Life. *13* Titus was so pleased to see the reborn love in all of you. *14* And he understood why I love you so much. *15* He sends his love and thanks to you again for your open welcome of him.

CHAPTER 8

1 We want you to know, dear sisters and brothers, the Divine Love granted to the Macedonian Communities. *2* How their deep love moved them to give so generously even in their poverty. *3* Their poverty has over flowed into a wealth of love. *5* They outdid themselves in generosity to God and to us.

6 We now turn to you who have grown in so many ways. *7* Be as generous now as you have been in the past. *8* For Jesus being rich, came among us in poverty, to invite us into the richness of his Love. *12* For gifts given in Love always return to us increased by God's Love.

13 Share fairly with all. *14* When you have abundance, you should share with those who don't, so that they may share their abundance when you experience a need. *15* Balance always leads to peace.

16 We thank God that Titus loves you as much as we do. *17* He went off on his own accord to share with you the opportunity of giving. *18* We are sending along a brother whose virtue is known to all the Communities. *19* These Communities have appointed him to minister with us, and assist with this great collection. *20* For we want to make sure that all of this is done in the Light of the Love, *21* and the clear view of all. *24* So show proof of your love by the generosity of your giving.

CHAPTER 9

6 For you know that the more generous the sowing, the greater the harvest. *7* So give with a loving heart. For God has a special love for those who give joyfully. *8* And the more generous the giving, the more generous the receiving. *9* God's Love can never be out-given. *10* Generous giving on the human dimension always brings generous receiving on the Divine Dimension.

CHAPTER 12

1 Let us talk now of Visions and Revelations from Spirit. As hearts open, these always increase. When Jesus first came to me, this opening began. *2* Fourteen years ago I was taken up as far as the Third Heaven where I was told things beyond words. *3* In this intimate presence of the Divine all human senses fail. *4* This presence fuses with one's identity and only Love is left. *5* Experiencing Oneness with God brings one's heart to its knees in humble gratitude. Divinity does not inflate, but rather humbles the heart in Love.

6 And I want to be very clear that this was not given to me because of any personal greatness, but because of my Call to teach the Message of Jesus. *7* This Oneness with God is the Good News he preached, and called me to preach. I received a thorn in my side to remind me of this. *8* Three times I asked Jesus to take this from me, and three times he said, "My Love is strong enough for you to do this, for my strength shines forth the best when people are aware of their weakness." *9* So I am happy to admit my weakness so the power of Jesus' Love for me may shine forth. *10* For it is when I face my weakness that I become strong in God, and can face all the hardship and tribulations that surround my life. *12* I showed you all the signs of being called to be an apostle with many miracles and acts of this power through Jesus.

14 I am getting ready for my third visit to you. *15* I am willing to give up everything so that you may open to Jesus. *16* I believe I have already shown you this. *17* I sent you Titus and another brother to help you find Jesus. *19* I have always acted as Jesus' representative to help you grow in faith.

CHAPTER 13

1 When I come you will see again that Jesus speaks through me. Jesus will continue his mighty work in you. *2* His Divine power will fill you with Divine Life. *3* We may feel weak, but he is always strong. *4* And as his Life and our Life melt into one, his Message will incarnate in the world one heart at a time. *5* Look at our hearts and see if the face of Jesus smiles back at you. *6* Jesus' Life is always visible when it incarnates in us.

11 Finally, my dear sisters and brothers, I say: Goodbye. May the God of Love and Peace be with you. *12* Greet one another with a holy kiss. All the saints here send their greeting to you.

13 May the grace of Jesus, the Love of God, and the fellowship of Spirit be with all of you.

GALATIANS

CHAPTER 1

1 Paul, an apostle not chosen by any human person, but by Jesus himself, *2* and all the sisters and brothers here with me, to the Communities of Galatia. *3* Love and peace to you from God our Dad, and Jesus our Brother, *4* who gave himself to help us overcome our fears, and to see God as our Dad.

6 I urge you to stand firm, united with our brother Jesus and his **Gospel of Good News**. *7* Some will try to distort or dilute what I have taught you, but don't listen to them.

10 All I want is to serve Jesus and his Message, *11* which I received directly from him through many glorious revelations, *12* and not from any human person.

13 You have heard of how I persecuted the Communities before Jesus came to me. *14* And how I tried to destroy them because of my zeal for the law. *15* But when he came to me in vision and revelation, having been set apart even in the womb to preach him and his Message to the Gentiles, *16* I did not talk to anyone about this, *17* nor go to Jerusalem to talk to those apostles before me. Instead Jesus called me away to the desert in Arabia to teach me his Message, and then I came back to Damascus.

18 Then after three years I went up to Jerusalem to get acquainted with Peter and stayed with him a couple of weeks. *19* But I didn't see any of the other apostles, only James, the brother of Jesus. *20* I swear to you that this is true. (*He says this because Acts had said he went back to Jerusalem to consult with the apostles right after his vision.)

21 Then I went into the regions of Syria and Cilicia, *22* but did no ministry in Judea. *23* Some of those in Judea talked about how the one who had been persecuting the Communities was now trying to build them up. *24* They marveled at God's ability to work in us.

CHAPTER 2

1 Then fourteen years later I went up to Jerusalem again along with Barnabas. *2* Jesus asked me to do this in a revelation and to lay before the apostles there the Good News I was preaching to the Gentiles.

3 And Titus, who was also with us, was a Greek and not a Jew, was not asked to be circumcised, as some had hoped, *4* in order to put the law back over Jesus' Message of Love. *5* We were adamant in opposing this imposition so that the true Good News might continue to be preached to you.

6 And the leading apostles did not try to add anything to the Good News of Jesus that I was preaching. *7* I would not have paid attention to them anyway, *8* since my Message had been given to me *directly* by Jesus himself.

9 So James, Peter, and John, who were considered the Church pillars, simply opened their hearts in fellowship to Barnabas and me to serve the Gentiles, while they would continue to serve the circumcised. *10* The only thing they asked is that we remember the needy, which actually we were already doing.

11 But later when Peter came to Antioch we had a strong confrontation. *12* Peter had been eating with the Gentile converts until a delegation from James arrived. Then he stopped eating with them for fear of the delegation. *13* The other Jews also stopped eating with the Gentile converts, which seemed like hypocrisy to me since they had all been doing that before James' delegation arrived.

14 So I said to Peter in front of everyone, "If you, who are a Jew, have lived as a Gentile, how can you require Gentiles to live like Jews?" (*15* It needs to be remembered that Gentiles eat food that Jews believe is unclean.)

16 We already realized that keeping the law does not bring us closer to God. Only by believing Jesus when he says that God is our Dad, can we change our relationship with God and come closer to him. The Way to God is Love and not law.

17 Then what happens if I love, and yet do not keep a law? If I love, I am always in God since God is Love. *18* True laws may be guideposts to happiness. So if I break a True Law I may limit my happiness, but not my connection with God, with Love, since that is impossible.

19 Otherwise my actions are stronger than God's Love! So we keep the true laws, not to keep God's Love, but to keep our own happiness.

20 I have become One with Jesus. My old self has died with Jesus on the cross, and my new self has been raised with him. *21* So now it is not I who live, but the Jesus who gave himself to me, who now lives as me. When I look in the mirror of faith, I see the Jesus I have become.

CHAPTER 3

1 My dear Galatians, did you receive the Spirit from works of the law, or from believing Jesus' Message of Love? *5* Do you believe Spirit works in you because you keep the law or because you Love? Before Jesus came with his Message, God was seen as closely connected with law, but now we know that he is Love.

6 Abraham did indeed keep the law, *7* but his motivation was always Love. *8* When fear is what motivates us to keep the true laws, we have walked out of Jesus' Message of Love. *9* We have gotten stuck again in the valley of fear. *10* Those who depend on keeping the law to be pleasing to God, suffer under this curse of fear. *11* God doesn't want us to fear, since fear distances us from God, who is Love.

12 When Jesus came down from the cross, he left fear nailed to it. He wants us to leave it there to rot back into the nothingness that it really is. *13* The God of Love is the one who rose on Easter morning. *14* The Spirit, the risen Jesus, leads us on the Path of Love to the God who is Love.

15 Sisters and brothers, if we look at human custom, we see that no one can change a person's last Will. *16* And the Covenant of God was given to Abraham and "his offspring," in the singular, which refers to Jesus. *17* This is the point I am getting at, the law which came four hundred and thirty years later, could not change the Covenant of God, the Will of God. *18* The Covenant of God came before the law of Moses.

19 Then the question is: why was the law given in the first place? *20* The law was given to guide us to Love, to open our hearts for the coming of Jesus. But when it passed into human hands and was written down, it was changed into a tool of judgment and condemnation. Its original glory was overshadowed by the addition of fear.

21 Jesus was sent to resurrect the law back into the Love of the Covenant of God, so it could again be seen as loving guidance rather than harsh judgment. The Covenant was meant to reestablish an intimate relationship between God and us. *22* Anything in scripture that is not reflective of this is not a true revelation from God, who is Love. Law gives guidance; Love gives Life.

23 Before Jesus came we were locked under the law, through this misunderstanding. *24* Jesus did not change reality; he simply revealed it more clearly to us. He freed us from our misconceptions of the law, *25* and restored the intimate Covenant we had with God. *26* He became our brother, to show us that we are daughters and sons of God. He restored the Family of God! *27* The washing away of these misconceptions of the law has allowed us to realize we are a part of the heart of Jesus, and thus part of the Family of God. The Covenant of Love has been restored.

28 So now there are no longer Jews or Greeks, slaves or free people, women or men, because we are literally all One in Jesus. *29* When we are in Jesus, we are the true offspring of Abraham, and so heirs of the Covenant of Love.

CHAPTER 4

1 Another way to understand this is to compare it to an heir who is still a minor. While the person remains a minor there is no access to the inheritance until the time stipulated by the deceased parent. *2* Until that time, everything is handled by guardians or trustees. *3* This was in some sense our situation until the time when Jesus came. *4* But when God sent us Jesus, born of a woman, born in the time of the law, *5* he reminded us of the Covenant, so we could move out from under the law and experience the "adoption" as daughters and sons of God. *6* And because we now realize we are indeed daughters and sons of God, he has sent forth the Spirit of his son Jesus into our hearts, so we can cry out to God in unison with Jesus: "Abba! Dad! *7* So you are no longer under the law, but through our brother Jesus, you can now know that you are a daughter or son of God, and as such an heir to the Covenant which established the Family of God.

8 Before that, however, when you did not know you were part of the Family of God, and therefore God, you felt you were under the law of judgment. *9* Now you should realize you are under the Love of God. So why do you not now live as such, rather than slipping back to observing laws that you have been redeemed from? *10* You sometimes make me feel that I wasted my efforts teaching you the Good News of Jesus, *11* the liberation from the law.

12 I beg you, my dear sisters and brothers, to become like me, for I became like you to lead you to a closer intimacy with Jesus. *13* Remember now I first brought you the Good News of Jesus, because I could not travel due to my physical difficulties? *14* But you accepted and loved me with all my limitations, and even welcomed me as an Angel of God, even as Jesus himself.

15 What has happened to this love whereby you would even have plucked out your eyes and given them to me? *16* Why do you listen to those who want to put you back under the law of judgment? *17* Those who are trying to do this are not your friends.

18 I beg you to live the Good News of Jesus even when I am not with you. *19* My dear children, I once more feel the birth pains of bearing you into Jesus. *20* I long to be present with you right now to try again to present the Good News to you.

21 Tell me, you who want to be under the law again, what did I not explain well? The law divides, but Love unites. And I long for a greater unity among all of you.

22 We know that Abraham had two sons, one with a slave woman, and one with a free woman, his wife. *23* The one born of the slave woman was born in the natural way, while the one born of his wife was born in a supernatural way, through the Covenant with God. This is an allegory referring to the two covenants. *24* One is the covenant through Moses on Mt. Sinai, which connects with slavery; and the other is the Covenant through Abraham on the Mountain of God, which connects with freedom. *25* The first connects with the Old Jerusalem and the slavery to the law; *26* the second connects to the New Jerusalem and the freedom of the Covenant of Love. *28* And you, my dear sisters and brothers, are like Isaac, children of the Covenant. *31* And as such are children of freedom.

CHAPTER 5

1 Jesus opened this freedom for us, so stand firm in it and don't slide back under the slavery of the law. *4* All of you who believe the law will bring you closer to God, have not understood the Good News of Jesus. *5* But if we can open more fully to his loving Spirit, this will bring us to the intimacy with God that we long for, *6* and we will see faith manifesting in Love. *12* You have been called out of law and into freedom, my sisters and brothers, *13* and this freedom must always be exercised in Love. *14* Because the entire law can be summed up in this one phrase: "Love your neighbor as you love yourself."

16 I ask you to behave in a Spirit way. *17* Your call from slavery to freedom, from law to love, must radiate through your whole life, and not just your external life. *18* The inner feelings of your body are natural and can also be spiritual. *19* They need to be honored as God–given. *20* You did not design your body; God did, and he doesn't make mistakes. *21* It may be hard to move out of enslaving your feelings into honoring them, without ending up in some troublesome activities.

22 Jesus became a human person to bring Divine Wisdom into human actions. *23* Sexuality and Spirituality are the two sides of human creativity. *24* We need Love between these two, just as we need love between each other. *25* This is going to take time to work out since we have been slaves under the law for so very long. *26* But Jesus worked it out, and so he can teach us how to work it out.

CHAPTER 6

1 My dear sisters and brothers, be gentle with those who have trouble once they leave the law and have not yet really arrived at Love. Those who get to Love first should support those who are still on the way. *2* Take care of one another as happens in any loving family. Help others carry their burdens as Jesus helps us. *3* Be humble as he was. *4* Look at the fruits of your actions to help you know your intentions. *5* For how we sow is how we will reap.

6 Share generously with those who teach the Word of God; for they help you carry your load. *7* Only Divine Life lasts forever so make that your first priority. *8* Reverence your human life because it is a blessed gift, but it is not eternal. *9* Look for ways to sow love, so you can reap a good harvest of God. *10* Love everyone as Jesus has asked us to. *12* As I have said before, reverence your human body, but realize it is transitory.

14 Let us die in the heart of Jesus, *15* that we may rise with his Love in our hearts. *16* Let us proclaim the Good News with our Love. *17* May the Love of Jesus be always in your Spirit, my dear sisters and brothers. *18* Amen!

EPHESIANS

CHAPTER 1

1 Paul, an apostle of Jesus by the will of God, to the saints in Ephesus, *2* Love and Peace to you from our Dad God and brother Jesus. *3* Blessed be the God and Dad of our brother Jesus, *4* who has graced us with every possible blessing in the world of the Divine, through Jesus. *5* In love he called us to be his daughters and sons, *6* together with our beloved brother Jesus. *7* In him we were called out of fear and into Love, *8* which he poured out on us. *9* He made known to us the secret of his heart, *10* that everything in heaven and everything on earth be brought together into One.

11 Through Jesus we have regained our birthright, as was God's plan to re-establish his Family, his Covenant. *12* So our Call was simply to spread his Good News that God is Dad of everyone. *13* Through Jesus you too have accepted this Good News of Spirit, who is the Spirit of Family, the Spirit of Covenant, the Spirit of Love, the Spirit of God. *14* This is the glorious Oneness that Jesus prayed for; the Oneness that he came to bring. He is the answer to his prayer.

15 When I hear about your faith in Jesus and your love for each other, *16* I never fail to give thanks for you in my prayers, that the God of Jesus, *17* our loving brother, might give you a Spirit of wisdom and revelation, that you might truly understand him. *18* That you might truly have eyes of the heart to see our glorious call to reestablish the Family of God, the Family of Jesus, the Covenant with Dad. *19* Could there possibly be any greater Good News? Could there possibly be a more loving Dad, a more loving brother, a more loving Spirit?

20 When Dad raised our brother Jesus from the dead, he restored his Covenant, his Family, his Love. *21* He broke the chains of death, of law, and restored the Oneness that was felt to be broken at creation. *22* When he pulled us out of law into his Love, creation began again! *23* Fear died; Love rose! And the original plan of God was restored.

CHAPTER 2

6 When Dad raised Jesus, he also raised us to the heavenly realm, and set for us a family table to eat of his Love. *10* Once we had eaten of this Love, we have the energy to do his will.

14 Jesus is our Love. Jesus is our peace. And as such he helps us take down all the barriers between peoples. *15* By abolishing the law he freed himself to bring peace to all. *16* Now we are again the One Family of God. *17* Jesus always preached peace, and called us to always live peace. *18* Through the "Spirit of Jesus" in us, we all have direct access to Dad God. *19* Therefore you are no longer strangers or neighbors, but members of the Family of God. *20* You are now built on the foundation of the apostles and prophets, of which Jesus is the cornerstone. *21* This whole building, built by him, is the house of God, the "Family of God."

CHAPTER 3

1 Because of this I, Paul, a prisoner of our brother Jesus on behalf of you Gentiles, was called by God to this ministry, *2* and given the secret of the Good News by direct revelation. *3* I wrote you a brief letter about this before. *4* If you reread it you will understand this secret, *5* which was not made known in former generations, but is now revealed by Spirit to the apostles and prophets. *6* And the secret is that you Gentiles are joint heirs of God, and part of the Family of God. *7* I was called to share this wonderful secret with you. *8* I, the least of all the saints, was called to preach this fathomless wealth of Jesus to you Gentiles, *9* and to bring to you the Light and Love that has been in the heart of Dad God forever.

10 And so the radical wisdom of God can now be made known through the Communities, to the rulers and authorities of the earthly and heavenly dimensions. *11* This is in accord with God's eternal purpose which he carried out through Jesus, *12* in whom we now enjoy the glory of unreserved access, as with any true Dad. *13* So don't lose courage in any affliction because we can always go to him for comfort and wisdom.

14 I am eternally grateful to Dad for this, *15* for he is Dad not only for those in heaven, but also for us here on earth. *16* I pray that you may open your hearts and be empowered by the strength of his Spirit. *17* So that you may truly know that Jesus lives in your hearts, so that you may always be rooted in this Love. *18* And so that you may all have the power to understand what is the breadth, the length, the depth and the height of God's Love for you. *19* Even to know the Love of Jesus, which surpasses all knowledge, and that you may be completely filled with the Divinity that you are.

20 Now to him who works within us to do everything immeasurably beyond what we pray or think of, may our hearts turn with infinite love and gratitude, in our Communities, in our Families, forever. Amen!

CHAPTER 4

1 So I urge you as one totally committed to Jesus, to conduct yourselves worthy of the calling you have received. *2* Be humble and patient with one another. *3* Make every effort to preserve the unity of the Spirit in the bond of peace. *4* Unity is the core of our faith. We together form one body in Jesus; there is also only one Spirit, *5* just as you received your call with one hope, *6* one Brother, one faith, one baptism, one God and Dad of all of us, who loves us all, and is in us all, as our true self.

7 Divine Life is a Gift from Jesus to us. *8* When he rose from the dead, he ascended all the way to the heavenly realms, taking us with him to infuse us with this Divine Life. *9* As Jesus had been God, even before this, so were we, but it was not evident. *10* When he ascended, he filled the whole universe with Divine Love.

11 Through this New Life he has appointed some apostles, others prophets, some to be evangelists, and others to be pastors and teachers, *12* so that his presence and activity could continue in his new Earthly Body; until we have all arrived at the Oneness of faith and Love. *13* This happens as we truly understand that we are literally daughters and sons of God; which frees us from the cocoon of fear and releases us into the Life of Jesus.

14 And as a result of this we should grow up in every possible way. *15* Toward being the Jesus who is our heart, and from whom the entire Body receives the Life Blood of Love. *16* So that we may live and act from his Divinity, which has now become our own.

17 So I tell you this as from Jesus himself, begin living your Divine Life. *18* Don't live anymore in the darkness of believing you are only human. This false belief has caused many to live far from their Divine Life. *19* Failing to see this Truth they have turned their sacred bodies into toys for pleasure rather than means of creating the Divine.

20 This is not the way to live the life of Jesus. His life can become your life, if only you open your heart to him. *21* Take off your old habit and put on Jesus. *22* He does not judge how you have lived, but only longs for you to live in the joy and peace and Love of his life. *23* Clear your mind of untruths, and accept Jesus as the real Truth. *24* Jesus is like a magnet who will draw you into him, if you only get a little closer to him.

25 So be drawn into Truth. Lies come from fear and fear can drive out love. And since we are Love, fear tries to make us less than Divine. *26* See anger as a call to remember your Divinity; that you are Love. Negative actions are always requests for Love. *27* When we Love, we become more Divine, and help those around us become more Divine. That is our call in Jesus.

28 When we realize our Divinity, we realize there is nothing more that we need, but we continue to work, so we will be able to share. *29* Speak only from Love for this will build up those around you. *30* Try every day to open more fully to Spirit acting and loving through you. *31* Get rid of anything that does not come from Love and Truth. Be patient and kind with everyone as Jesus is with you.

CHAPTER 5

1 Therefore imitate God as his beloved Children, *2* and live always in Love as Jesus loves us.

3 Act always in Love as is proper for saints. *4* And always be thankful. *5* Don't fall into greed for that is worshipping money rather than God. *6* Treat your bodies always as sacred temples. *8* Live as children of the Light. *9* And Light consists of goodness, holiness and truth, *10* which manifest your inner Divinity.

17 Seek always to do the will of God, *18* and be filled with Spirit. *19* Share psalms and hymns and spiritual songs with each other. Sing from your heart, and make music to God. *20* And at all times give thanks to God, our Dad, and our brother Jesus.

21 Honor one another just as you would honor Jesus. *22* This is especially important for husbands and wives. *25* Husbands, love your wives as you love Jesus. *26* Wives, love your husbands as you love Jesus. *27* There has never been a greater example of the Love we are called to than that of Jesus.

28 One who loves his wife loves himself. One who loves her husband loves herself. *29* This is simply the reality of our Oneness. *30* As Jesus treats his Communities, we are to treat one another, for we are members of his Body. *31* Husbands and wives should have as deep a unity with each other as Jesus has with his Communities, and with each one of us.

32 Only hearts totally open to Spirit can understand the depth of our call to Love. *33* Only hearts totally open to Jesus can live it.

CHAPTER 6

1 Children, listen to your parents and do what they tell you. *2* Honor them as you would honor God. *4* Mothers and fathers, honor and love your children as you would honor and love your God.

10 In conclusion, be strong in God in the strength of his Spirit. *11* For he will protect you from all attacks. *12* There are energies still stuck in the darkness of fear who are jealous of our Light. *13* We must walk both with caution and with Love among them, for we must protect ourselves while always being open to their walking into the Light.

14 So stand in faith and stand in Truth, knowing that Jesus has freed us from fear, and that his Love will eventually free all from fear, *15* so universal peace may finally come to the world and to the universe. *16* Fight only with Love, to bring all to Love, their true identity. *17* Use the Word of God in this struggle for it carries the Life of Truth. *18* Prayer allows for this Word to bring the Divine into our lives and struggles. Walk in faith, knowing that Jesus always walks with us. *19* And please pray for me that when I open my mouth I may proclaim fearlessly the marvelous secrets of the Good News of Jesus. *20* Pray that I always present the Good News freely, as is my Call.

21 In order that you may know about me, I am sending this letter with Tychicus, our beloved brother and faithful minister of God. *22* He will let you know all about us and encourage your hearts.

23 Peace and Love to you, my dear sisters and brothers in the faith, from God our Dad and Jesus our brother. 24 Grace to you who have an ever increasing love for Jesus.

PHILIPPIANS

CHAPTER 1

1 Paul and Timothy, servants of Jesus; to all the saints in Jesus that live in Philippi, with the bishops and deacons. *2* Love and peace to you from God our Dad and Jesus our brother.

3 Every time I think of you I thank God. *4* Every time I pray, I pray for all of you with joy *5* for your fellowship in furthering the Good News from the first day of our mission. *6* For I am sure that He who has begun this good work in you will bring it to completion, as Jesus becomes our life more fully each day.

7 It is right for me to give thanks in this way, since I have you in my heart. We share together the Divine Life, whether in prison or in sharing and confirming the Good News. *8* For God is my witness that I long for you with the Love of Jesus.

9 And this is my prayer, that you may grow ever richer and richer in real knowledge and truth, *10* and that you may do the better things and walk closely with Jesus, so that your holiness that comes through Jesus may give glory and praise to God.

12 I want you to understand, dear sisters and brothers, that my being in prison has helped spread the Good News. *13* For throughout the imperial guard and everywhere else it has become known that my imprisonment is because I belong to Jesus.

14 And the majority of the sisters and brothers in Jesus have been encouraged by my imprisonment, to be far more daring in proclaiming the Message of Jesus fearlessly.

15 Some, of course, preach Jesus for the wrong reason; *16* but others out of good will; others indeed out of pure love for Jesus, for they see by my example how totally dedicated I am to the Good News.

18 I am happy that Jesus is preached for whatever reason. *19* For I know that all this will eventually turn out well through your prayers, and the immense blessings of the Spirit of Jesus. *20* For I really hope not to be put to shame after all, but that I may continue being bold in honoring Jesus in my body, either through living or through dying. *21* For to me to live is Jesus and to die is even better.

22 If, however, I can continue to serve by staying alive, I don't know which to choose. *23* My heart is divided. I long to die and so completely live in Jesus, for that would be so much better. *24* But it seems necessary that I stay alive for your sake. *25* I know that for now I will continue to be with all of you, so that you may progress in the faith and have the great joy that comes from that. *26* And so that through my coming to you again, your pride in Jesus, may be even greater.

27 I ask you to live in a manner

worthy of the Good News of Jesus that you have heard, so that whether I come to you or not, I may hear that you are standing firm in the oneness of Spirit. *28* And that you are not intimidated by those who persecute you. *29* For you have walked with Jesus even to the point of experiencing persecution as he did. *30* So you are experiencing the same inner conflict that I am, that of wanting to die and live fully with him, or stay and help spread his Message.

CHAPTER 2

1 We all love Jesus so very much, that this draws us to love one another. *3* So don't do anything out of selfishness or conceit, but rather serve all with humility. *4* Look out for the good of all and not just your own. *5* Learn to think and love as Jesus did. He was God and yet did not hesitate to also become human, *6* even to the point of being willing to serve others. *7* For a time he seemed almost to walk out of his Divinity, so he could walk into our humanity. *8* He walked into our humanity even unto death, death on a cross.

9 Dad, therefore, raised him up as an example of what his daughters and sons can do, *10* so that when we look on Jesus we can see our own calling, *11* and realize the glory Dad has called us to.

12 And so, beloved, live the Good News whether I am with you or not. It was given to you to bring you back into Divine Life. Although you can never really leave it, since

it is what you are. *13* Divine Life is God at work within you, God fusing your Identity and Will with his own. *14* This was what Jesus prayed for. That you be one with God, and God be one with you.

15 In the beginning God created you. And then God rebirthed you, to establish the Family of God, with you being his true Daughters and Sons. *16* Now *you* are rebirthing God, by allowing him to be reborn in you. Thus God can be reborn as your Father, as your Dad.

17 So in the midst of this, if my lifeblood must be poured out as an offering, I am happy to do it, and happy that you are a part of it. *18* An even greater happiness would be that you continue to share in this with all the other sisters and brothers.

19 Trusting in our brother Jesus, I hope to send Timothy to you shortly, so that I may be cheered up with news from you. *20* For I have no one else here who shares my deep love for you. *21* Many are looking out for their own interest, and not those of Jesus. *22* But you know Timothy's sterling qualities, *23* how as a son with his father, he has served the Good News with me. *24* And I have confidence in our brother Jesus that I too shall be able to come to you soon.

25 I am going to send you my brother and coworker Epaphroditus, whom you sent as your messenger, and to minister to my needs. *26* He misses you and is concerned that you heard he was ill. *27* And he was indeed ill, even to the point of death; but God took pity on him, and on me as well, so I would not suffer another grief. *28* So I am sending him back to you so that you may be glad and feel more relieved. *29* So welcome him with great joy in our brother Jesus. *30* And honor him, since he was so willing to give his life to make up for the service you could not do for me.

CHAPTER 3

1 Finally, dear sisters and brothers, be glad always in Jesus. I don't mind repeating myself because I want to be as helpful as I can. *3* Remember that our Covenant with God comes from our heart and not our circumcision. *4* But even if we were to look at externals, I would come out among the best.

7 But everything I used to consider important, doesn't mean anything anymore to me because of Jesus. *8* In fact I consider everything as loss in comparison to the immense blessing of knowing Jesus, my brother. For his sake I have lost everything and now consider it all rubbish, because I have found Jesus who is much more valuable. *9* And I have found my true self in him, not by following the law of Moses, but the Good News of Jesus. For the Good News of Jesus teaches us that our values, our very Identity, come not from keeping the law, but by being Jesus. By being re-adopted by God we have been reborn into the Family of God. When Jesus told us God was Abba, our Dad, the Covenant of Love with God was reborn.

Gone was the need to follow the law in order to be loved by God. The door of Love, the door to God, was reopened; and love always draws us into right action. The Good News of Jesus teaches us that Love is our birthright; Love is our essence, and so God is our essence. The Good News of Jesus did not change reality; it simply revealed reality.

Thus God does not need to redeem us, but simply to remind us that we have always been his beloved daughters and sons. That the Covenant of Love made with Abraham, has always been true; we simply had forgotten it.

When our minds and hearts open to this wonderful News, the immense fact of Jesus' Resurrection becomes our *own* Resurrection into the Truth, into Jesus. *11* Opening to Truth often involves suffering, since false Truths have to die, but this always leads to resurrection.

12 I do not want to pretend that I am completely reborn. I still suffer from birth pains. *13* But I press onward in the hope of a total rebirth in(to) Jesus, as he has already been totally reborn in me. *14* And so, dear sisters and brothers, I forget my past and reach out to my future. My past was the law, my future is God, opening to God and to being God.

15 Let those of us, then, who have already experienced our rebirth, share the Good News of our experience with our sisters and brothers.

Jesus will continue the Revelation of His Truth within us. *16* Truth is a Relationship; it is a Oneness with God which we must hold on to.

17 So please join me on this Path to Truth; follow my example and become an example of how reborn Love lives. *18* I now tell you with tears in my eyes, that if you don't do this, you will never be happy. *19* For happiness comes from being who we are, and we are Love and Truth. *20* When we live this Divine Reality, we proclaim the Good News of who we are, who everyone is. *21* Jesus has delivered us from our mistaken Identity, and restored our Divine Identity. *22* Let us share this Good News with the entire world!

CHAPTER 4

1 Now then, my dear sisters and brother, I want you to know how much I long to visit you, and how much I want you to stand firm in our brother Jesus.

4 Be joyful in Jesus; let me say that again, be joyful in Jesus. *5* Let people see how much you love one another so they will know that God is near. *6* Don't worry about anything. Talk to God in prayer as you would talk to a loving Dad. *7* This will bring you a peace that is deeper than understanding, because it rests in your hearts.

8 Finally my sisters and brothers, open your minds and hearts to whatever is true, whatever is honorable, whatever is fair, whatever is lovely, whatever is gently spoken, whatever is lofty, and whatever is praiseworthy. *9* This will invite the God of peace to be with(in) you.

10 I am so very happy that recently your great thoughtfulness toward me has been shown again. You are always interested in my well-being, but often lack a way to show it. *11* I don't mention this because of need, since I have learned to live on what I have available. *12* I know how to live simply, and I know how to enjoy prosperity. I am familiar with having plenty and with going hungry. *13* Jesus gives me strength to live in any situation.

14 It was so nice of you to be generous with me in my time of trouble. *15* And you Philippians know that when we began to preach the Good News, you were the only ones that contributed to this ministry. *16* For even when I was in Thessalonica, you sent me help a number of times. *17* For me this is not simply about your generosity, but about your growing in Love, growing in God.

18 Now that I have received your generous gift from Epaphroditus; my heart is happy and I know God's heart is happy. I now have more than enough of everything. *19* And as you have taken care of me, God will take care of you in our brother Jesus.

21 Greet every saint in Jesus. The sisters who are with me send you greetings. *22* All the saints greet you, especially those of Caesar's household. *23* The Love of our brother Jesus be with your Spirit.

COLOSSIANS

1 Paul, an apostle of Jesus by the will of God, and our brother Timothy, to the consecrated sisters and brothers of Jesus at Colossae: *2* Love and Peace from God our Dad and Jesus our brother.

3 We constantly give thanks to God, the Dad of our brother Jesus, as we are praying for you. *4* For we have heard of your great faith in Jesus and your great love for the saints. *5* This helps you realize that heaven is within us, as Jesus proclaimed and told his friends to proclaim. *6* As you have come to live this Truth, it is now spreading across the world. Our hearts long naturally for heaven, and to be told that heaven is already inside us, that God is already inside us, is indeed Good News.

7 Epaphas helped you learn this marvelous Truth, he who is also bound to Jesus as his faithful minister. *8* He has told us of your great love in Spirit. *9* From the day he told me this I have never failed to pray and petition for you, that you might be filled with all spiritual wisdom and insight so that you might understand his glorious will for you. *10* And so that you might live a life worthy of your Divinity, being completely One with your God, which manifests in your service to one another, and your spiritual knowledge.

11 We pray that you may be invigorated with complete power from God's power, and be filled with unlimited patience and perseverance. *12* Be very thankful that Dad has made you aware of your inheritance of his Divinity through his son's Message.

13 Dad has rescued us from the darkness of fear, and brought us into the home of his beloved son, *14* from whom we have received our Divine Blood(line). *15* Jesus revealed Dad's love to us and showed us our participation in it. *16* For through him all things created have Dad's Divine stamp on them and his Divine Life in them.

18 Jesus is also the Heart of his Body, the Communities, and as such is to be their Life. So that everything that happens in them is to flow from his Heart through his Spirit. *19* For Dad endowed him with his complete Divinity, which we as his sisters and brothers also have received, even though this marvelous Truth is still not totally realized.

20 When he died on the cross, he rose in us. The blood that he shed there, ended up in our hearts, and calls us to be (like) him and act always with his Love.

21 You, too, who once felt estranged from God in your thoughts and actions, should now feel the joy and peace of knowing you are an integral part of Dad's Family. *22* Jesus' presence with us brought

Dad's presence to us, to transform us into the Divine Family. *23* If you remain always grounded in this Truth and settled in this Faith, my ministry of spreading the Good News of Jesus will have been accomplished.

24 Until the Good News incarnates as fully as Jesus did in the world, there will be suffering. There is no need for suffering, but rather the need to accept the Truth of our Divinity as Jesus' Risen Body. Jesus' Risen Body is the Communities, or better, the Communities that live the Good News, since he never intended to set up a Kingdom or "Church."

Jesus was reborn in us and as such continues to suffer as we suffer since we are now One. When his Communities really live his Message, suffering will subside. When all the world lives his Message, suffering will end as True Oneness begins.

25 I have become a minister in his Communities by divine appointment, and yet I continue to suffer because his Message is not universally lived. The Mystery of our being truly daughters and sons of Dad God, is still young in the world. As it matures, violence will cease and love will reign; divisions will cease and unity will abound, fear will die and be reborn as Love.

26 We are all called to midwife the birth of this Good News. And although the Good News is from Jesus, it is about Love; so that even those who never hear of Jesus can birth their Divinity by Loving. That is the glory of the Good News: God is Love; we are God, so we are Love. And we live out our Divinity to the extent that we love.

27 God wants everyone to hear this Good News. God wants everyone to incarnate his Love. Jesus was Dad's model for all his daughters and sons to follow. "Love God" was Jesus' commandment, but even more importantly, it was his description of his Dad and our Dad.

28 I say again, when we look in the mirror and see only Jesus, the Good News will have become incarnate, the Risen Jesus and our reborn selves will have become One as Jesus prayed. *29* This is what I long for, this is what Jesus and his Spirit give their Energy for.

CHAPTER 2

1 I want you to know how very much I pray for you and for the Laodicean sisters and brothers, and even for those I haven't met. *2* I pray that their hearts may be welded together in love, and that their hearts may also be welded to the heart of Jesus, *3* the fountain of faith and wisdom, the very secrets of God.

4 This is the way to avoid the confusion of worldly logic. *5* And I want you to know that even when I am not present with you, my heart is welded to yours in Spirit, especially when I hear of the firmness of your faith in Jesus.

6 So as you realize that Jesus is truly your brother, live in intimate union with him, even to the point of being him. 7 This will cause your hearts to overflow with thanksgiving.

8 Beware of anyone trying to keep you captive by philosophy and worldly wisdom, rather than the Good News of Jesus. 9 For in him all the wisdom and Life of God dwells. 11 In him you were covenanted with Dad. 12 When you were buried with him in baptism, you were then raised to Divine Life with him through this Covenant with Dad.

13 And you who were dead in your fear of the law, he brought to life, by the teaching of the Good News and by nailing the law to the cross.

16 Be assured that there is no longer any validity to laws about what you should eat or drink, or how you are to keep the Sabbath. 17 These are ancient shadows of things to follow; but now we are to follow only Jesus. 18 Let no one teach you differently; but rather keep your focus on the Heart of our Communities which is Jesus, 19 who draws us into his own Divine Life.

20 If you have died with Jesus to worldly wisdom and values, why continue to live under worldly control? 21 Don't touch this! Don't eat that! 22 All these laws will simply eat you up; 23 their concern is material things rather than the way of growing into a Divine Life with Jesus.

CHAPTER 3

1 If then, you have been raised to Divine Life with Jesus, set your hearts on the things of heaven, where Jesus is with Dad. 2 Think about those things; not earthly things. 3 For you have died with Jesus and now live in his heart. 4 When Jesus, who is our very Life, appears, we shall appear with him, because we are him.

5 So let everything that is not of Jesus in you simply pass away. 7 For even though you have been addicted to these things in the past, Jesus will now fill their places in your hearts. 8 So let his Love fill those places that used to hold anger, bad temper, malice, and slander. 9 Always speak the Truth since Jesus is Truth. 10 Let your pre-Covenant habits pass away while you become (like) the God who created you. 11 There's no longer any difference between Greek and Jew, covenanted and un-covenanted, barbarian and saint; but Jesus is all and in all.

12 Therefore as God's Beloved, clothe yourselves with tenderness of heart, kindliness, humility, gentleness, and patient endurance. 13 Bear with one another and always forgive one another, having only Love in your hearts. 14 Let Love wash over everything and form the perfect bond of Oneness. 15 And let this Love, to which you were called when you entered into Community, arbitrate everything between you. And be always very thankful.

16 Let the enriching Message of Jesus have ample room in your lives and hearts as you teach and admonish in all wisdom and love.

Celebrate this with psalms, hymns and spiritual songs that are sung to God in a thankful spirit. *17* And whatever you do, do it all in the Spirit of our brother Jesus, through whom you do it to God our Dad.

18 Wives, love your husbands. *19* Husbands love your wives. *20* Children, be obedient to your parents in every respect, for this is what will make you happy, and teach you to live in the Covenant of the Family of God. *21* Parents, love your children, open your heart to them.

23 Whatever any of you do, do it all and always for God and the Communities. *24* For this is part of the Covenant of the Family of God. And this is how you live your Divine birthright as his daughters and sons.

CHAPTER 4

2 Keep faithful in prayer, our connection with our God and with ourselves. Give thanks for our Dad and for our Brother. *3* Ask them to open my heart more fully every day to understand the Message of Jesus, for which I am in prison, and that I may be able to explain it well to all.

5 Conduct yourself wisely with those not (yet) in the Covenant. Use your time the best way possible. *6* Always speak to everyone from Love and Wisdom.

7 I am sending you our beloved brother Tychicus, a faithful minister and friend of Jesus, who will tell you all about my affairs. *8* He will tell you what is happening here and encourage your hearts. *9* He will be accompanied by Onesimus, another of our faithful and beloved brothers who is one of you. They will bring you up to date on all that is going on here.

10 All here send you greetings and prayers, *12* especially Epaphras, one of your own, who prays constantly that you may stand firm in Jesus, *13* together with the sisters and brothers of Laodicea and Hierapolis.

14 Luke, the beloved doctor, sends his greetings too. *15* Extend our greetings to the sisters and brothers in Laodicea, also to Nympha and the Community that meets in her home.

16 When this letter has been read to you, please arrange that it may be read to the Laodician Communities, while you read the letter I sent to them. *18* My greetings in my own handwriting. Keep me in your prayers. Love be with you.

FIRST THESSALONIANS

CHAPTER 1

1 Paul, Silvanus, and Timothy, to the Communities of the Thessalonians in God our Dad and Jesus our brother: Love and Peace to you.

2 We give thanks to God for all of you in our prayers, *3* and always remember your wonderful faith, your works of Love, and your enduring hope that rests on our dear brother Jesus.

4 Sisters and brothers, beloved of God, we are well aware of his choice of you, *5* for the Good News came to you not only in words but also in the power of Spirit. You saw the kind of life you were called to by witnessing the kind of life I lived. *6* So you began to imitate our example and become followers of Jesus, fueled with the joy that can come only from Spirit. You opened your heart to him even though it caused you great affliction. *7* So you in turn became an example to all the believers in Macedonia and Achaia. *8* For not only did Jesus' Message echo from you in Macedonia and Achaia, but news of your marvelous faith has spread everywhere, and your witness has made my ministry very easy.

9 So many talk about how we brought the Good News to you, and how you turned your lives over to Jesus and turned you back on worldly values. *10* They talk about how they see the Love of Jesus in you, and service to the sisters and brothers in your lives.

CHAPTER 2

1 For you are aware, sisters and brothers, how effective our ministry was with you. *2* And you know that after the persecutions and suffering we endured in Philippi, how very blessed we felt when God helped us so much to bring the Good News to you. *3* People know that our motives are pure and honest, and that we have been called by God to spread his Good News, *4* and that we rejoice in being able to do just that. *5* We never put up a false front. *7* Instead we walked humbly among you and treated you tenderly like our own children. *8* We were so willing to share not only the Good News with you, but even our lives, because you had become so dear to us.

9 You will remember, sisters and brothers, that we worked day and night so as not to be a financial burden to you, while we preached the Good News of God to you. *11* You know that we were like a father to you, encouraging you to open to the Divine Life of God and let it shine through you, *12* so that his loving Covenant with you would be obvious to all.

13 We constantly thank God that you accepted the Good News as really coming from him and not from us. *14* For you, sisters and brothers, have become known as friends of Jesus in his Communities in Judea. *15* And because of this you were persecuted by those around you, just as Jesus was. *16* But take heart that your faith is based on such a solid conviction.

17 For we, sisters and brothers, tried so very hard to see you even when the Jewish leaders forbad us to teach you the Good News, or even to be with you. *18* But you have always been present in our hearts, *19* for who but you is our hope and happiness? For you are our glory and joy.

CHAPTER 3

1 So when we could not stand it any longer, we sent you Timothy, our brother and God's minister of the Good News, while we stayed behind in Athens. *2* We sent him to support you in your faith and encourage you, *3* so that you would not be so concerned about our afflictions. *4* For even when we were with you, we told you about the troubles we were going to have.

5 I sent Timothy to make sure of your faith, so that no one could take it from you. *6* And now that he is back and has brought us the wonderful news about your faith and love for each other, and how you keep us constantly in your prayers, and long to see us just as much as we long to see you, *7* we have reason, sisters and brothers, to be encouraged by all this in spite of our distress and affliction. *8* Because now we have these examples of faith to keep us going.

9 How can we ever repay God for you in view of all the happiness we enjoy because of you, in the presence of our God? *10* Day and night we keep praying that we may see you face to face to make up what is lacking in your faith.

11 May God our Dad and Jesus our brother answer our prayer to visit you. *12* May Dad make your love for one another and for everyone overflow, as does ours for you. *13* And may your hearts be so strong and your faith so deep, that you may incarnate Jesus in your very lives, with all the other saints.

CHAPTER 4

1 And so, sisters and brothers, we beg of you in the name of our brother Jesus, to keep living the way we taught you, that each day you may shine more fully with his Divine Life in you. *3* This is God's will: that you manifest in your life the Jesus that lives in your hearts.

4 Learn to love your spouse more fully, *5* not like those who do not know that God is Love, and that he calls us to mirror this in our lives; that all may learn this Truth. *6* Treat all the sisters and brothers with respect and honor, *8* for Jesus has asked us to reincarnate him in our lives to manifest the powers of Spirit.

9 It is not really necessary, sisters and brothers, to teach you about Love, since you have learned how to do this from Love himself. *10* And you are practicing it toward all the sisters and brothers of Macedonia.

11 But we appeal to you to grow in Love every day, so you can live in peace with everyone, and mind your own affairs. *12* Remember what we said about everyone having their own work, so you don't have to depend on anyone.

13 We want to be very clear, sisters and brothers, about those who have died, so you don't grieve for them as others do who have no hope. *14* For if we believe that Jesus died and rose again, we know that we will do the same. *15* We tell you this as it was told to us by our brother Jesus. When he reincarnates in us, he will come into the world the second time. The first time was in Bethlehem; the second time will be in our hearts. This will announce the end of the world of fear, and the beginning of the world of Love, the world of God.

16 As the Fire of Spirit spreads across the world, it will be like Angels trumpeting this Second Coming. *17* As hearts open and are reborn into Jesus, even the dead will rejoice in Divine Life. *18* We will experience being drawn into the heavenly realm even while we are alive. Encourage one another with this Great News.

CHAPTER 5

1 Jesus came to bring us the Good News, *2* and now we have *become* the Good News. *3* Where two or three really gather in the name of Jesus, we have a Second Coming of Jesus. *4* His Love exploded into the world as a child in Bethlehem, and now our lives are to explode with his Second Coming. *5* Sometimes it will be earth-shattering (changes), sometimes it will be a gentle breeze. There are no laws around how Jesus will come the second time, except the one saying he will come again (as us). When Jesus was buried in his tomb, he was also buried in our hearts. We decide when he will rise from there into our lives. *6* The sign of this second rising will be the Love in our lives and Spirit in our actions.

7 As the Gifts of Spirit pour across the world, the Angels will sound the trumpet of Joy to those with ears to hear. *8* The birth pains of his Second Coming have begun. *9* The persecutions against us are part of this; but when birth pains begin, the birth is assured. *10* We can resist this and continue in the pains of fear, or we can open our Divine womb and let Jesus be born again through us and from us!

11 But you, sisters and brothers, already know this Great News. The Good News of Jesus points to the Great News of his Second Coming through us. And, thanks be to God, this has already started. Pentecost was its beginning; total Oneness in Love will be its end. Encourage one another with this Great News.

12 We beg you, sisters and brothers, to open to all who bring you this News. *13* Hold them in high esteem because they point the way to true happiness, joy, peace, Jesus. *14* Help the weak open to this joy, by loving them more each day.

Love is all you need to reach Jesus, since Jesus is only Love. Be careful of anyone who teaches any other doctrine.

15 See to it that no one pays back evil with evil; instead always try to be helpful to one another and everyone. 16 Always be cheerful. 17 Pray unceasingly. 18 Always be thankful, for such is Dad's will for you in our brother Jesus.

19 Do not resist the actions of Spirit coming through you. 20 Open to prophetic utterances, 21 but also check them out with the Community, and retain those which are Truth. 22 Change evil into Love. 23 This will make you holy through Love Himself, for the secret to holiness is opening to Love. 24 He who calls you (to) Love will accomplish It in you.

25 Sisters and brothers, pray for us. 26 Greet each other with a holy kiss. 27 I ask you to have this letter read to all the sisters and brothers. 28 The grace of our brother Jesus be with you.

SECOND THESSALONIANS

CHAPTER 1

1 Paul, Silvanus and Timothy, to the Communities of the Thessalonians in God our Dad and Jesus our brother: *2* Love and Peace to you from our Dad and our Brother.

3 We are always thanking God for you, sisters and brothers, because your faith is growing so much and your love for each other abounds. *4* We tell all the Communities of God here about your fortitude and faith amidst the persecutions and distresses that you endure. *5* Jesus has brought you into his Covenant, and it is on account of this great blessing that you are suffering. *6* You can expect nothing less as Jesus is reborn in you. *7* Your relief from this will come from him who is being reborn in you, and not from what happens outside of you.

8 Those who reject the Good News of Jesus don't realize that they are actually rejecting themselves too, for we are all One even if we don't accept that Truth. *9* We pray they open their hearts to themselves, *10* so as to rejoice in being who they are, in Oneness with Jesus, as we have witnessed so often to you.

11 It is for this that we constantly pray for you too: that as you are born in Jesus you may accept your place in the Family of God, so that Jesus may be seen by how you live, as you reveal the love of God and our brother Jesus.

CHAPTER 2

1 Now I beg of you, sisters and brothers, with regard to the Second Coming of Jesus, and our becoming One with him, *2* don't be afraid of this or let anyone upset you. *3* Don't believe anyone who says that if Jesus is reborn in you that you will die. The simple reason is that Jesus is not someone else; he is *your* own very essence. When he becomes us, our real self becomes his real self, and the Truth of Unity begins to sparkle. *4* Unity with God brings peace and joy and Love. Being (one with) God used to be called blasphemy. The Good News of Jesus tells us it is simply reality. Facing this reality is the Path to (being) God.

5 Don't you remember when I told you this when I was with you? *6* This radical Good News of Jesus replaces the old law with Love. *7* Belief in law as the way to God actually keeps us from God. *8* Laws are for human order, not for reaching God. *8* Law may be the foundation of order, but Love is the foundation of Life. *9* How can God who is Love be squeezed into law? *10* Those who try to do this, end up living very unhappy lives. *11* Love brings Joy. *12* Love is our birthright; Love is our very selves.

13 We give thanks that most all of you already know this. You know you are beloved by God just as you are. *14* The Spirit of Love has called to you, and you have heard the Good News that we have preached. *15* You now know you share the identity of God. So stand firm in this Truth, sisters and brothers, and share it with others as I have shared it with you.

16 And may our brother Jesus himself, and God our Dad, who has always loved us and given us his Divine Life, *17* strengthen your hearts so that you may manifest the Divine Life in every good work and word.

Chapter 3

1 And now finally, sisters and brothers, pray for us, and that this Word of God may overflow into all the world and be lived as it has been in you. *3* God is faithful and will give us the strength to live out his Call. *4* So through him we have confidence in you, that you are practicing what we have taught you. *5* And may God direct your hearts into his Love and the patient expectation of Jesus' rebirth in you.

6 We charge you, sisters and brothers, to form Communities so strong that no one can impede their Love. *7* There are always some who resist their own happiness. Try to love them into it.

8 All of us are called to participate in creation by the work we do. You saw how we did this among you and paid our own way.

10 For while we were with you we always said, "Those who can work, must work; otherwise they are not to eat from the Community table." *11* Being God does not mean that we are no longer human, and subject to the human need to work. *12* So we insist that all live by doing their own work, earning their own living.

13 As for you, my dear sisters and brothers, don't get tired of following Jesus. *14* Love even those who don't, *15* as you would Jesus himself.

16 And may the God of Peace himself grant you peace at all times and under all circumstances.

17 The greeting in my own handwriting. I sign all my letters this way. *18* The Love of our brother Jesus be with you all.

FIRST TIMOTHY

CHAPTER 1

1 Paul, an apostle of Jesus, called by God to this ministry, *2* to Timothy, my dear son in the faith: Love, Peace and Joy from God our Dad and Jesus our brother.

3 As I asked you when I was on my way to Macedonia, please stay in Ephesus to help keep the Good News there pure; *4* so that people don't argue about things that don't have anything to do with the faith *5*. We must always keep centered on Love that flows out from a pure heart, a clear conscience, and a profound faith. *6* Some have strayed from this, *7* wanting instead to be teachers of the law rather than of Love.

8 For the law is for unbelievers. *9* If we truly believe in Love, in God, there is no need of law, *10* other than those which bring order to our external world. *11* But we have the Good News of our beloved God to guide us, and which I have been entrusted to share.

12 I am grateful to Jesus our brother, who considered me faithful, and gave me the strength to fulfill this service; even though my life before his Call was lacking so many things. *13* But he looked beyond these because I had not yet heard the Good News; *14* and when I opened to it, he filled me with his own faith and love.

15 It is this Jesus—present in my life, who has lifted me up into my own Divinity. The rebirthing into my True Self is what we are all called to. *16* Or perhaps a better way to put this would be our call to be reborn into our other self, our Jesus Self. *17* May our hearts always give thanks for this Divine Self that Jesus came to reveal to us.

18 So, my dear son Timothy, be faithful to Jesus, and the amazing prophesies about you. *19* Rebirth Jesus in yourself and in those you serve. This is your Call, this is your life.

CHAPTER 2

1 First of all then, remember always to pray. *2* Join your will to that of Jesus, to bring peace and love to all layers of society, to those considered important and to those considered unimportant. *3* This is the Life Jesus came to bring. *4* Then we will be living in and of the Truth. *5* For there is one Truth and that is Jesus, *6* who incarnated to reestablish the Oneness of all. *7* I was appointed to preach this Truth, this Good News.

8 So I want everyone to live a life of prayer in harmony with everyone. *9* We are Divine, so there is no need to impress others with what we have or how we dress, *10* but rather by how we live.

11 If we all understood and lived our Divinity, we could walk humbly through the world in service and love. *12* Some struggle to be great, not realizing they are already God.

Chapter 3

1 Those who feel called to serve as bishops have a good intention. Those who don't feel called to serve, don't have a call to be bishop. *2* Above all a bishop must have a good heart, know how to love, know how to live in peace and to bring peace, be honorable and honest, and a good teacher. *3* The present family of a possible bishop is a good indication of the future Community of the person. *4* Jesus needs to be a bishop's treasure, not money, prestige or power. *5* An open heart and gentle spirit is the foundation of all callings. *6* A good name comes from a good life.

8 The same is true of deacons, who are called especially to serve the needy. *9* Give them a chance to live their call for a while before validating it.

11 The spouses of those called need to have the same attributes, *12* if not the same talents, as those called. *13* For we are all called to reincarnate Jesus in our lives and in the lives of those around us.

14 I am writing this advice to you in case my visit is delayed. *15* We need to be quite concerned that the house of God reflects the Love of God. *16* All our communities must reflect the Good News of Jesus. *17* This is the secret to Communities being loving.

Chapter 4

1 Do not be heartbroken when people slide away from the faith. *2* Those who do always feel miserable, even when they lie and talk of feeling liberated. *3* Some become so bent that they say marriage is bad, and sex is worse. Our bodies are Divine Incarnations and enjoying marital bliss can open the door to our own Divinity. Even enjoying healthy food can help us connect with the Universe. *4* For everything created by God is a part of God, and is not to be rejected, but received with thanksgiving. *5* When we see that all is consecrated, we are a step closer to seeing the Unity of All.

6 If you teach this Truth to the sisters and brothers, you will be a faithful minister of the Good News of Jesus, to whom you have given your life and service. *7* Don't pay any attention to anything else. *8* Train yourself to be Divine. *9* Physical training is helpful for our time on this earth; but Divine Training leads to eternal life. *10* This is what we have struggled so hard to have, to live, and to preach.

11 This is also your calling, as you well know. Don't be concerned about your youth, for maturity does not come from the years we live, but from the service we render. *12* Become an example of what you preach, an example of faith, of hope, of love, and purity of heart.

13 Until I arrive, devote yourself to public readings of exhortations, to preaching and teaching. *14* Use your special gifts, revealed through prophecy, and bestowed by the laying on of hands by the elders. *15* Practice these things so that your spiritual growth may be evident to everyone. *16* Live what you teach; teach what you believe, and believe what we taught you.

CHAPTER 5

1 Be gentle with older men and treat them as you would your own father, treat younger men as your own brothers; *2* older women as your own mother, and younger women as your own sisters. *3* Jesus wasn't concerned about a new religion, but about a new Family. *4* Loving relationships are the core of his Good News. *5* Honor all true widows and widowers who have no children to take care of them. *6* You must become their faith in God.

7 Teach those things so that all may live in and as the Family of Jesus. *8* Always take care of your dependents; be they children or parents.

9 Take special care of those who have taken special care of others. *15* The service roles of our Communities of Faith are mainly toward those who have no one. *16* In this way we become their family and bring them into the glorious Family of God.

17 Elders who have served well are worthy of special honor, especially those who have labored in leading, teaching and healing.

18 Never let our Communities degenerate into institutions. Communities, or extended families, are held together by love; whereas institutions are held together by laws. Families take care of their own; institutions take care of those who pay them for their service.

19 Do not recognize a charge against an elder unless it is supported by a second witness. *20* Correct those who have gotten off the path of Jesus, with the love of Jesus.

21 Follow what I have presented here in all circumstances. *22* Lay on hands of ordination only after a time of discernment. *23* Always follow Spirit in this regard.

24 With time it is fairly easy to tell those who still walk in the dark, and those who have found the Path of Jesus.

CHAPTER 6

6 Be happy with who you are, *7* how you are, *8* and what you have. *9* The Love of money is the path away from God, since God is Love itself. *10* The love of money is the darkest idolatry, since it takes us away from not only God, but also from our sisters and brothers, since where does excess money come from if not from them? Some believe that money will bring them happiness only to find out too late that it has only brought them sorrow.

11 But you, man of God, avoid this trap and walk instead toward a holy life, a Divine Life; full of faith, love, patience and gentleness.

12 With God as your heart and

Jesus as your guide, *14* walk in the radiance of Love until you become Love, become God. *15* Then Jesus indeed will have come again into our world. *16* The Second Coming of Jesus is our becoming Jesus.

17 Tell those who are rich that they need to become humble. *18* That they need to put their hope in God who is eternal, and not in money which always passes away. *19* Urge them to do good, to be rich in good works, to be generous givers, to practice sharing, so that they may take hold of the life that is truly Life.

20 My dear Timothy, guard the precious gift that has been given to you. Don't let it be diminished by discussions of what is false knowledge. Keep your eyes and heart always on Jesus. Grace be with you all.

SECOND TIMOTHY

CHAPTER 1

1 Paul, an apostle of Jesus by the will of God, with the promise of Divine Life; *2* to Timothy, my beloved son: Grace and peace from God our Dad and Jesus our Brother.

3 I thank God for you as I pray day and night. *4* I know that things have been tough for you since I have seen you. I long to see you again that I might be perfectly happy. *5* I remember the deep faith that lived first in your grandmother Lois, then was born in your mother Eunice, and now has grown so strong in you.

6 It is on account of this that I would remind you to live the flame of God's gracious gift, which you have through the laying on of hands. *7* For Jesus has given us a spirit of courage, of power, and of love. *8* So be bold in bearing witness to our brother Jesus and about me, his prisoner. For my sufferings help me crystallize the Good News, by virtue of the power of God, who has called us to this dedication. He does this not because we are so special, but because he is so loving. He has graced us with a call beyond human understanding. A call from all eternity to help us grow into eternity. Now his will has appeared as Jesus, who overcame fear by overcoming death. He brought us to eternal life, to his own Divine Life through his Good News for which I have been appointed a preacher, an apostle and a teacher. *12* It is for this reason that I am in prison, but I am not ashamed for I know Jesus will grant me ultimate freedom when my day comes.

13 Hold to the sacred teaching that you heard from me. Fortify your faith and love in Jesus. *14* Let Spirit be the guardian of the sacred gifts that have been entrusted to you.

15 You know that all those in Asia have deserted me. *16* But may God bless the family of Onesiphorus, who was always a joy and aid to me. *16* And who was not ashamed that I was a prisoner. *17* The first thing he did when he came to Rome was to search me out. *18* I know that Jesus loves us all completely and totally, but I also believe those who have helped spread his Good News have a special place in his heart.

CHAPTER 2

1 And so, my son, be strong in the grace that is Jesus. *2* Teach what I taught you to others, who will in turn also teach it. *7* You will be able to do this well, for Jesus will grant us understanding in everything. *8* Always keep Jesus in your heart, risen from the dead, descended from Dad, to bring the Good News that I too preach; *9* and for which I suffer punishment like a criminal even to shackles; but the Good News cannot be shackled. *10* I endure all this for the sake of the sisters and brothers that they also may welcome our brother Jesus into their lives and so receive his Divine Life.

11 This is important to remember: if we have died to our former selves together with Jesus, *12* we shall also rise with him and share in his own Divine Life. *13* He will never abandon us, for how could he abandon his very self?

14 Never tire of preaching this glorious Truth. *22* Always seek after integrity, faith, love, peace; and be in fellowship with all those of God's Family. *24* A sister or brother of Jesus must not quarrel, but instead they must be respectful and kind to everyone, skilled in teaching and willing to suffer wrong. *25* In a gentle way they should correct those who have strayed from the Truth, *26* for the Truth is Jesus.

CHAPTER 3

1 Be aware that as the Good News spreads, opposition to it will also spread. *2* Let this not shock you. *3* Be careful in your dealings with those who have strayed from Jesus, *4* but always remember that they too are children of our same Dad, even though they refuse to admit or accept this Truth. *5* For opposition does not change Truth. *6* Opposition to Jesus does not change our call to love our enemies. *7* But always live in a faith community to support you when things get rough, *8* and to rejoice with you when things go well.

10 I give thanks that you have always been faithful to my teachings, my way of life, my faith, my love, my steadfastness, and my patience. *11* You were with me even in my persecutions and sufferings and everything that happened to me in Antioch, in Iconium and in Lystra. *12* All who follow in Jesus' footsteps should expect to be treated as he was. *13* Loved by many, persecuted by a few.

14 Be faithful to what you have learned, and to those from whom you learned it. *15* For from childhood you have known the sacred writings that teach you wisdom and faith in Jesus. *16* All writings inspired by God are helpful to teaching, correcting, and training in holiness. *17* So that those in the Family of God may live as God.

CHAPTER 4

1 I charge you in the presence of God and Jesus, to preach the Good News when convenient, and even when it is not convenient. *2* Use it to correct and exhort with gentle patience and continual teaching.

3 For the time is coming when some will walk away from the Good News. *4* Keep writing so that even those you do not see may hear your words. *5* Keep faithful to your Call to be a minister.

6 For I feel that the time of my service is done and that the time of my passing has come. *7* I have fought the good fight; I have finished the race; I have kept the faith. *8* And now it is time to go to a deeper presence of our brother Jesus, together with all the sisters and brothers already there.

9 So please try to visit me soon. 10 For Demos has left me and gone to Thessalonica; Crescens has gone to Galatia; and Titus to Dalmatia. 11 Only Luke is here with me. 12 Find Mark and bring him with you, for he is always very helpful to me in my ministry.

13 When you come bring the coat I left at Troas with Carpus, and also the books and especially the parchments.

16 When I was first charged, no one came to my defense. 17 But Jesus stood by me and gave me strength, so that I might bring the Good News to all the Gentiles. 18 He rescued me from the lion's jaws and delayed my coming fully into his presence so I could continue to proclaim his Message here on earth.

19 Please give my greetings to Prisca and Aquila, and to the family of Onesiphorus. 20 I left Trophimus in Miletus for he was too sick to travel. Please do your best to come before winter.

21 Eubulus, Pudens, Linus, Claudia and all the sisters and brothers send you greetings. 22 May Jesus be (with) your Spirit. Grace be with you.

TITUS

CHAPTER 1

1 Paul, a servant of God and an apostle of Jesus, to Titus my true son in the faith. *2* We were called to foster the faith in all the daughters and sons of God, and to usher them into the Divine Life we are (can have) as daughters and sons of God and sisters and brothers of Jesus. *3* We were called to bring this Good News to all. *4* Love and Peace to you, Titus, from God our Dad and Jesus our Brother.

5 You know that I left you in Crete to take care of the problems there and to appoint elders in every town. *6* These elders are to be outstanding people whose children believe and live the Good News. *7* For the bishop must take care of the Family of God. As any parent, the bishop must lead an exemplary life so as to teach by example, and not be stubborn, arrogant, given to drink or greedy.

8 Bishops must have a gracious and welcoming heart, a gentle spirit and a holy life. They must believe and live the Good News of Jesus, which they are to impart through Spirit-filled teaching, *9* being able to deal with those who have yet to accept this Good News.

10 So Titus, my dear son, be sure to insist that those who have been Jews not impose old laws onto new converts. *11* Jesus led us out of the law, but not into lawlessness. *12* Love is gentle but no less demanding.

13 Law deals with actions, whereas love deals with the heart, a much deeper part of us. *14* This is so very important because the deeper we get into ourselves, *15* the closer we get to Jesus, and the more the Good News incarnates.

CHAPTER 2

1 Teach the older sisters and brothers with love and with patience, to be temperate, easygoing, and sound in their faith. *2* They should realize their Call to teach the younger sisters and brothers of the Community by word and example. *3* The younger sisters and brothers should look to their elders as to their parents, for wisdom and guidance; that they may grow into the fullness of faith. *4* From the very beginning all young children must be taught that they are also the daughters and sons of God, *5* so that they may grow up realizing and living their birthright.

11 For this very reason our brother Jesus came to remind us that our God is our Dad, loving and looking out for us as the best of Dads do. *12* Jesus taught us that the foundation of our faith is the Family of God, *13* always inviting us to love more deeply and serve more willingly. *14* Not as a sacrifice, but as a privilege. *15* Not as a law to keep, but as a love to celebrate.

CHAPTER 3

1 Remind them to respect any valid authority, and be ready for service of any kind. *2* They should know not to slander anyone, even their enemies; but to be gentle and humble toward all people. *3* For Jesus showed us these things by his wonderful loving example. *4* He taught us how much God loves us and that his love was to be our example of life. *5* When we feel we cannot love as he did, we must remember that his Spirit, the Spirit of love, is now fully within us to help us. *6* So when we open to Jesus, we open to the grace of love as he did (and does). *7* This demonstrates that he is our brother, that God is our Dad; and that we have their own Divine Life in us now, as our own Life.

8 This is the core of what Jesus taught us and so must be the core of what we teach. *9* From this Divine Life in us comes love and service, and we must always be open to these manifestations of this new Life. *10* Love those who do not follow this teaching, *11* but let your main associations be with those in the Communities who follow it.

12 When I send Artemas or Trychicus to take your place, try to visit me in Nicopolis, for I have decided to spend the winter there. *13* Please supply Zenas, the lawyer, and Apollos, with what they need for their trip. *14* And have our people dedicate themselves to honorable work to meet our needs. *15* All those with me send you greetings. Greet those who love us. May grace be with you.

PHILEMON

1 Paul, a prisoner of Jesus, and our dear brother Timothy; to Philemon, our beloved co-worker, *2* and to our sister Apphia and our brother Archippus, and the Community that meets in your home. *3* Love and peace from God our Dad and Jesus our brother.

4 I always give thanks to God when I mention you in my prayers, *5* for I hear of all the love and faith you practice toward our brother Jesus and all the saints. *6* I pray that all the love and service you have in your Community may help in the spreading of the Good News. *7* For the deep love you have shown your sisters and brothers has overflowed onto me and brought me such joy and comfort.

8 Therefore, even though, as your spiritual father, I feel free to give you direction, *9* I prefer to ask you a favor as a brother because of our love. *10* So I, Paul, an old man and prisoner of Jesus, appeal to you for my son Onesimus, whom I adopted while in prison. *11* Once he was useless to you, but now he is helpful both to you and to me. *12* I am sending him back to you, and my heart with him. *13* I would prefer to keep him here with me, so that he might serve me while I am in prison for the sake of the Good News, *14* but I do not want to do anything without your permission, so that your graciousness may come from your heart. *15* For perhaps he was parted from you for a time so that you might have him back forever. *16* Not as a slave, but as a brother. This seems obvious to me and I pray it does to you in our brother Jesus.

17 So please receive him as you would me. *18* If he has wronged you, or owes you anything, put it down on my account. *19* I, Paul, now write this with my own hand to swear that I will return it, not to mention that you owe me your very self for the new life I gave you. *20* Yes, my brother, I am very happy of what I have done for you since it has brought us both closer to Jesus.

21 I am writing to you, confident that you will listen to me, and knowing that you will do even more than I ask. *22* Meanwhile, please prepare a guest room for me, since I hope through your prayer to be able to visit you.

23 Epaphas, my fellow prisoner in Jesus, sends his greetings. *24* So do Mark, Aristarchus, Demas and Luke, my fellow workers.

25 The grace of Jesus be with your Spirit.

HEBREWS

CHAPTER 1

1 Dad spoke to our ancestors in various times and in different ways through his prophets. *2* Finally he has spoken through his son, our brother Jesus, telling us of his love for us; and that we are all members of his Family. *3* Jesus is a perfect reflection of his Dad and calls us to be the same. He cleansed us of our old ideas of God, and continues to do so even to this very day.

4 Jesus became a son to teach us that we too are daughters and sons of Dad. *5* He asks us to listen carefully in our heart so that we can hear Dad say, *6* "You are my beloved daughter, my beloved son," *7* and "I will be your Dad, and you will be my daughter, my son."

8 The Good News is all about family, all about God's Family. *9* The Good News is all about relationship; relationship with our Dad, and with our sisters and brothers. Nothing is as important as this. *10* Not power, not rank, not money; those were all melted away by Jesus, to be replaced with Love. *11* A God of Love could do nothing else. *12* A God who is Love established Families (Communities) of Love. *13* The Good News replaces law with Love; and temples with homes, with hearts. *14* Temples are for a distant God; homes are for a loving Dad, who is ultimately in our heart.

CHAPTER 2

1 We must keep our eyes and hearts on this wonderful Truth. *2* The Spirit will keep reminding us of it until it sinks into our bones forever. *3* It is so different from what our ancestors thought that it may be hard for the mind to adjust to it, but the heart will recognize it as the Truth it has been longing for. There will be such joy as this Truth lights the world on fire with love. Pity those who can't adjust to it, keep loving them until they too can walk into it and rejoice. There is more Good News in Jesus than in all the prophets of old. They lead the way, but Jesus *became* the Way.

When you see the Gifts of Spirit at work, you will know that Love is present. For Spirit is Jesus disincarnated. The Spirit is Jesus resurrected, and the invitation to resurrect with him into our own Divine Life, our own inheritance from our Dad. Dad has called us to be his daughters and sons, and as such to be his Gods, to continue the marvelous work that his son Jesus began. Let no one tell you differently. The psalms and Jesus himself have said, "You are Gods." But be sure to remember that God is Love and God is Service. That he is never distant, and never judging.

In a way, we were born through Jesus, since he opened the door to the Family of God for us. When we walk through that door, and are welcomed by our God Dad, we are recreated, reborn into his very essence.

11 Every person has the same Dad, the same Divine Bloodline. By this Bloodline we are made holy, just as Jesus was made holy. He began to really live the Divine Bloodline, which will transform the world when it is recognized and lived by all. That is why Jesus is proud to call us sisters and brothers, and to say to our Dad, "I have told my sisters and brothers what you have told me, so that together we may give you thanks."

Jesus incarnated Dad's Covenant with Abraham, and brought it out of the law it was stuck in for centuries. We now see that the Covenant of Abraham was the precursor of the Family of God. We must always keep everything based on Family. When Jesus died in his humanity and rose in his Divinity, he established the Divine Family to perpetuate the Divine Bloodline of Love.

CHAPTER 3

1 So my holy sisters and brothers, beloved members of the Family of God, set your minds and hearts on Jesus, the Brother of all our Communities. *2* He was faithful to what our Dad asked him. *3* For this he deserves honor for pointing out our path to the Family of God. *4* Every family begins with a mother and father. Then comes the eldest child, which is Jesus in the Family of God. *5* It should be noted that our

God is big enough and broad enough to be both Mother and Father, already experiencing total Oneness. A oneness to which we all are called. *6* A Oneness that Jesus prayed for, and we know Jesus' prayers will always be answered. And we are invited to be a part of this answer.

7 Therefore, as the Sprit says in our hearts, "Today when you hear his voice inviting you into his Family, open to it, walk into it." *12* Be careful not to miss this opportunity, for even though he continually speaks out this invitation, a hardened heart can block our hearing it.

13 Those who have hardened their hearts can sometimes not hear God, so don't be hesitant to extend this invitation yourself to those you love and those you meet. *14* For even though we can never really lose membership in the Family of God, we can lose the joy that comes from feeling loved.

CHAPTER 4

1 So let us be very careful to listen daily for the Voice of our Dad and our Mom in our hearts. This is basic in any family, and more so in the Family of God. *2* For we have heard the Good News inviting us into this Family and accepting our Divine Bloodline. When we believe this, we enter that glorious family and rest in its love. There is no joy that surpasses this, so never tire of inviting all into it. Joy always increases as it is shared.

Some believe that there are those

unworthy of entering the Family of God. What true mother or father would ever believe that? What true sister or brother ever rejects a sibling? Jesus came to save us from that view. Jesus reestablished the Family of God as he preached the Good News of Dad's Love for all. Dad doesn't want us to fear him, but to come to him in love. To do this we have to believe the Good News, and forget all the bad news we were told before. This is hard; this demands a real death to self, to our old ideas of God; but Jesus has shown us the power(possibility) of resurrection. Death has been the deepest fear of humankind since the world began. Jesus walked through death to take away that fear, to open us to our God of Love.

The old belief was that death was the gate to heaven, the Good News now is that Divine Life is the gate to God's Divine Presence and can be had by simply opening to it! Jesus shed his blood so that it could enter us. This had absolutely nothing to do with the sacrifices of the Old Testament; but everything to do with changing our belief about God-Dad.

As his blood enters our body, our being, and we accept this Divine Bloodline, the Good News is born (in us). That is why part of the Good News is the ceremony he gave us wherein we remember to drink his Blood. At the end of which he says, "Do this to remember that you are me!"

12 This Word of God is a two-edged sword. It cuts deeply into old beliefs; but they have to die if the Good News is to rise. "It is love I want and not sacrifice," as Hosea says so wonderfully, clarifying Dad's desire. The blood we drink to follow Jesus' command, has nothing to do with sacrifice and death, and everything to do with Life. He knew it would take time for us to really believe our new Bloodline so he gave us this ceremony as a constant reminder of it.

By having this ceremony during a meal and in a home, Jesus moved religion from the temple to the home. He changed religion from the worship of a distant God, to an intimate gathering with a loving Dad-Mom and Brother. This eliminated a need for a mediator between us and God. So the new priests are prophets proclaiming the Good News that we are all priests, that we **all** can talk and walk directly with Dad and with Brother.

CHAPTER 5

1 We need to talk further about this huge change that Jesus taught and lived. He tried to be a prophet for the Jewish people but many wrote him off as a rebel. Even worse, they considered him a threat. And indeed he was a threat to the old religion of a distant God that demanded sacrifice for sin.

When he brought religion back into the home, where it was always meant to be, he upset the priests who considered themselves to be very special people. The Good News tells us all, that we are very special people; so special, that we belong to the Family of God. Jesus longs for us to realize and believe this marvelous teaching of his. In some way he died as God to be resurrected in our hearts. Hearts are the new temples.

This is why Jesus' very first instruction to his apostles was: "Tell people that God is within." Jesus as God died, so that people would stop always looking for God outside. People would see him outside after his resurrection, but they would feel him inside. And this feeling would grow into a being, always present with them. We would move from wanting to be near God to wanting to be God, not in the former way of an all-powerful being, but in the way of a friend who loves and serves.

CHAPTER 6

So let us go deeper into the core of the Good News and deal with the struggles to live it. The new "religion" of Jesus is relationship. He talked about the basic three relationships: Love of God, Love of Neighbor, and Love of Self. In doing this he pointed to the deep interconnection of those three. If we don't love ourselves, we cannot love our neighbor or our God. If we don't love God we can't really love our neighbor or ourselves.

Please teach your children this with deep respect and profound love. Don't criticize them, invite them to grow. Don't punish them; love them into right actions. Remember that children's image of God is based on their image of their Mom and Dad. Religions that teach a vengeful God allow parents to be vengeful. The Good News does away with all this bad news. But the problem is that we have heard so much bad news for so long, we can believe the Good News is simply a fantasy.

That is why some are very excited about the Good News, but use the bad news as its foundation. So after some time they feel misled and go back to the bad news, mistaking it for Truth. We need a constant Pentecost to avoid this. We need a constant drinking of our Bloodline to overcome centuries of bad news.

You are God! You have Divine Life in you. You will live forever. You have a Divine Family to support you. If you don't feel supported by your Community, change it or leave it. Find a new Community or start a new Community, not to rule, but to serve. The Good News is very simple: Live in the Family of God and be God, a God who loves, a God who serves.

CHAPTER 7

So we come now to the question of priesthood in the Good News. In the old law a priest became such by simply having priestly blood, the blood of Levi. This was when it was believed that the only way to the distant God was through sacrifice. We sinned, so we sacrifice, and thus we appease the angry God who will then allow us a little closer to him, but not close enough to love.

Jesus changed all that. He chased the animals and money changers out of the temple to physically teach: "I want Love, not sacrifice." But the teaching of Hosea was heard and then ignored because it was too far from what was being taught by the priests. It would also take away their livelihood. So in time this Word of God spoken through Hosea was totally ignored. To be resurrected by Jesus.

So if we take away the need for sacrifice, we seem to take away the need for priests. And on some level that is exactly right. But that is when "priest" is seen as the executioner of sacrifice.

In the Good News, Jesus teaches that we are God. How can God possibly have a need to do sacrifice? That old law died when Jesus died. That is why right before he died he established a new priesthood, not for temples, but for homes. Not for institutions, but for families. When Jesus said, "Do this" he was referring not only to the actions but also to the place where they were to take place. Today we keep this custom, but those with the Gift of Prophesy know that the time will come when priests will again build temples and make their livelihood working in them.

The Last Supper was the first meal of this new priesthood. Sacrifice is no longer needed, but nourishment is. The Breaking of the Bread points back to the Manna from heaven; to Dad feeding his Family. The drinking of the Blood points to our need to be regularly reminded of the Divine Bloodline Jesus reminded us of.

Dad had tried for centuries to get this Message through to us. David heard it and put it in one of his Psalms. But people never took it seriously. So Jesus came with that main Message, and it set fire to the world, until it was quenched by greed and the desire for power.

Many are still alive who heard Jesus preach about the Divine Bloodline, this Divine Life, this Eternal Life; but few are those who have grabbed ahold of this Truth with Faith. Many laugh when you preach this Good News, even in Communities that say they follow Jesus. Until we take money and power out of our expression of faith and our Communities, the Good News cannot catch fire again. It has been watered down too much.

So my dear sisters and brothers, let us have family gatherings where we feel fed by Dad-Mom and receive a blood transfusion. Those who do this with us are the true priests of Jesus. I received my priesthood directly from Jesus. Let us honor others who receive this grace by the laying on of hands, as taught by the other apostles. I myself believe in *both* ways of being called to love and serve the Family of God.

So whether your call to service came from my laying hands on you, or by simply acknowledging the call already in your heart, stand firm in the model of priesthood shown to us in the Good News.

CHAPTER 8

8 Before Jesus came, Dad said, "The days are coming when I will make a new Covenant with my daughters and sons, not like the one I made with their ancestors when I brought them out of Egypt. *10* In this new Covenant I will fix my will in their minds and my love in their hearts, and I will be their God and they will be my people. *11* No longer will my daughters and sons need to be taught about me, for they will all know me through our intimate relationship. And I will have this intimate relationship with everyone, from the young to the old."

CHAPTER 9

Let me say one more thing about the death of Jesus. People look at this as such a tragedy, and all suffering obviously is in some sense. But to become heirs, the person bestowing that must first die. The tragedy of the crucifixion is also the Trumpet Call announcing that his Bloodline has now passed to us. Announcing that through his death we have inherited his Life. Perhaps an odd way to affect this, but all Dad's previous efforts at this had not brought the result he planned.

CHAPTER 11

1 Let us now talk about faith, and people of faith. Faith can be seen as an assurance of things hoped for; or as a conviction about things we cannot see. *3* By faith we believe that the universe was created by God out of nothing.

6 Faith is a wonderful help in our relationship with God. We generally do not see him, but we can often feel him. That is because his essence is more energy than physical matter. *7* At the beginning it is very important to have faith in the existence of God. But after we have experienced God, this type of faith is no longer needed because we now *know* God.

8 By faith, Abraham listened when God told him to go to an unknown place that would become his inheritance. For a time he wandered about with no idea of where he was going. By faith he lived in the Promised Land as in a foreign country, living in tents, as did Isaac and Jacob who were joint heirs of this promise.

11 Also by faith, Sarah received the power to conceive even though she was way past the age for that, because she believed what God had said. *12* And so from one important couple came descendants like the number of the stars in the sky or the grains of sand on the seashores. *13* These all died in faith without seeing what had been promised them, *14* but they nevertheless believed that Dad already had a special place prepared for them.

16 That is why God drew them to his heart. His Heart, his Love, is the real Promised Land!

17 Abraham's faith had another severe test. He was seemingly asked to sacrifice his beloved son. And he responded by taking Isaac with him up the mountain as a sacrificial offering, *18* even though God had promised him descendants through Isaac. *19* Abraham believed that God could bring back Isaac even from the dead, which in some way he did.

29 By faith, the Israelites crossed the Red Sea as though on dry land, and yet the Egyptians pursuing them drowned. *30* By faith, the walls of Jericho fell down after the Israelites marched around them for seven days.

32 I could go on and on with so many examples of faith from the Scriptures, but I believe I have made my point about the supreme importance of faith.

CHAPTER 12

Let us bask in the marvelous light of these many witnesses to faith. Let us open our lives completely to this light, so that we may clearly see how to let the Good News of Jesus totally envelope us. Breaking out of the law-mentality is extremely difficult because for centuries we have thought it was the true way, the ultimate truth.

But now we know that Jesus is the Truth, and since the Truth is a person rather than a set of laws or rules, we have to open our faith to him from the very beginning.

So let us fix our eyes on Jesus, and start down this new path mapped out for us. The Path to Jesus, the Path of Love gets extremely narrow at times. You may feel it is too narrow to get through, but what is impeding your passage is not the narrow Path but the baggage you are carrying. So you will often have to make tough decisions: drop the baggage that impedes your going ahead or go back, and look for a wider path. But that wider path never leads to happiness.

If you heart is open, Jesus will give you enough glimpses of himself to urge you to keep going/coming. Our problem is that we consider our baggage to be ourselves and so don't want to leave it behind. To leave it behind feels like we are denying ourselves, but in fact it is the only real way of becoming our true selves. Jesus will not lead us astray, nor will he allow us to continue in our lies about who and what we are. Lies keep us from the Truth, and so they can't be allowed on the Path to Truth.

Jesus' Path to becoming the Truth was not easy either. He walked his humanity through the same narrow Path he now invites us to follow. He is a gentle lover, but also an insistent lover, only because there is no other option to growth. So be very careful of those offering you baggage for your trip.

If we return now to our image of Family, we see that parents are like this Path. They sometimes must tell their children to take off different bags that they have picked up along their way. To limit the amount of these bags, parents must always speak the Truth, for a bag of lies is often very hard to get rid of. And they must always act from love, since a bag of fear is even harder to leave behind.

12 So courage, my dear sisters and brothers, on this Path. And even if you begin to limp don't slow down and allow the joint to be completely dislocated. Rather keep your eyes straight ahead on Jesus, and he will heal you.

14 And as you go, seek peace with everyone you meet, for this will keep the road smooth. And to those who won't give you peace, give them love, for love covers a multitude of bumps. 22 In this way we will arrive at Mt. Zion, the City of the living God, the New Jerusalem, the City of Jesus, the City of Truth.

CHAPTER 13

And finally, let us talk of Love, the center of everything. "May God let love continue to grow each and every day among the sisters and brothers." 2 Be quick to offer hospitality, for in doing this, some have welcomed Angels into their homes without even knowing it. 3 Remember those who are in prison, as though you were in prison yourselves. The same with those who are being mistreated.

4 Let couples live in deep respect and love for one another, and be faithful to one another. 5 Love God much more than money. Be satisfied with what you have, for Dad has said, "I will always be with you." 6 And so we must always say, "Dad is the one who takes care of me; I will not be afraid. What can anyone do against me?"

7 Keep in mind your pastors, who gave you God's Message. Follow their example of how to live and what to believe. 8 For Jesus Christ is the same yesterday, today and forever.

9 Do not be led astray by anyone who teaches anything but Love. For only Love can really give us strength. Only Love is our real nourishment. 10 Let the heart of Jesus be our only altar. 11 Let the Love of Jesus be our only guide.

12 Jesus has walked ahead of us on the Path of Holiness. He is our holiness. 13 So let us walk only with him, even when that means bearing insults and persecutions as he did. 15 With his strength, let us always be thankful; let us only love.

16 Always remember to walk the righteous Path and be generous on it, for this is pleasing to God. 17 Always follow your good Pastors for they look out for you. Be supportive of them as you would be of me. 18 Pray for us that we may always live and act honorably. 19 And pray that I may be able to visit you soon.

20 May the God of Peace who can resurrect us out of thoughts of anger along our way be our Good Shepherd. May he continue to deepen our Covenant with him, by

working in us through Jesus. *21* And may Jesus always be our strength and our guide.

22 I ask you sisters and brothers to listen patiently to what I have written here. *23* I want to let you know that our brother Timothy has been freed. If he can come here I would love to visit with him. *24* Give our greetings to all your Pastors and to all the saints. The Italian sisters and brother send their greetings.

25 Love be with you all.

JAMES

Chapter 1

1 I, James, a servant of our Dad and our brother Jesus; to the twelve tribes in the Diaspora: Greetings.

2 When you have trials, my dear sisters and brothers, consider it an occasion of completing you. *3* For the trials that are endured and overcome increase our faith and make us strong. *4* And the stronger we get the easier it is to walk with Jesus.

5 If you have questions, ask God for the wisdom to understand more fully. He gives generously to everyone, whatever we ask of him in faith. But we should ask in faith without a doubt; *6* for those who doubt are like the waves on the ocean that are tossed around by the wind.

7 Remember, faith is the flower of Love. When we have been loved and taken care of, we have faith. *8* So always love and take care of yourself and those around you.

9 Let everyone be considered equal, from those who have been considered lowly, to those who are rich. *10* For wealth always fades away in the end, even if one can hold onto her money. *11* And if we try to hold onto God with one hand, and money with their other, when it comes to the heart a decision has to be made, for we have only one heart with which to love.

12 When trials come they can get us down, or they can lift us up if we walk through them with the strength of God. Our God, our Dad, is always trying to help us, even when it doesn't seem that way. *13* Temptations never come from Dad but from ourselves. When they come we can either react to them with fear or with faith. *14* Fear is caused by a lack of faith. Faith allows us to walk more fully into our Divinity, which is pure faith, because it is pure love. *15* So let's not blame Dad for what we feel, but rather walk in faith knowing that with his strength we can face and overcome any trial.

16 Be well aware, my dear sisters and brothers, of how gracious and generous our Dad is. *17* He pours down his abundant love on us with no exceptions. *18* He birthed us from Love so that we might be Love.

19 Also understand this, my dear sisters and brothers, how important it is to listen, and how slow we should be to speak *20* or to get angry, since anger comes from fear and not from God. *21* So purify your hearts and minds, so that in humility you may hear the Word of Dad. *22* Be doers of his Word, and not simply listeners, *23* for those who hear and do not respond are the same as those who are deaf. *24* But those who hear the Word of Dad and follow it, *25* will find real joy in their lives. *26* Those who believe they are religious and yet talk against others are deceiving themselves and practicing a useless religion. *27* Pure and undefiled religion in the eyes of God our Dad is this: to look after orphans and widows in need, and to keep free from worldly values.

CHAPTER 2

1 My dear sisters and brothers, in Jesus there are no distinctions and no room for partiality. When we walk with him there is no room for snobbery. *2* So if a rich person dressed in fancy clothes and gold jewelry comes into your home, as well as a poor person in rags, they should be treated as equal sisters and brothers in our own brother Jesus. *3* If you say to the rich person, sit here beside me and to the poor person, sit over there on the floor, you are the worst type of snob. *4* We are not to judge anyone, but to love everyone equally.

5 For has not Dad chosen the poor of the world to be rich in faith and his special heirs? *6* But if you act in this way, you have dishonored the poor. Do not the rich often walk all over you and drag you into court? *7* Do they not slander your good name? *8* You will do well if you keep the Love Rule of Jesus: "Love your neighbor as yourself." *9* But if you are a snob, you are not acting as Jesus asked us to.

10 We cannot pick and choose among the things Jesus has asked us to do, for they form an integral whole. *11* We cannot love some and hate the rest, for everyone is sister and brother to us. *12* Speak and act in a way consistent with how Jesus spoke and acted. *13* If we judge, we become subject to judgment; but if we love we are subject only to love.

14 For judgment comes from the law, and brother Jesus taught us the Good News that we are not under the law, but under love, since we are already daughters and sons of Dad. *15* From Love comes faith; from faith comes the call to serve others in Love. *16* This continuous circle from love to faith to service to love, cannot be broken without destroying our happiness, and the very essence of who we are. *17* For God is Love, and we are God and therefore also Love.

18 Those who object to this are objecting to God. *19* Those who do not see it this way need only to listen again to the Good News of Jesus. *20* For what he taught was not simply his opinion, it was the incarnation of Truth.

CHAPTER 3

1 Be slow, my sisters and brothers, to become teachers, for it involves grave responsibilities. *2* What we speak with our tongue is our connection to the Truth. *3* When we put bits into horses' mouths to guide them, we guide their whole bodies. *4* And we can guide ships with a small rudder even in violent winds. *5* So the tongue, though a small organ, can speak big things, as a forest can be changed radically by a small spark of fire. *6* The tongue is also a fire, and can destroy many things. It can also transform many things and do immense good, depending on the speaker's heart.

7 Most every kind of animal—bird, reptile, sea creature—has been tamed by humankind. *8* But many humans have not tamed their own tongue. *9* We can praise God our Dad with it, and yet curse his daughters and sons. *10* From the same mouth comes blessings and curses, and as we have said before, we cannot pick and choose those whom we will love and bless.

11 The spring does not bring us sweet and bitter water at the same time, does it? *12* Nor is it possible, my sisters and brothers, for a fig tree to bear olives, or a grapevine to bear figs, is it? Salt water cannot produce fresh water.

13 Who among you are wise and understanding? Let them show this by their good behavior, for wisdom and good behavior are two sides of the same coin. *14* So if you cherish bitter jealousy and rivalry in your hearts, you are showing your lack of wisdom and understanding. *15* Such wisdom does not come from God, but is mixed in with worldly values.

17 But the wisdom that comes from God is first of all pure, then peaceable, courageous, congenial, impartial, sincere, and full of mercy and love. *18* And the harvest all this brings to peacemakers, comes from what they have sown.

CHAPTER 4

1 Where do conflicts and fighting among you come from? On a human level they come from worldly passions and desires. *2* Because on the Divine level, unity and peace come from believing the Good News of Jesus that we are all God. This Good News could not be taught openly at first because blasphemy was a capital crime. But a part of all of us knows that we are Divine, and when we cannot find a door to Divinity in our religion, we turn to money or power to quench this hunger to realize our Divine Identity. To be Divine we must first seek the Divine, and then everything else will fall into place. If our life is in disorder, it is because our values are in disorder. If we are trying to become anything other than Divine there will always be disorder in our lives. Prayer, closeness with God, is the solution to everything; since it makes us who we are, and allows us to show this Love to the world. This allows the Spirit in us to shine out from us.

11 So on a more practical level, do not malign your sisters and brothers, for how can you possibly malign God? Let us look anew at the Good News and begin following it.

CHAPTER 5

1 Let me speak now to you wealthy people. I will begin by apologizing for when the Good News of our Divinity was not preached, so that you felt it necessary to accumulate wealth to quench your desire to realize your Divinity. This path may have caused you to walk over many people, so I would ask you in turn to apologize to any you may have mistreated and make restitution to them.

What is yours is your Divinity; the money that you have belongs to all the sisters and brothers, since the means to obtain it was their work too. Ask for guidance in prayer on how to distribute what is not yours to the poor and needy. This will give you the happiness that you seek, since Gods are always generous because all are Love. The money you keep must be sensed as a call to stewardship under the inspiration of Spirit.

Begin to love everyone, since they are indeed your sisters and brothers. In turn you will be loved. Jesus will come to you more easily when you begin to act like him. This is the result of his Spirit being in us, as us. And finally, my dear sisters and brothers, be aware of the immense healing power that comes from the Spirit of Jesus dwelling in us. *13* So when you are suffering, ask in prayer for help from the Presence of Jesus within. And when you are happy, rejoice even more in this inner Presence with Psalms and joyful song.

14 When anyone gets sick, call in the elders of the Community; because Jesus, through his Spirit has empowered them to heal, just as he did to his apostles. *15* The prayer of faith will heal the sick and Dad will raise him up. And if his time has come, he will be welcomed home.

16 Be honest with one another. Ask for help when you need it since we are all weak at times. When you fall, ask your sisters and brothers to help you get up. Live without judgment in total love. There is immense power in prayer, especially the prayer of a Community of Love. *17* The powerful prayers of the prophets are an example of what we too can do, since they were human just like us. *18* We simply need to realize we are Divine, as they on some level knew that they were.

19 My sisters and brothers, if anyone strays from the Truth, realize they have strayed from Jesus. Help those return to the Person who loves them. *20* This will help you too in your walk with Jesus.

FIRST PETER

CHAPTER 1

1 I, Peter, an apostle of Jesus, to the exiles of the Diaspora in Pontus, Galatia, Cappadocia, Asia and Bithynia, *2* chosen by God our Dad and consecrated by the Spirit to be obedient to Jesus: Love and peace to you in increasing measure.

3 Blessed be the God and Dad of our brother Jesus, who according to his great love has given us new birth into our Divinity, through the resurrection of Jesus into us. *4* We now have an imperishable inheritance through being daughters and sons of God, our beloved Dad.

6 You rejoice now in the Good News of Jesus even though you are suffering trials. As you endure or overcome these trials your faith will grow; *7* and faith is more precious than even gold. *8* For this faith allows you to love Jesus even though you perhaps have never seen him, *9* but I know you have felt him in your hearts and sensed him in your minds.

10 We are now passing through the special time many of the Prophets of old spoke of, "a time of trials, but also a time of extraordinary blessings." *12* This is the time of Good News, preached to you by means of the Spirit whose mystical presence was sent to replace Jesus' physical presence. Things are indeed happening now that even the Angels long to stoop down and watch.

13 I walked with Jesus; I talked with Jesus, and I heard him explain how he was going to come back in us, as us. *14* I did not understand that, but I have seen this humble servant of his doing the same things that he did, so I now am certain that he lives in me. *15* And I hope you are ready for his coming (in)to you. Then even amidst all the trials, there will be an inner peace and joy that is unshakeable, because Jesus is unshakeable, and it is his presence in us that brings us these things. *16* This is the true meaning of the phrase: "You shall be holy, because I am holy."

17 Call God "Dad," call Jesus "Brother" to make more real the love between you. *18* The first time I called Jesus "Brother" I thought my heart would jump out of my mouth. I realized later that I had been given a marvelous teaching, that only the love of Jesus was to come out of my mouth.

19 This will happen to you too, my dear sisters and brothers, if you remember always to open your heart before you open your mouth. *20* The glory of the Good News is that we are all the same, there are no differences. All the blessings I have received are available to all of you who simply open your hearts and let Jesus in. *21* This has been the plan of God forever, it is simply now being realized.

22 Love one another fervently

from the heart. *23* For you have been born again into the Divinity of the risen Jesus. *24* This is the Good News that has been preached to you.

CHAPTER 2

1 So lay aside anything in you that is not Divine. *2* Be (like) the new-born Divine babes that you are. Be thirsty for the best spiritual milk, so that you may grow more fully into your Divinity. This Divine Life is your destiny, it is your essence.

4 Come to Jesus, a living stone rejected by human builders, but chosen by God. *5* Allow Spirit to build you up into a powerhouse of Love and Service.

6 Scripture says, "See, I place in Zion a chosen, precious corner-stone, and these who believe in him will never be put to shame." *7* This obviously refers to Jesus. He is to be the cornerstone of this powerhouse, since he is the Love and Service that is the essence of the Good News. *8* Those who don't believe in Jesus, don't believe in themselves; since they are God too. *9* Remember you are a royal priesthood, a holy people of God, by rebirth into your Divinity. *10* You who once felt lost, now feel like you are members of the Family of God.

13 Be respectful of every just and rightful government. *16* Enjoy the liberty of the daughters and sons of God and act as such. *17* Treat everyone honorably without exception. Love your sisters and brothers as you love your God, your Dad.

23 Remember the example of Jesus, who did not return an insult when he was insulted, and who did not threaten when he was abused.

CHAPTER 3

3 Keep your values straight so that you know always that your best adornment is a loving heart, and not fancy clothes or jewelry. *4* Remember the noble quality of a gentle and loving spirit. Nothing can surpass this. *7* This is especially true in marriage where this makes your Divinity obvious for all to see and imitate.

8 To summarize all of this: live always in harmony, loving as sisters and brothers; be deeply compassionate, and humble-minded. *9* And don't return evil for evil, but quite the contrary, when you see what looks like evil, simply use it to **remind** you of your Divinity and your Love Essence. Invite others into love and out of their fear, since it is always fear that causes what we call evil.

10 Don't ever speak against anyone, and speak only the truth. *11* Try always to do your best, and that will bring peace. *12* Be one in mind and heart with God.

13 Who can really hurt you if you do all of these things? *14* And even if you suffer for doing what is right, you will be blessed. *15* So always reverence Jesus in your hearts and be ready to explain to others the joy and hope you feel in your hearts because of him, but always do this gently and reverently. *16* Keep your actions pure so that if you are slandered, people will realize it is a lie. *17* And even if they don't, it is better to suffer for doing what is right than for doing what is not.

18 For Jesus suffered and died to teach us death is nothing to fear, and that true life is eternal. *19* He died in his humanity to rise in our Divinity. *20* Our Divinity is his Good News. Our Divinity is why he became human.

CHAPTER 4

1 So accept this call to continue the life of Jesus on earth, and live as the God you are, *2* remembering always that God is Love and Service. *3* You may lose friends for living this way, but you can continue to love; *6* just as God can love into holiness even those beyond the grave.

7 The time has come to incarnate the Good News and keep Jesus' Message alive. *8* These things will help you do that. Pray every day and in every way; cherish intense love for one another, for love covers a multitude of mistakes. *9* Practice hospitality toward one another without grumbling. *10* Let everyone serve others to the best of their abilities, as good stewards of God's gifts. *11* Talk of the messages God has given you; serve with the strength he supplies through his Spirit, so that all is centered on God and his son Jesus, our brother.

16 If you suffer as a Christian, do not be ashamed, but praise God that you bear that glorious name.

CHAPTER 5

1 Therefore as a fellow elder, and as one who was privileged to walk with Jesus, *2* I ask you to really pastor the flock entrusted to you. *3* Do this with a willing and loving heart, and not because you have to, as we used to do when we believed in the law. Do it for joy and not for greed; not for power, but for a chance to serve and give an example of the Good News. *4* All of this will bring you into the heart of God where true happiness originates.

5 The younger ministers should learn from those with more experience, with everyone pastoring with humility. *6* If you walk down this road of humility, it will be Jesus who raises you up, just as it was Dad who raised him up. You have to do a lot of dying if you really want to do a lot of living. I urge you to follow Jesus as he walks the Path to Calvary, so you can continue walking with him into his resurrection. *7* Throw all your anxiety on him, for his first concern is you.

8 Exercise self control, not as a following of law, but as a walk into freedom. *9* Stand firm in your faith, based on your love, so as to resist those pointing to something other than Jesus.

10 Dad of all Love will hold your hand through all your suffering and pull you into that Love, as you let go of lesser goals. *11* When you are firmly established on the rock of Love, your example will be a beacon for those on the Path to the Good News.

12 I have written this letter to you, with the help of our dear brother Silvanus, to encourage you, and to share the wisdom I have been blessed to receive from Jesus.

13 My son Mark sends you his greetings. 14 Greet one another with a kiss of love.

Peace to all of you in Jesus.

SECOND PETER

Chapter 1

1 I, Peter, a servant and apostle of Jesus, chosen by our Dad and our brother Jesus, send greetings to those with a faith as precious as ours. *2* May love and peace be yours in abundance through knowing and loving our Dad and our brother Jesus. *3* For his love has bestowed on us everything we need to live a life in union with him.

4 He has granted me such amazing blessings, some for me and some to share with you, that you might share in his own Divine Life. *5* For this very reason strive to increase your faith with virtue, your virtue with knowledge, and knowledge with self-control, your self control with patience, your patience with holiness, your holiness with love for all, and your love for all with Love Himself. *8* For if you have these qualities and grow in them, you will also grow in your knowledge of, and union with, our beloved brother Jesus.

10 Urge yourselves on this path, sisters and brothers, to continually move closer to the Good News we have received through Jesus and those he has chosen to spread it. *11* This will lead to your eternal and Divine Life in the Trinity where you long to live.

12 I will continue to remind you of these wonderful truths even though I know you already walk in them. *13* Still I believe it is my duty to encourage you by reminding you as long as I live. *14* For I know that my time here is short, and even after I leave this world, *15* I will try my best to continue to remind you, *16* because when I told you about the coming of our brother Jesus into our world and his marvelous teachings, I was not talking about something I had simply heard. On the contrary, I was an eyewitness to all that he did and all that he said. *17* I was even there when he was transfigured on the mountain so we could actually see his Divinity, and hear Dad say, "This is my beloved son, whom I love so very much." *18* We heard his voice boom down from heaven when we were on that very sacred mountain.

19 So we had the prophetic messages confirmed in our very presence, and urge you to pay attention to them as you would to a light that shines in the dark until dawn comes, and the Daystar rises in your hearts. *20* We want to be very clear that the prophetic Scriptures cannot be explained by reason, *21* because prophesy does not come from willing it, but rather from God revealing it, though Spirit.

Chapter 3

1 This, my dear friends, is my second letter to you. *2* I am trying to remind you of what the holy prophets have said, and the teachings of our brother Jesus, given to you by your apostles.

3 I would also like to explain again a most important part of what Jesus taught us. The very first time we went out on a Mission he told us to tell the people: "God is within you." Many have had trouble understanding this; others have forgotten it. Without this core teaching of Jesus, many of the prophesies seem erroneous. Jesus never planned to be a king in the outer world, but rather in our deepest hearts. He never planned to come again in the outer world, or to bring an end of the world; but rather to come into our hearts to help us end our previous ways of living. So the talk about his Second Coming should not be in the form of a threat, but as the need for us to be prepared for this coming as we would for anyone who is going to visit us. Only his visit will be very different in that it will be permanent and will melt his presence into our presence.

The Second Coming of Jesus will be when we open our hearts so completely to him that his entire self can come into us. The Second Coming of Jesus will be when we ourselves become Jesus, when there is an end in us of everything that is not Jesus. This will fulfill the prophesies of a new heaven and a new earth.

So do your best, dear friends, to open to his coming, to be at peace with him and with his marvelous teachings, as our dear brother Paul has also written to you.

Grow in Love and in Jesus every day.

Pray for me as I do you.

Love me as I do you.

FIRST JOHN

CHAPTER 1

1 We are writing to you about the Heart of Life, who was from the very beginning. We have heard him with our own ears; we have seen him with our own eyes; and we have even touched him with our own hands. *2* Indeed, Life has been revealed, and we have seen It, and are bearing witness to It. We are announcing to you the Divine Life, who existed with Dad before becoming our brother. *3* We saw him and heard him, and are now telling you, so that you may be united to him as we are, in union with Dad and his son Jesus, our brother. *4* We are writing this so that our joy in him may be your joy in him.

5 The Message we heard from him and pass on to you is that Dad is Light and that there is no darkness whatever in him. *6* So if we say we are walking in Jesus, and are still walking in the dark, we are kidding ourselves. *7* But if we walk in the light, then we walk with him, for he himself *is* the Light, and we (can) become one with him and with one another. Then the very blood of Jesus becomes our blood and our being daughters and sons of Dad is made manifest.

8 As sisters and brothers of Jesus we must walk always in the Truth, since Jesus is Truth; otherwise we are trying to walk out of the Family of God.

CHAPTER 2

1 I write you these things to keep you secure in the Family of God. If for some reason you feel you have already walked out of the Family of God and want to return, Jesus will put his arms around you and welcome you home. *2* He is the welcome-home-party for the Family of God, which includes the whole world.

3 By this we can be sure we know him, that we live as he lived. *4* Those who say they know him and do not walk with (as) him are kidding themselves. *5* But those who truly walk with him in love have reached spiritual maturity. *6* Again, if you claim to walk with him you must live as him.

7 Dear friends, what I have written to you is nothing new, but simply what Jesus taught from the very beginning. *8* But now I want to tell you something new, although many of you have already heard this from Jesus or from your Divine Self. And it is this, the darkness is passing away, and the Light is already shining brightly in many of you. *9* Those who claim to be walking in the light, and yet still hate their sisters and brothers are still walking in darkness. *10* Those who love their sisters and brothers are walking in the light, and we generally don't stumble in the light. *11* But those who hate their sisters and brothers are walking in darkness; they don't even know where they are going since they can't see in the dark.

12 I am writing you, dear children, so that from the very beginning you will know how deeply Dad loves you. *13* I am writing you young people so you will continue to open your hearts to Dad's Love. *14* I am writing to you parents so that the first thing you teach your children is how much they are loved by Dad, as you show by your actions how much you yourselves love them.

15 Place your hearts first in God, and the world can be an aid to your loving him. *16* But if you please your heart first in the world, it is extremely hard even to open your mind to God, let alone your heart. *17* Your physical connection to this world is a passing experience, so unless your heart is in God, you will feel lost when this physical experience ends.

18 Let me be very clear about the extreme importance of where your heart is placed. *19* If you follow the example of many of those around you, you may put your heart in a place where it will become locked in. Jesus is the key to this lock, but how will you find him when your heart is locked away?

20 You already have Jesus living in you and know all these things, if you only open to them. *21* The reason I am writing is not that you don't know these things, but to encourage you to live them. You have the Truth, Jesus, living in you; all you have to do is live him!

22 Since Jesus is the Truth, to deny him is to deny the Truth; and to deny the Truth is to deny him. A life lived without the Truth is chaos, confusion and misery. *23* If this is how you feel, then you now know what you need. You need to begin living in Jesus.

24 Live what I have been telling you from the beginning. As you live this you will be living in Jesus; you will be living your Divine Life. *25* And this is what Dad has promised all his daughters and sons.

26 When you do this no one can deceive you. *27* The anointing you have received from Jesus puts you in direct connection with the Truth, so you don't need anyone else to teach you. All you need to do to walk the Path of Truth is to stay in union with the Truth.

28 And so, dear friends, stay in union with him and let his Truth flow through your actions. This will give him a way to come into the world again. *29* And when you see his Truth flowing through the actions of others, you will know they are in union with Jesus.

CHAPTER 3

1 See what a wealth of Love Dad has lavished on us, that we should be called his daughters and sons, as indeed we are. This is true even though those with a worldly perspective are blind to it.

2 Beloved friends, we now know

that we are Dad's daughters and sons, *3* and as such the sisters and brothers of Jesus. *4* We also know that when we are reborn as seeds of Dad, we will have the same Divine Nature as Jesus did and still does. *5* This new identity can only be known as it is experienced, since it is beyond human comprehension. *6* When we have been reborn as God and have learned to walk as such, *7* our entire reality will be changed. *8* Some fear this as a loss of self, when it really is becoming our true selves. *9* Our old selves were thought to be under law and judgment; our new selves will be Love just as God is Love. *10* Our new Divinity will purify our old humanity so much that we will always act out of our true nature, out of Love. *11* This will move us into the City of Love, the City of God. *12* And Jesus' incarnational work will be finished.

13 Do not be surprised, sisters and brothers, if the world hates you. *14* We know we have moved into Divine Life when we love the sisters and brothers. *14* Those who do not love, do not yet live their Divine Life. *15* Everyone who hates his sisters and brothers, hates himself because there really is no "other." Whether we realize or accept it, we are all One. When we walk with Jesus there is no "I", there is only "we."

16 We understand the true meaning of love by Jesus' example of laying down his life to take away our fear. We in turn ought to lay down our lives for our sisters and brothers. *17* Those who possess resources, whether material or spiritual, and see their sisters and brothers in need, and do not share with them, don't yet know what love is, what God is, nor that their sisters and brothers are God. In fact many guard their resources so that God—their sisters and brother—does not get them!

18 My dear friends we must keep Love and Truth always united as One. God is Love, Jesus is Truth— Love spoken—so Truth is Love. The core Message of Jesus is that we are God, which means we are Love and we are Truth. *19* When I love I show my belief that my sisters and brothers are God. When I don't love them, I have become an atheist, because I don't believe in them—I don't believe they are God. Those who don't love their sisters and brothers don't believe the Good News, don't believe the Message of Jesus.

I do not say this to condemn anyone, but to call everyone to Life. True Life is Love! True Love gives us Life, this is the Truth of Jesus.

19 So let us rest in Truth, in Him. This will bring us peace (eventually). *20* For even if our hearts seem to condemn us; Love is greater than hurts, and will heal us into who we already are: God-Love.

21 And if we are already at peace, we know we have walked into our Divinity. *22* When we walk into our Divinity, we do Divine things; we do loving things, so it is obvious to us.

23 Dad wants us to put our faith in Jesus, and put our Love in our sisters and brothers. We know we are God when we act like God. 24 And when we act like God, we know God-Jesus is in us. This is the promised Spirit.

CHAPTER 4

1 My beloved sisters and brothers, do not believe everything that you hear. Always compare it with what Spirit has said in your hearts and what you have heard from us. 2 We know Spirit always talks about how our brother Jesus was sent by Dad, and any Spirit that does not teach this is not the real Spirit. 3 There are false prophets around who try to (mis)lead us away from the Truth, away from Jesus.

4 You are God, dear friends, by the fact that Jesus lives in you, as you. 5 There are others filled with the world, so their views are from the world and not from God. 6 We are from God. Those who are from God listen to us, because we are on the same wavelength. Those who are on the wavelength of the world cannot even hear us.

7 Beloved, let us love one another, because love springs from God and as we love we are (re)born of Love and become God. 8 Those who do not love do not know God; since God is Love. 9 The love of God was revealed to us by the fact that he sent his beloved son to become us and invite us to become him.

11 Beloved, since God has loved us so very much, we too ought to love one another. 12 We generally don't see God, but his presence is manifested as we love, and as we love his presence becomes our identity. 13 From this we can easily know when he is in us, and we are in him, by the way we love. 14 So we ourselves bear witness to Dad's love as we love our sisters and brothers. Love is what makes Dad, his son, our brother, and ourselves, all One.

15 Those who believe that Jesus is the son of Dad have opened their hearts to the Truth. 16 We ourselves have come to know and believe the immense love which Dad has for us. God is Love, and when we are in love we are in God, and God is in us.

17 We know that we have become Love, become God; when we have no fear, since perfect love eliminates fear. Fear was the basis of law, which Jesus overcame with Love. 18 When we have become God we have become All; so there is nothing outside of us to be afraid of. When fear ceases to exist, creation will be complete. We will all be Jesus; we will all be Love; we will all be God. We will have become what God has always been, which was the original plan of creation.

20 Those who say, "I love God but not my sisters and brothers" are still walking in the dark, 21 since in the light we can clearly see that there is no difference between God and our sisters and brothers.

CHAPTER 5

1 All who believe that Jesus is a Christ have been reborn of God. And all who love Dad will love his Son, our Brother. *2* This is how we will know we are daughters and sons of God: when we act as God. *3* For to love God is to act as God, and God always loves. *4* All who have been (re)born of God have overcome the fear of this world. This is the inheritance we have from Dad.

5 Jesus was born of a woman who had already realized her Divinity; and so came into a Family (of God) that had no fear. *6* He was aware of his Divine Bloodline even before his birth. *7* Those who believe this become this, and witness to it, not only by their faith, but also by their life (of Love).

9 And because of this Divine Transformation, those who believe in Jesus have the proof of their belief within themselves, that is, the Jesus who they are. *10* Those who do not believe Jesus have only to look at the lives of those who do, and they will see the actions of Jesus.

11 For God has granted Divine Life to all who believe in his son. Those who have the Son (in them) have Divine Life. *12* Those who don't have the son have not yet realized the Divine Life in them.

13 I am writing this to you who have Jesus in your hearts so that you may know that you have Divine Life. *14* And we know that whatever we ask that is in accordance with his will, will be granted. *15* Anything we ask from the heart of Jesus will be granted.

16 If you see anyone acting without Jesus in their hearts, tell them this Good News. Tell them the joy you feel in walking with Jesus. *17* Invite them to also walk with Jesus so that their prayer may also be answered and their hearts may be at peace. *18* We know that all those who have the Divine Life in them act as God would, otherwise God would not be God. *19* It is hard at times to walk in the world and yet live as God. *20* And yet we know that Jesus has come into the world and into us; that we are him and he is us; that we truly have Divine life, and that **we are God!**

AN AFTERWORD FROM THE SCRIBE

I want to share a personal word with you here at the end. Scribing this *New* New Testament was the hardest thing I have ever done in my life. It was also the thing I resisted most.

Yet...it was also the **Greatest Blessing** of my life.

There were many days as I scribed this, in which I could not write a word as I tried to adjust to what Jesus was telling me. Other days I could only cry for what had been put into the "original" New Testament.

And finally, I really want you to know that I have done nothing unusual or special. We all can listen to Jesus and hear him speak to us in our hearts. We have only to listen and then do what we have heard.

Please do this, if you don't already do it!

My guess is that for you too it will be the hardest thing you will ever do, but also the **Greatest Blessing** you will ever have!

—A Friend of Jesus

CPSIA information can be obtained at www.ICGtesting.com
Printed in the USA
236368LV00002B/4/P

9 781618 060006